Lecture Notes in Computer Science 6712

Commenced Publication in 1973
Founding and Former Series Editors:
Gerhard Goos, Juris Hartmanis, and Jan van Leeuwen

W0246058

Christos Xenakis   Stephen Wolthusen (Eds.)

Critical Information Infrastructures Security

5th International Workshop, CRITIS 2010
Athens, Greece, September 23-24, 2010
Revised Papers

 Springer

Volume Editors

Christos Xenakis
University of Piraeus, Department of Digital Systems
Karaoli and Dimitriou 80, PC 18534 Piraeus, Greece
E-mail: xenakis@unipi.gr

Stephen Wolthusen
University of London, Department of Mathematics, Information Security Group
Royal Holloway, Egham, Surrey TW20 0EX, UK
E-mail: stephen.wolthusen@rhul.ac.uk
and
Gjovik University College, Department of Computer Science
Norwegian Information Security Laboratory
2802 Gjovik, Oppland, Norway
E-mail: stephen.wolthusen@hig.no

ISSN 0302-9743   e-ISSN 1611-3349
ISBN 978-3-642-21693-0   e-ISBN 978-3-642-21694-7
DOI 10.1007/978-3-642-21694-7
Springer Heidelberg Dordrecht London New York

Library of Congress Control Number: 2011929369

CR Subject Classification (1998): K.6.5, E.3, B.4.5, C.2, D.4.6, J.1

LNCS Sublibrary: SL 4 – Security and Cryptology

Typesetting: Camera-ready by author, data conversion by Scientific Publishing Services, Chennai, India

Printed on acid-free paper

Springer is part of Springer Science+Business Media (www.springer.com)

Preface

The present volume contains the carefully revised proceedings of the 5th International Workshop on Critical Information Infrastructures Security (CRITIS 2010), held during September 23–24, 2010, in Crown Plaza Athens City Hotel, Greece. The workshop was organized by the Department of Digital Systems, University of Piraeus, Greece, in conjunction with the European PKI (EuroPKI 2010) workshop and the European Research Consortium in Informatics and Mathematics' (ERCIM) Security and Trust Management (STM 2010) workshop, and took place just after the 2010 European Symposium on Research in Computer Security (ESORICS 2010), which was also held in Athens (September 20–22). By doing so, it was facilitated to bring together not only researchers of the critical infrastructures community, but also of adjacent research communities. This continuation of the series of successful CRITIS workshops has once again allowed the research and stakeholder community from academia, research institutions, industry, and government entities to meet and exchange views covering the key areas facing critical infrastructure protection. This was reflected in the carefully selected full research papers, but also in panel discussions and the poster talks. To this end, each of the 12 out of 30 submissions was peer-reviewed anonymously by at least three independent technical experts before presentation, and the research papers contained in this volume further reflect the feedback and discussions at the workshop. Similar care was also applied to the two poster presentations; the research papers on which these were based are also included in the present volume, but marked as poster papers.

The joint format of the workshops facilitated the invitation of speakers from the critical infrastructures community, and provided a wide-ranging but topical choice of invited talks by distinguished speakers. We were fortunate to have a talk on "Data Privacy in Outsourcing Scenarios" by Pierangela Samarati of the Department of Information Technologies at the University of Milan on the first day, with the second-day keynote provided by Gustav Kalbe, the Deputy Head of Unit Trust and Security at the European Commission discussing the European policy on trust and security with a particular perspective on upcoming research and development in the 8th Framework Programme, while the third day's keynote talk on "Enhancing Europe's Critical Information Infrastructures—ENISA's Resilience and CIIP Program" was given by Udo Helmbrecht, the European Network and Information Security Agency's (ENISA) Executive Director. We would like to once again express our gratitude to these keynote speakers.

The CRITIS workshop was, moreover, able to host a special session organized by ENISA, during which Demosthenes Ikonomou of ENISA provided an overview on the activities of ENISA in the areas of technologies with the potential to enhance resilience. This session also included a review of a cyber-security and cyber-warfare exercise conducted in Greece, by Dimitris Gritzalis of the

Department of Informatics, Athens University of Economics and Business, enti-
tled "Cyberwar Ante Portas! Identifying the Role of the Academic Community
in National Cyber Defense Exercises," as well as a talk by Piotr Cholda of the
Department of Telecommunications, AGH University of Science and Technology,
on resilience metrics followed by a spirited panel discussion.

A year that has seen the security of control systems and particularly their use
in cyber-warfare become a major concern even in mainstream media with the
widespread propagation of the *Stuxnet* worm has validated many of the concerns
that have been discussed in the critical infrastructure protection community for
a long time, and it remains to be hoped that the problems identified in the
research arena and discussed over the course of the workshop will be acted
upon in a timely manner so as to prevent major incidents. It is precisely this
combination of blue-skies research and analysis with more pragmatic technical
solutions and engagement with stakeholders that makes the CRITIS workshops
valuable to the community, and we hope that the 2010 instance was only one
in what will continue to be a primary venue for this community both within its
customary base in Europe and beyond.

Realizing such a workshop, however, does not happen in a vacuum, and it
is first and foremost the authors and workshop participants with their original
research contributions and interactions with speakers and panelists that shape
the character and success of the CRITIS workshops. We would also like to thank
the Technical Program Committee members whose timely and thorough reviews
helped ensure not only the high quality of the research contributions, but also
provided valuable insights to authors. The General Chairs, Javier Lopez of the
University of Malaga and Sokratis Katsikas of the University of Piraeus, provided
important guidance and stability as did the members of the standing CRITIS
Steering Committee. Finally, Eleni Darra and Nikos Vrakas contributed to the
successful organization of the workshop by serving as the Local Arrangements
Chairs.

September 2010   Christos Xenakis
                                                    Stephen Wolthusen

Organization

Program Committee

General Chair

Javier Lopez	University of Malaga, Spain
Sokratis Katsikas	University of Piraeus, Greece

Program Committee Co-chairs

Christos Xenakis	University of Piraeus, Greece
Stephen Wolthusen	Royal Holloway, University of London, UK and Gjøvik University College, Norway

International Program Committee Members

Alcaraz Cristina	University of Malaga, Spain
Baiardi Fabrizio	Università di Pisa, Italy
Bloomfield Robin	City University London, UK
Bologna Sandro	ENEA, Italy
Carvajal Jose Fernando	INDRA, Spain
Casalicchio Emiliano	Università di Tor Vergata, Italy
Chavarri Daniel	S21SEC, Spain
Clemente Roberto	Telecom Italia, Italy
Deconinck Geert	K. U. Leuven, Belgium
Dritsas Stelios	Athens University of Economics and Business, Greece
Eckert Claudia	Fraunhofer SIT, Germany
Garber Richard	DRDC Centre for Security Science, Canada
Gelenbe Erol	Imperial College London, UK
Geneiatakis Dimitris	University of Piraeus, Greece
Geretshuber Stefan	IABG, Germany
Gheorghe Adrian	Old Dominion University, USA
Gritzalis Dimitris	Athens University of Economics and Business, Greece
Gritzalis Stefanos	University of the Aegean, Greece
Hadjsaid Nouredine	L.E.G Grenoble Institute of Technology, France
Hämmerli Bernhard	Acris GmbH, Switzerland
Johnson Chris	Glasgow University, UK
Klein Rudiger	Fraunhofer IAIS, Germany

Lambrinoudakis Costas   University of Piraeus, Greece
Lansard Pierre-Dominique   France Telecom, France
Lewis Paul   Technology Strategy Board, UK
Luiijf Eric   TNO Defence Security and Safety,
                             The Netherlands
Masera Marcelo   EU Joint Researh Centre, EU Commission
Nadjm-Tehrani Simin   Linköping University, Sweden
Ntantogian Christoforos   University of Athens, Greece
Okamoto Eiji   University of Tsukuba, Japan
Panzieri Stefano   Università di Roma Tre, Italy
Rannenberg Kai   Goethe University Frankfurt, Germany
Rome Erich   Fraunhofer IAIS, Germany
Sanders William   University of Illinois, USA
Setola Roberto   Università CAMPUS Bio-Medico, Italy
Shenoi Sujeet   University of Tulsa, USA
Solms Sebastian   University of Johannesburg, South Africa
Suri Neeraj   TU Darmstadt, Germany
Suter Manuel   ETH Center for Security Studies Zurich,
                             Switzerland
Svendsen Nils   Gjøvik University College, Norway
Taute Barend   Council for Scientific and Industrial Research,
                             South Africa
Trushell Paul   Attorney General's Department, Australia
Tsoumas Bill   Ernst & Young and Athens University of
                             Economics and Business, Greece
Zhou Jianying   Institute for Infocom Research, Singapore

Table of Contents

Inter-dependency Assessment in the ICT-PS Network: The MIA Project Results

Emiliano Casalicchio[1], Sandro Bologna[2], Luigi Brasca[3], Stefano Buschi[4],
Emanuele Ciapessoni[3], Gregorio D'Agostino[2], Vincenzo Fioriti[2],
and Federico Morabito[1]

[1] University of Rome Tor Vergata – Dep. of Comp. Science
casalicchio@ing.uniroma2.it, federico.morabito@gmail.com
[2] UTMEA-CAL Unit, ENEA, Rome, Italy
{bologna,fioriti,dagostino}@enea.it
[3] SSE - Power System Development Dept., ERSE Spa, Milan, Italy
{ciapessoni,brasca}@erse-web.it
[4] Booz & Company Italia, Milano, Italy
stefano.buschi@booz.com

Abstract. Inter-dependency evaluation through quantitative approaches is one of the open challenges in Critical Infrastructure Protection. The incapability to conduct appropriate networks inter-dependencies measurements undermines the possibility that the Critical Infrastructures protection programs can correctly assign resources and efforts for mitigation solutions targeted to the most important risks.

This paper describes the approach and metrics used in the "Methodology for Interdependencies Assessment" EU Project to asses interdependencies in ICT and Power System networks. The major project finding, metrics applicability results and scalability issues are described in the paper.

1 Introduction

Current context of network inter-dependency analysis for energy, transportation, communication, oil, gas, water and ICT networks, the so called Critical Infrastructures, has developed insights on the magnitude of the potential risk but has had great difficulty, given the innate complexity, in developing appropriate practical methodologies for measuring dependencies. The incapability to conduct appropriate networks inter-dependencies measurements undermines the possibility that the Critical Infrastructures protection programs can correctly assign resources and efforts for mitigation solutions targeted to the most important risks. The "Methodology for Interdependencies Assessment" (MIA) EU Project[1] aims to assess measures of inter-dependencies between the ICT and the electricity generation/transmission (PS) network.

---

[1] The MIA Consortium (http://www.progettoreti.enea.it/mia/) is formed by ENEA (coordinator), ERSE, TERNA, TELECOM, ENEL, Booz&Co. With the support of the "Prevention, Preparedness and Consequence Management of Terrorism and other Security-related Risks Program" European Commission - Directorate-General Justice, Freedom and Security.

C. Xenakis and S. Wolthusen (Eds.): CRITIS 2010, LNCS 6712, pp. 1–12, 2011.
© Springer-Verlag Berlin Heidelberg 2011

Into the MIA project we committed ourselves to achieve the following goals: (i) identification of the most suitable models for ICT-PS inter-dependencies representation; (ii) identification of the most suitable set of metrics for the quantification of the inter-dependencies between ICT and PS infrastructures; and (iii) evaluation of the models and metrics applicability and scalability.

The MIA project relies on some of the main results from the inter-dependency modeling and analysis literature, however the selection of the models is dictated also by the expertise of the MIA consortium partners and by the "best practice" nature of the project. Two of the three models adopted to reproduce ICT-PS coupling bring with them mathematical tools used to define inter-dependency metrics. Moreover, the MIA project proposes also inter-dependency metrics that are independent from the system model adopted and that can be used to characterize time series obtained from historical data, direct measures and simulation experiments. The proposed set of metrics is evaluated by means of three case studies to provide procedures, algorithms and tools for the calculation of metrics on realistic scenarios and to give evidence of the results. The metrics evaluation is not intended to be comparative but it is oriented to provide insight into metrics applicability and scalability.

The purpose of this paper is to give a general overview of the MIA methodology, to describe a subset of the metrics we propose and to show and discuss major results obtained applying the metrics to realistic case studies. For lack of space this paper does not provide neither a detailed description of the inter-dependency models implemented in the case studies and of the underlining modeling theory; nor a detailed description of the large set of experiments conducted for the purpose of metric evaluation. An exhaustive discussion of this aspects can be found on the project documentation (available on-demand from the MIA consortium).

The paper is organized as follow. Section 2 introduces the MIA framework for inter-dependency models and metrics evaluation. Section 3 describes the inter-dependency models adopted as basis for inter-dependency assessment. Section 4 presents the metrics proposed and evaluated in the project. Section 5 introduces the case study used for metrics evaluation and discuss the major project findings. Section 6 conclude the paper discussing metrics and model applicability as well as open issues.

2   The MIA Framework

Metrics are tools designed to facilitate decisions making, tracking performance and directing resources through collection, analysis, and reporting of relevant data. Metrics should be based on problem specific objectives and must yield quantifiable information (percentages, averages, and numbers). Moreover, data supporting metrics needs to be readily obtainable and only repeatable processes should be considered for measurement. The MIA metrics, designed to measure the ICT-PS coupling along specific dimensions of analysis, were implemented taking in mind the above principles.

Inter-dependencies can be classified on the base of their nature (physical, geographical, cyber, logical) and can be analyzed along their temporal scale [1].

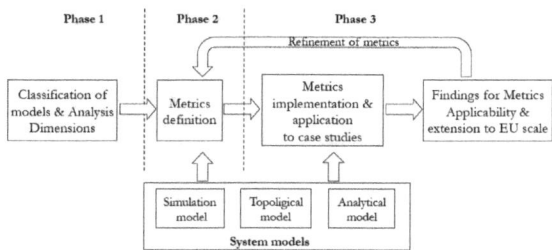

Fig. 1. The three phases of the MIA framework for metrics definition and implementation

In the MIA framework the above mentioned characteristics has been used as a main driver for both model and metrics selection. The MIA framework, sketched out in Figure 1, is organized in three main phases:

1. *Classification of models.* Models are created to reproduce inter-dependencies among infrastructures and to extract measures of such inter-dependencies. Historical data, typically extracted from case histories of utility failures, where used to create workload models and to parameterize infrastructures models.
2. *Definition of metrics.* The second phase is the development of a set of metrics which permit the quantification of ICT-PS coupling along the dimension of analysis we consider (physical, cyber, geographical and temporal). Metric definition consider also the modeling approach used and the mathematical tools them provide to measure the model behavior.
3. *Metrics Implementation Process.* The third phase is related to the metrics implementation. Procedures, algorithms and tools to calculate the selected metrics are provided and described. The output of this phase evaluates also the feasibility of metric implementation and its applicability, therefore it should be intended as feedback to phase 2.

In the remaining of the paper we discuss the model selected in the first phase, the metrics defined and implemented, the results obtained.

3   Inter-dependency Models

Among all the models that can be used to reproduce ICT-PS systems behavior and their coupling, the MIA consortium chose the ones it is familiar with and that allow to reproduce the dynamic of physical, cyber and geographical characteristics of the system under study. The models we considered are the Topological (based on graph theory approach), the Analytical (based on transfer function representation of inter-dependent systems) and the Simulative (based on discrete event simulation). Table 1 summarizes the capability of the selected models versus the dimensions of analysis of ICT-PS coupling. As reported, each model has different capability at the price of implementation costs and scalability.

Table 1. Capabilities of the inter-dependencies modeling approaches selected versus the inter-dependencies characteristics

Models	Dimensions of analysis			
	Physical	Cyber	Geographical	Temporal
Topological	YES	YES	NOT Explicitly	NO
Analytical	YES	YES	NOT Explicitly	YES
Simulative	YES	YES	YES	YES

Of course, more detailed is the model finer the grain of the information that can be extracted and larger the set of inter-dependency characteristics that can be measured. Despite their advantages, detailed models have the drawback to be costly in term of model building and model parameterization. Another important observation is that formal modeling approaches such as the topological and the analytical, that are based on a sound theory, bring with them tools to measure the model behavior and that can be used to measure inter-dependencies, as we will describe in the next section.

In the following we give an overview of the inter-dependency models features. A detailed description of the modeling methodology is contained in the project deliverable (available on-demand from the MIA consortium).

3.1   Topological Model

The topological approach adopts models of the inter-dependencies between the nodes of the power grid and of the communication infrastructure at the level of the network topology and its structural properties. The topological approach constructs a representation of the two infrastructures adopting graphs models and theory. The proposed graph model [2,11,10] is built trough a process called Perimetring, by which a system consisting of a network requiring an other one network for normal or exceptional operations is represented by the two networks, where the first network will be named *behaving* net while the second will be named *auxiliary* net.

The two networks are then constructed by using the data from the stakeholders (the public power utility and the Telco provider), specifying the analysis on a particular region or area of interest. Two main assumptions are then considered to make the model more easy and tractable, which are the logical coincidence between the Primary Station or Substation node and ending point of the Telco network and the existence of *radius of influence* of each electrical node for the network nodes as the radius of an circle delimiting an (ideal) area powered by that node (not considering the existence of Uninterruptible Power Supply systems).

After the two networks have been built, the approach performs robustness test to assess the topological level of inter- dependencies of the two networks.

The robustness test consist of a stochastic removal of nodes and on the computation of the node unreachability probability. From this dependency index will be computed the ICT-PS coupling metric denominated *Topological robustness metric* and discussed in the next section.

3.2   Analytical Model

The analytical approach is a quantitative method based on the use of the dynamic control system theory, namely it uses the transfer functions and the correspondent frequency responses as an approach to achieve a methodology to assess the interdependencies among critical infrastructures.

System theory permits to build an analytical model representing the ICT and PS coupled systems trough the definition and characterization of the transfer functions of the systems and subsystems composing the ICT and PS infrastructures [3]. With the introduction of the transfer functions, the analysis of the inter-dependencies can be done using common tools taken from the control system theory (e.g Bode and Nyquist diagrams, the system stability analysis, and so on) for the study of the coupling of the ICT and PS infrastructures.

Both ICT and PS infrastructures and their components are described by the transfer functions that express the input/output relationship of the system into the domain of Laplace (or in the domain of frequency). After the identification of the components of the infrastructures to be considered are determined the relationships of connectivity (in terms of input and output signals) between each component and to determine the values for the parameters specifically of the identified components (from TSO and stakeholders). By the application of the Mason's formula (which computes the transfer functions regarding the input signals and the output ones along a path which is considered of interest), it is possible to define a global transfer function and the corresponding frequency response along the path of interest.

3.3   Simulation Model

In literature are proposed different simulation model to analyze interdependencies: SimCIP, DIESIS, I2Sim, CISIA, FederatedABMS, to cite few. A good and extensive discussion the simulative approaches to the study of CI is reported also in [12].

The MIA project uses the SimCIP [6,7] simulator that models the Telco PSTN and GSM networks of Rome and the distribution power grid of Rome. The simulator was used to deepen the understanding of critical infrastructures and their inter-dependencies as well as to identify possible problems and to develop appropriate solutions. In order to simulate specific domain behavior, an electrical and Telco simulators were considered and interfaced with SimCIP. SimCIP uses a geo-referenced representation of the infrastructures and it allows to study the dynamics of the behavior of power grid and Telco system when failure events (on the infrastructures components) are introduced. Data collected from simulation must be post processed to compute inter-dependencies indexes and metrics.

4   Interdependency Metrics

In the second phase of the MIA framework we have proposed a set of dependencies and inter-dependencies indexes [4]. The more significative coupling indicators are here reported, our choice is driven by the necessity to have at least metrics for inter-dependency assessment along the physical, cyber and time scale dimension of analysis:

- Topological robustness, that measures the intensity of cyber and physical dependencies.
- Module and phase of frequency response and the poles placement, that measure the cyber and physical dependencies from a dynamic point of view.
- The ratio of being a cause of miss-behavior to being affected by miss-behavior, that measures the cyber and physical dependencies both from a static and a dynamic point of view. Such metric has also the capability to measure geographical dependencies but not test and validation has been performed.
- Temporal scale of the inter-dependency, that measures the time scale and therefore the dynamic of cyber and physical dependencies.

Of course, the list above presented does not pretend to be an exhaustive one. In the literature as been proposed many interdependency metrics on what our work is inspired on (see the related work section in [4]). In the project we have also proposed a geographical inter-dependency index and an economic scale inter-dependency index, that were no further investigated because of low priority in the project commitment. However, the way forward (also behind the project) is to improve the proposed inter-dependency metrics as to define new indexes capable to cope with all the dimension of inter-dependency analysis.

4.1 Topological Robustness

To measure the global dependence of the electric system with respect to the Telco network (or vice versa the dependence of the Telco network with respect to the power system) has been selected the *Topological Robustness Metric* (TRM). $TRM =< 1 - P_2 >$, where P_2 is the probability that each electrical nodes resulted to be unreachable upon the removal of two Telco nodes (or vice versa a Telco node is not more powered upon the removal of two power grid nodes). We remark that the larger the probability P_2, the higher the dependency between network nodes. Therefore TRM, that is the average value of the probability $1 - P_2$, is a measure of the network robustness and lower its value higher the independence of a network respect with the injection of failure in the coupled infrastructure. On the contrary, an high value of TRM means the coupled networks are highly dependent.

4.2 Module and Phase of Frequency Response and the Poles Placement

The analytical model allows to naturally evaluate the following measures, that can be used as valuable inter-dependency metrics. The *module of the frequency response*, that is a natural metric of the coupling between the infrastructures modeled by the resulting transfer function $G(s)$. $|G(s)|$ measures how much the input is amplified or attenuated by the system for every frequency in the range $[0, \text{infinite})$. Greater the value of $|G(j\omega)|$ in an interval of frequency stronger is the inter-dependency. On the other side, a low values, e.g. $|G(j\omega)| < 1$, reveals low intensity of the coupling between the considered input and output.

The analysis of *phase of the frequency response* between input signal and output signal in different frequencies interval can be useful to make some considerations and remarks on components and subsystems in response to input change. E.g. higher the phase of $G(j\omega)$ larger the potentiality of changes in the output signal, with respect to the input, which should be analyzed to assess the coupling.

The poles of the transfer function provides a direct measure of stability margin of the system At the last, the existence of at least one pole with positive real part in the transfer function $G(s)$ indicates that the overall system is unstable, which is an element of great significance for the analysis of inter-dependencies.

4.3   Ratio of Inter-dependency

Inter-dependencies in the context of events effecting more than one infrastructure were quantified by Zimmerman [9] as an *effect ratio*, which compared different types of infrastructures with respect to the direction of the impacts. The work by Zimmerman is oriented at the analysis of historical data. Inspired to this work we propose the *ratio of inter-dependency* as the ratio between the number of malfunctioning in a set of infrastructures (at least one) and the number of malfunctioning occurring in another infrastructure. A malfunctioning in an infrastructure is intended as the deviation from the normal behavior and it can be represented by arising failures, outages or more in general Quality of Service (QoS) level degradation. In the MIA project we consider as malfunctioning only the QoS degradation of the service level provided by an infrastructure.

To define the ratio of inter-dependency is introduced the concept of rate of malfunctioning $N(\cdot)$ that is defined as the number of time, over an observation time frame T, the QoS level provided by an infrastructure deviates from the agreed level. The definition of QoS level depend on the infrastructure considered and on the service or set of services provided.

Considering two infrastructures i and j the ratio of inter-dependencies $rd(i,j)$ is defined as $rd(i,j) = \frac{N(i \mid j)}{N(j)}$ where $N(i \mid j)$ is the rate of malfunctioning in infrastructure i due to malfunctioning in infrastructure j, and $N(j)$ is the rate of malfunctioning in infrastructure j. $rd(i,j)$ is an indicator which can portray the direction of the inter-dependency considering that the root of cause is in infrastructure j. Moreover, $rd(i,j)$ takes into account the coupling between i and j in both direction, and therefore it is an inter-dependency metrics. Indeed $N(j)$ counts also the QoS degradations in j that have root in i (feedbacks). The ratio $rd(i,j) \in [0, \inf)$ and its meaning differs if its value is greater, less or equal to 1. Let us consider the three cases in fig. 2. In *Case 1*, $rd(i,j) < 1$ means that i has a weak dependence on j and more the ratio goes to zero weaker is the dependence. In the example, while there is a cascade effect in infrastructure j ($N(j)$ increase) the QoS degradation in infrastructure i is moderate. In *Case 2*, $rd(i,j) \geq 1$ means that i has a strong dependence on j. In the example A failure injected into infrastructure j produce a cascade effect on infrastructure i. On the contrary, the

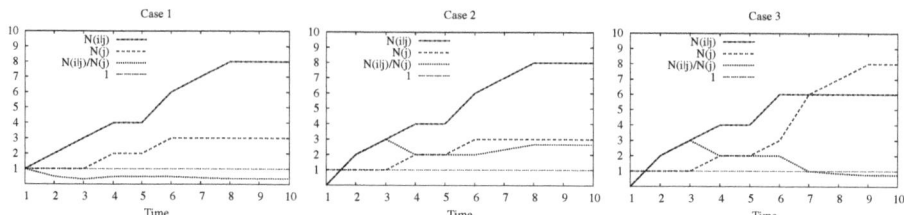

Fig. 2. Three example of evolution of $rd(i, j)$ measured over ten consecutive time intervals $T = 1$

number of QoS violation in infrastructure j is moderate. *Case 3* is an example where the absolute value of $rd(i, j)$ is misleading and it is worth to evaluate the evolution of $rd(i, j)$ over time. Indeed in fig. 2, the absolute value of $rd(i, j)$ is initially greater then one and finally less the one. In this case, the analysis of the time series of $rd(i, j)$ give a more in depth knowledge about the direction and the intensity of inter-dependency phenomena. Actually, infrastructure i and j are interdependent: at time $t = 7$ the QoS level in j start degrading more than the QoS level in infrastructure i, as side effect of infrastructure i QoS degradation. Hence, while an evaluation of the dependency degree considering only the $rd(i, j)$ value at $t = 10$ reveal a medium low inter-dependency $(rd(i, j) = 0.75)$, the analysis of $rd(i, j)$ for $t < 7$ indicates a strong dependency of i on j.

The measure of interest for the ratio of inter-dependencies metric are the following: the value, $rd(i, j)$ computed over a time interval T (as by definition of $N(\cdot)$); the average value over n observation defined as $\overline{rd(i, j)} = \sum_{k=1}^{n} rd(i, j)_k$, where $rd(i, j)_k$ is the ratio of dependency observed in the k-th time interval.

4.4   Temporal Scale of Inter-dependency

The *temporal scale of inter-dependencies* (*td*) is a metrics developed for take into account the temporal characterization of the inter-dependencies. *td* examines the ratio of the duration of an outage of one infrastructure to the duration of the cascading outage of another impacted infrastructure. Zimmerman and Restrepo [8] developed a simple measure of inter-dependency in the context of electric power outages and their effects on other sectors, the relative duration of cascading, which measures the electric power outage duration $T(e)$ and affected i infrastructures outage duration $T(i)$. Then ratio $T(i)/T(e)$ is a measure of the Temporal scale of the inter-dependency: it quantifies the intensity of the dynamics of a cascade phenomena, and it gives a direct interpretation of the direction of the cascade.

To extend the concept to two generic infrastructure i and j and to compute the relative duration we introduce the measure of duration of outages $T(\cdot)$ defined as the time interval the QoS level provided by an infrastructure deviates from the desired level. Therefore, the temporal scale of inter-dependency between two infrastructures i and j is defined as $td(i, j) = \frac{T(i \mid j)}{T(j)}$ where $T(i \mid j)$ is the duration of miss behavior in infrastructure i due to malfunctioning in infrastructure j, and $T(j)$ is the duration of miss behaviors in infrastructure j. $td(i,j)$ takes into account the coupling between i and j in both directions. Indeed $T(j)$ counts also the QoS degradations in j that have root in i (feedbacks). The generalization to more then one infrastructure is straightforward.

If $td(i,j)$ is less than 1 it means that the dependent infrastructure i has self healing properties or the recovery or protection mechanisms from the faults are very fast, that is it is capable to rapidly recover from the failure by them selves and then that it is capable to mitigate the dependency effect. On the contrary if the ratio $td(i,j) \geq 1$ the dependent infrastructure is strongly coupled with the root of failures.

4.5 Scale of Criticality

In the MIA project we have decided to introduce a Scale of Criticality, intended as a a comprehensive framework that orchestrates the optimal use of different models and metrics. There are two main reasons to introduce a scale of criticality. First, the results of metrics must be normalized in a standard scale that makes easy to understand the severity of inter-dependencies and the associated potential impacts and conditions for the verification of the events causing the interdependencies. Second, decision maker (often familiar with risk analysis concepts) should be abstracted by the physical meaning of a metric.

In the MIA project we use the five colors scale of criticality defined as follow: *Low* (Green), routine procedures are implemented to preclude inter-dependencies; *Guarded* (Blue) general potentiality of an activation of inter-dependency with no specific conditions; *Elevated* (Yellow) elevated potentiality of an activation of inter-dependency with no specific conditions; *High* (Orange), high potentiality of an activation of interdependency in relation with some events/conditions; *Severe* (Red) an inter-dependency has occurred or credible can be imminent. This condition is declared for a specific critical situation.

The mapping of metrics values into the grade of criticality is a process that requires interaction with the stakeholders and the definition of the thresholds values depend on the specific infrastructure. In the MIA project we have proposed threshold values for each metric (except for analytical approach metrics) with the only purpose to show how the scale of criticality concept can be applied.

5 Metrics Evaluation

The MIA consortium, being costly and out of the project commitment to setup a unique real test-bed for metrics comparison, has agreed to evaluate the proposed metrics on the following three case studies (for more details see [4]).

The *Rome area* case study reproduces the power generation network of the Rome province area and a realistic but not real communication network connecting power grid nodes in the same area. This case study is modeled using the topological approach and the cyber and physical dependencies are evaluated by means of the Topological Robustness Metric.

The *Rome mini-telco black-out* case study is the same adopted in the IRRIIS project [6] and reproduce the portion of the telecommunication and power grid network that was effected by the flooding of a Telecom Italia major telecommunication service node has occurred in Rome on January the 2nd 2004. This case study is evaluated using a SimCIP simulation model and the cyber and physical dependencies are evaluated by means of ratio of dependency and time scale of criticality.

The *power plant* case study permits to put in evidence the interdependencies inside a single power plant connected to the transmission network and in the specific the cyber-interdpendency. In the case of the power plant the PS components involved in the analysis are the following. Three Control Systems: Automatic Voltage Regulator (AVR), Power System Stabilizer and Reactive load power and voltage regulator. An electrical infrastructure: the generator. Two Communication Network associated to the AVR and to the SART. This case study is evaluated using the Analytical approach.

5.1   Main Project Findings

Some results from metrics evaluation are reported in Tables 2.

First, is evident as the use of a scale of criticality allows to easily communicate to a decision maker (not necessarily aware of inter-dependency metrics and of the theoretical background behind them) that, for example, the ICT-PS system coupling is characterized by a mutual low/guarded level of criticality (that is a failure in one system impact with a very low probability the behavior of the other system). On the contrary, respect to the time to recover from failure, the criticality of ICT-PS coupling is classified as elevated.

Second, we observe that, independently from the models and case studies considered and the assumed simplifications on data and models, all metrics give more or less the same result: the ICT and PS networks have a Low/Guarded dependency in both directions (cyber and physical) and in the specific when the Telco network is N-1 robust.

Third, the Temporal scale of physical dependencies shows that the "time to recovery after the faults" assumes basically the same values for the Telco and Power infrastructure (for the specific case study). However, the value less then one shows that, in the specific case study, the PS infrastructure has a self-healing property and it is capable to recover from the malfunctioning earlier than the ICT infrastructure, that is the root cause of malfunctioning.

Table 2. Some metrics values computed in the case studies evaluation and mapped into the scale of criticality

Level of Criticality	Dimensions of analysis		
	Physical	Cyber	Temporal
Low	$TRM = 0.0076$	$TRM = 0.0019$ $TRM = 0.0014$	
Guarded	$rd(ICT, PS) = 0.205$		
Elevated			$td(ICT, PS) = 0.81$

Forth, the interdependencies among infrastructures are clearly represented by the transfer functions between the input of one infrastructure and the output of the other one. In fact, applying the dynamical system theory tools it is possible to analyze the frequency responses and the stability regions of interdependent system. These analysis allow characterizing the critical behaviors of the infrastructures.

Fifth, the modeling approaches and the metrics adopted are general enough that can be exported and applied to different networks bot at regional and national scale and also to other EU countries [5]. Of course the specific results obtained in the case studies can not be generalized neither at national level nor at international level.

Finally, concerning the model scalability, the modeling approach that scale up with the size of the network is the topological one. Indeed graph model of any size can be easily analyzed [5]. Of course the data gathering phase needed to parametrize the model and the parameterization of the model itself is more time costly than the model resolution. On the contrary, the analytical and simulation based models are, of course, less scalable. While the application at regional or national level it plausible, the application at wide european scale it's very difficult.

6   Conclusions and Outlook

The MIA project has contributed to the field of inter-dependencies analysis as follow. A methodology for inter-dependencies metrics quantification has been proposed. The ICT-PS coupling has been modeled using different theories and the proposed models has been evaluated on specific and realistic case studies. A set of inter-dependencies metrics has been defined. The proposed metrics are capable to measure physical and cyber dependencies, as well as the temporal scale of cyber dependencies. Not reported experiments (that will be bring to the conference if paper acceptance) show that there are also metrics capable to evaluate geographical dependencies and the economical impact of dependencies.

The MIA project is a first step toward the definition of a comprehensive framework for ICT-PS coupling evaluation. The proposed modeling approaches and related metrics are general enough to be exported to other case studied both at regional and national level. It is open the problem of EU scalability intended as the modeling of the entire EU ICT-PS network. To achieve EU scalability there are limitation both from a modeling and from a data gathering point of view. This two aspects are strictly related because the model selection and therefore the inter-dependency metrics that can be computed, depends on the the data available for model parameterization and workload characterization.

Acknowledgement

This publication reflects the views only of the authors, and the Commission cannot be held responsible for any use which may be made of the information contained therein. Authors gratefully thank G. Condorelli, C. Caruso, B. Di Carlo, G. Fiorenza, A. Gazzini and all co- workers of the MIA Project.

References

1. Rinaldi, S.M., Peerenboom, J.P., Kelly, T.K.: Identifying, Understanding and Analyzing Critical Infrastructure Interdependencies. IEEE Control Systems Magazine, 11–25 (December 2001)
2. Rosato, V., D' Agostino, G.: Determination of the topological properties of network structure and nature of interdependency couplings. MIA Activity 2 Report (2009)
3. Brasca, C.L., Ciapessoni, E.: Coupling identification and measurement methodology at the service level. MIA Activity 3 Report (2010)
4. Buschi, S., Casalicchio, E., Brasca, C.L., Ciapessoni, E., D'Agostino, G., Fioriti, V.: Definition of a Metric for ICT-PS infrastructures. MIA Activity 4 Report (2010)
5. Buschi, S., Casalicchio, E., Brasca, C.L., Ciapessoni, E., D' Agostino, G., Fioriti, V.: Extension of ideas & methodologies to EU networks. MIA Activity 5 Report (2010)
6. Klein, R., Rome, E., Beyel, C., Linnemann, R., Reinhardt, W., Usov, A.: Information modelling and simulation in large interdependent critical infrastructures in IRRIIS. In: Setola, R., Geretshuber, S. (eds.) CRITIS 2008. LNCS, vol. 5508, pp. 36–47. Springer, Heidelberg (2009)
7. Usov, A., Beyel, C.: Simulating interdependent Critical Infrastructures with SimCIP, vol. 4(3). European CIIP Newsletter (November/December 2008)
8. Zimmerman, R., Restrepo, C.E.: The Next Step: Quantifying Infrastructure Interdependencies to Improve Security. International Journal of Critical Infrastructures (2006)
9. Zimmerman, R.: Electricity case: economic cost estimation factors for economic assessment of terrorist attacks (2005)
10. Rosato, V., Issacharoff, L., Gianese, G., Bologna, S.: Influence of the topology on the power flux of the Italian high-voltage electr. network, arXiV:0909.1664.1664v1
11. Rosato, V., Tiriticco, F., Issacharoff, L., De Porcellinis, S., Setola, R.: Modelling interdependent infrastructures using interacting dynamical models. Int. J. Crit. Infrastr. 4, 63 (2008)
12. Bloomfield, R., et al.: Infrastructure interdependency analysis, Adelard (2009)

A Quantitative Risk Analysis Approach for Deliberate Threats

Nikos Vavoulas and Christos Xenakis

Department of Digital Systems, University of Piraeus, Greece
{Vavoulas,xenakis}@unipi.gr

Abstract. Recently, organizations around the world are becoming aware of the need to run risk management programs in order to enhance their information security. However, the majority of the existing qualitative/empirical methods fail to adhere to the terminology defined by ISO 27000-series and treat deliberate threats in a misleading way. In this paper, a quantitative risk analysis approach for deliberate threats is introduced. The proposed approach follows the steps suggested by the ISO 27005 standard for risk management, extending them in order to focus on deliberate threats and the different information security incidents that realize them. It is based on three-levels: the conceptual foundation level, the modeling tools level and the mathematical foundation level. The conceptual foundation level defines and analyzes the terminology involved, using unified modeling language (UML) class diagrams. The modeling tools level introduces certain tools that assist in modeling the relations among different concepts. Finally, the mathematical foundation level includes all the different mathematical formulas and techniques used to estimate risk values for each threat.

Keywords: risk analysis, quantitative, deliberate threat, risk estimation, risk identification.

1 Introduction

More and more organizations around the world are becoming aware of the need to run a risk management program in order to enhance their information security. *Risk management* includes coordinated activities to direct and control an organization with regard to risk [3][4]. Standardization organizations, such as NIST (National Institute of Standards and Technology) and ISO (International Organization for Standardization), have issued risk management guides [5][6], in an attempt to create a common language, providing both the definitions and the practical guidance necessary for assessing and mitigating risks related to potential information security incidents, identified within Information Technology (IT) systems. An information security incident is a single or a series of unwanted or unexpected information security events, which have a significant probability of compromising business operations and threatening information security. On the other hand, an information security event is an identified occurrence of a system, service or network state indicating a possible breach of information security, policy or failure of controls, or a previously unknown situation that may be security relevant [9].

C. Xenakis and S. Wolthusen (Eds.): CRITIS 2010, LNCS 6712, pp. 13–25, 2011.
© Springer-Verlag Berlin Heidelberg 2011

A risk may arise through three different kinds of threats: environmental, accidental or deliberate. The risk related to environmental and accidental threats in most cases, can be adequately described by empirical/qualitative data. However, the same data may not be able to describe adequately the risk related to deliberate threats. IT systems operate in a menacing environment that constantly changes and thus past data may not necessarily describe a present situation. Things may become even worse when dealing with threats that are realized through technological vulnerability exploitation. New vulnerabilities are discovered in a daily basis in both hardware and software, allowing new attacks, with no previous of occurrence and thus limited or zero data about them. CERT (Computer Emergency Response Team) has catalogued over 21000 vulnerabilities from 2006 to 2008 [7]. Moreover, older vulnerabilities may become easier to exploit through time, since technology advances and becomes cheaper or implemented controls are becoming inefficient. Finally, empirical data and attack statistics are scarce [8], since organizations are reluctant to publish information regarding the attacks on their systems, for fear that the same or similar vulnerability will be exploited by other attackers, or for fear of suffering reputational damage.

Deliberate threats also differ from the other two threat categories (i.e., environmental and accidental) as it is the only threat category, which involves a specific type of information security events: the attacks. Each attack is related with a different probability of occurrence and consequence value, and thus, a different risk value. In many cases a single threat is realized by launching more than one attacks. Therefore, in order to estimate the risk of a deliberate threat, all different attacks, attacks series and the relations among them should be examined. Deliberate threats are complicated by nature, with many unforeseen aspects and thus should be elaborated in details in order to get full results from the risk analysis process. All the above mentioned issues clearly show the need to develop and adopt quantitative risk analysis methods which can be used either as stand-alone methods or as enhancements to the current methods that use qualitative/empirical data.

In this work, an in-depth quantitative risk analysis approach for deliberate threats is introduced. The proposed approach follows the steps suggested by ISO 27005 standard for risk management [5], extending them in order to focus on deliberate threats and the different information security incidents that realize them. It is based on three-levels: the conceptual foundation level, the modeling tools level and the mathematical foundation level. The conceptual foundation level is achieved by using class diagrams of the unified modeling language (UML) that follow the risk analysis terminology defined in ISO 27005 [5]. This level is further facilitated by the modeling tools and the mathematical foundation level. The proposed modeling tools help in modeling conceptually the relations among different concepts. Finally, the mathematical foundation level includes all the different mathematical formulas and techniques used to estimate risk values for each threat.

The remainder of this work is organized as follows: Section 2 discusses the limitations of current risk analysis approaches that motivate this work. Section 3 presents the conceptual and mathematical background that this approach is based on, as well as the tools that uses. In section 4 the entire approach is described, step-by-step, while section 5 provides a theoretical example of this. Finally, section 6 outlines the conclusions and future work.

2 Motivation

ISO 27005 [5] is a standard of the ISO 27000-series concerning information security risk management. It includes definitions about the main concepts involved in risk management, as well as a detailed description of the processes involved. According to ISO 27005, risk analysis is a group of two distinct processes that are involved in risk management: risk identification and risk estimation. Risk identification is the process where the unwanted events that may cause potential loss are determined. On the other hand, risk estimation is the process where qualitative or quantitative values concerning the probability and the consequences of the identified events are assigned. ISO 27005 describes generically all the steps required to perform a risk analysis but it does not propose any specific qualitative or quantitative risk analysis approach.

Currently, there are several qualitative risk analysis approaches/methods such as CRAMM [10], CORAS [14], OCTAVE [15] etc., some of which are widely used. Most of these methods are either incompatible or partially compatible with ISO 27000-series in terms of the conceptual foundation, the results and the steps that should be followed in risk analysis, since some of these methods pre-existed ISO 27000-series and its ancestors (i.e. BS 7799 part one and part two). CRAMM is one of the oldest risk analysis methods, which lately has incorporated an add-on in its supporting tool (version 5) [10] that it maps the suggested countermeasures with the ISO 27001 and ISO 27002 suggested controls. However, CRAMM still remains incompatible with ISO 27000-series since it uses terms, such as risk management, with completely different meaning. The entire set of available risk analysis methods (i.e., including CRAMM) considers different types of threats using the same processing steps and a certain level of details. This can be proved misleading for deliberate threats, which usually present an elevated level of complexity (i.e. dependence among attack events, different threat-source capabilities etc.). Moreover, some of most widely used risk analysis methods focus on the business perspective regarding risk. However, in deliberate threats, attackers' perspective is also important, since what the organization wants to protect not necessarily identifies with what a malicious can/wants to attack. Furthermore, qualitative approaches do not provide a basis for a cost-benefit analysis making difficult to justify investments in control implementation.

Recently, a few quantitative risk analysis approaches have been proposed, that try to address some of the limitations of the aforementioned methods. Zaobin Gal et al. have presented a risk estimation methodology for information systems [11], which introduces a "through the eyes of the adversary" approach. In this work, they propose the use of an extended version of the Shneier's attack trees [1, 2]. An attack tree represents the attacks that realize a threat as a tree structure. The root node represents the goal of the attack, while the leaf nodes represent the different attacks needed in order to accomplish the goal. The extended version of attack trees covers the case of attacks launched under the condition that other attack(s) preceded. Another study that focuses on the risk assessment of VoIP call interception [12], proposes a formal risk assessment method, which includes two modeling techniques: attack trees and vulnerability dependency graphs. While attack trees are used to model the threat under examination (VoIP call interception), the vulnerability dependency graphs present the dependencies among the identified vulnerabilities and how these vulnerabilities interact to each other. Although, both of the quantitative approaches mentioned above provide an in-depth level of risk analysis for deliberate threats, they are attacker driven only, focusing on the probability of a vulnerability being exploited rather than the consequences that an organization would suffer. Furthermore, there are no ISO-compatible, limiting their use, and do not consider multiple attacker profiles. However, some of the ideas proposed in these approaches are adopted, extended and optimized in this work, in an attempt to make some steps towards a risk analysis method for deliberate threats, free of the limitations and deficiencies mentioned above.

3 Proposed Approach

The proposed risk analysis approach for deliberate threats consists of three distinct levels of details (see figure 1). The highest is the conceptual foundation level, which defines and analyzes the terminology involved using UML class diagrams. The intermediate is the modeling tools level, which introduces certain tools that help in modeling conceptually the relations among different concepts. Finally, the bottom level is the mathematical foundation level, which includes all the different mathematical formulas and techniques used to estimate risk values for each threat.

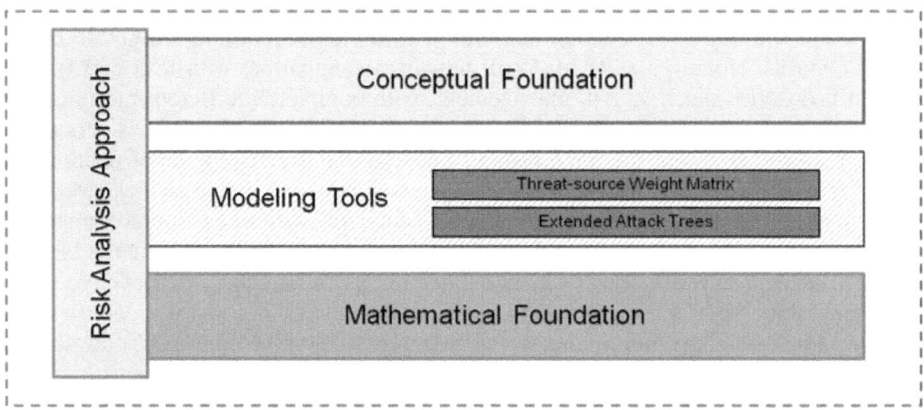

Fig. 1. The proposed three-level risk analysis approach

3.1 Conceptual Foundation

The conceptual foundation level achieves concept formalization using UML class diagrams [13]. The latter present, formally, how different concepts, involved in risk analysis, are related and which attributes of each concept participate in the risk estimation process. In order to create these diagrams, the concepts involved in the proposed risk analysis approach for deliberate threats should be identified and defined.

As mentioned previously, ISO 27005 classifies threats into three main categories: deliberate, accidental and environmental. Each of these categories is directly related to a set of concepts involved in a risk analysis process. An exception is the deliberate threats, which are related to an extra concept; the concept of "attack" (see Table 1). In the following, the concepts that are involved in the proposed risk analysis approach for deliberate threats, are defined according to the ISO 27000-series:

Table 1. Concepts related with different threat categories

	Environmental	Accidental	Deliberate
Asset	✓	✓	✓
Risk	✓	✓	✓
Vulnerability	✓	✓	✓
Threat-source	✓	✓	✓
Attack	✗	✗	✓

- Asset is "anything that has value to the organization" and which therefore requires protection.
- Threat is the potential cause of an unwanted event (i.e., an attack), which may result in harm of a system or organization.
- Vulnerability is a weakness of an asset or control (i.e., in ISO 27000-series, a control is a synonym of a countermeasure), which may be exploited by a threat. This general definition covers all threats categories. However, for deliberate threats, vulnerability is a weakness of an asset or control, which may be exploited by an attack to realize a threat.
- Risk is the combination of the probability of an event and its consequence.
- Attack is an attempt to destroy, expose, alter, disable, steal or gain unauthorized access to or make unauthorized use of an asset.
- Threat-source is anyone whose intention is to exploit an asset's vulnerability, launching an attack and thus, realizing a threat. Threat-source is a synonym of an attacker.

Figure 2, presents the UML class diagram of the concepts defined above using three different types of relations: association, aggregation and composition [13]. Association is represented with a simple line between two classes and denotes a simple relationship between two classes. Aggregation is represented with a transparent diamond shape and denotes a part-whole or part-of relationship between two classes. Finally, composition is represented with a solid diamond shape and denotes a strong life-death relationship between classes. Notation at the ends of each relation in the diagram is called multiplicity and indicates the number of objects that participate in the relation. For example, in figure 2 we can see that a threat may harm one or more (1...*) assets. On the other hand, an asset might be at risk by zero or more threats (0...*).

As illustrated in the UML diagram, deliberate threats are realized through information security incidents which involve the occurrence of one or more attacks. The latter exploit one or more of the asset's vulnerabilities to realize threats, and thus, harm the assets. The self-association of the attack class represents attacks series (i.e., a sequence of attacks) realizing one or more threats. Attack series may be either dependent events (i.e., occurrence of one affects occurrence of another) or independent events (i.e., occurrence of one does not affect occurrence of another).

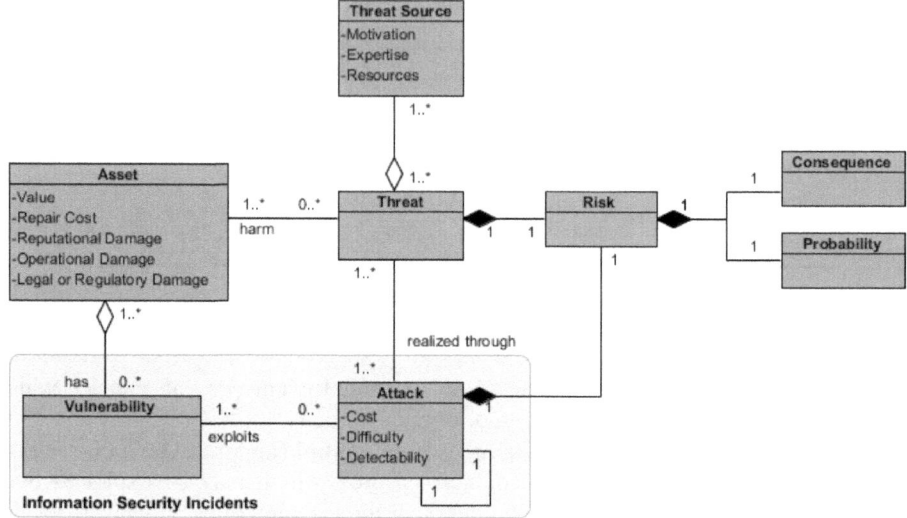

Fig. 2. UML class diagram for the proposed risk analysis approach

A threat may harm one or more assets and is related with one or more threat-sources. The aggregation relation between these two classes (i.e., threat and threat-source) denotes that if a threat is removed, then the same threat-sources may still exist for other threats. The risk analysis process estimates a risk value for each identified threat. This value is related to the probability of each threat to be realized and the corresponding consequences that occur. As mentioned previously, deliberate threats may be realized through one or more attacks, each of which has its own probability of occurrence and consequences, and, thus, its own risk value (Figure 2). The estimated risk value of a threat equals to the maximum risk value of all single attacks or series of attacks, which realize the threat. Consequently, risk values of the identified attacks and series of attacks should be estimated prior to estimating the risk value of the related threat. Since each threat is related with a unique risk value, if this threat is removed, then the corresponding risk value no longer exists. To represent this life-death dependency between the threat class and the risk class, as well as between the risk class and the attack class, the composition relation is employed.

Each of the concepts identified and modeled formally using the UML class diagrams, has certain attributes that should be considered during the risk estimation process. Some of these attributes are related to the probability of occurrence of a threat; while others are related to the consequences following the threat occurrence. However, not all of these attributes are always relevant with the threat under examination, and thus, each case should be studied separately. The attributes, which are included in the modeled concepts of the proposed approach and consider both business and attackers' perspectives, are:

- Threat-source
    - Motivation: what motivates a particular threat-source (or attacker) to launch an attack.

- o Expertise: the level of knowledge of a particular threat-source (or attacker) related to an attack.
- o Resources: the resources (money, equipment) that a particular threat-source (or attacker) has in its possession.
- Attack
  - o Cost: the cost of equipment needed to launch an attack.
  - o Difficulty: the level of expertise needed for someone to launch an attack.
  - o Detectability: the easiness or difficulty of an attack being detected.
- Asset
  - o Value: the value of a specific asset (it may also be considered as the cost of replacement).
  - o Repair Cost: the cost to repair an asset.
  - o Reputational Damage: the damage in reputation occurs if an asset is compromised.
  - o Operational Damage: the damage occurs in an organization's or system's operation due to the compromised asset.
  - o Legal and Regulatory Damage: the fines and penalties that will be paid because of the compromised asset.

3.2 The Modeling Tools

The modeling tools used in the proposed risk analysis include: (i) the threat-source profile matrix and (ii) the extended attack trees. The chosen tools link the conceptual with the mathematical foundation level of the proposed approach, as explained bellow.

The Threat-source Profile Matrix. The threat-source profile matrix is a two-dimensional matrix, which contains the weights of the attributes involved in an attack probability estimation (i.e. cost, difficulty, detectability) for all different threat-sources. The UML class diagram of Section 3.1, shows that a threat is related with one or more threat-sources. Each threat-source has each own motivation, resources and expertise level and thus there is a different probability for each threat-source exercising a specific attack. For example, the high cost of an attack wouldn't be for a professional hacker as deterrent as it would be for a script kiddy. In other words, while the cost attribute does not carry too much weight in the attack probability estimation for a professional hacker, it does for script kiddies which have limited resources. In order to reflect this diversity in probability values for different threat sources, profiles are created by assigning weight values for each attribute taking part in an attack probability estimation.

The Extended Attack Trees. Attack Trees [1] [2] represent a formal method of representing the varying of attacks that a system is exposed to, using a tree structure. The root node of the tree symbolize an identified threat, while the leaf nodes stand for the information security events (single attacks or attacks series) that realize the specific threat. The intermediate nodes of the tree can be either alternative subgoals, each one satisfying the parent goal (OR Nodes), or partial subgoals, whose composition satisfies the parent goal (AND Nodes). In a compound system there are several threats and consequently, attack trees, which form an attack forest. Attack trees can be illustrated both graphically and textually. However, graphical representation is not appropriate for composite systems, due to the enormous size that the tree could reach. In the proposed risk analysis approach, an extended version of the attack trees [11], which incorporates the CAND (Conditional AND) node is used. The classic attack trees cannot formally represent all the previously described information security incidents. Although the AND nodes of a tree can be used for depicting attacks series of independent events, they cannot be used for attacks series of dependent events, where the attacks occur under certain occurrence conditions. This is achieved by adding the CAND node (i.e., extended attacks trees). The CAND relation between nodes represent that the upper node is accomplished if all sub-nodes are attained under certain conditions.

3.3 Mathematical Foundation

As mentioned previously, the risk is the combination of the probability of an attack event and its consequences. In this approach, the risk value of an attack is derived by multiplying the probability of occurrence value of the attack with the estimated consequences, as shown in equation (1):

$$Risk(Attack) = P(Attack) \times C(Attack) \tag{1}$$

In order to estimate the attack probability value, utility curves from the multi-attribute utility theory are adopted that convert the attribute values into utilities. In the current approach, the utility curve chosen is the $U(x)=1/x$. We chose this utility function because the probability attributes are in inverse proportion with the probability itself. Furthermore, it can accurately represent residual risk as the probability can never become equal to zero. Risk can only become equal to zero if the consequences are equal to zero or the corresponding vulnerability is removed. Each utility is then multiplied by the corresponding weight of the threat-source under examination and summed up to the probability value, as shown in equation (2):

$$P(Attack) = W_{cost} \times U(cost) + W_{diff} \times U(diff) + W_{dete} \times U(dete) \tag{2}$$

Where:
cost = Cost of an attack,
diff = Difficulty of an attack,
dete= Detectability of an attack,
Wcost = weight of the attack cost for a specific threat-source,
Wdiff = weight of the attack difficulty for a specific threat-source,
Wdete = weight of the attack detectability for a specific threat-source,
U(x) = utility function of the attributes.

The consequences of an attack equal to the sum of the related asset attribute values, as shown in equation (3). These attributes are: the asset value, the repair cost, the reputational damage, the operational damage and the legal damage, as defined in section 3.1.

$$C(Attack) = assetValue + repaCost + repuDam + OperDam + LegalDam \quad (3)$$

In order to estimate the risk of a specific threat, a risk aggregation over the constructed attack tree is required. Starting from the leafs and moving toward the root of the tree, the total risk value is aggregated according to the following:
In the OR nodes, the total risk value equals to the maximum risk value of its sub-nodes (SubN), as shown in equation (4):

$$Risk(N) = MAX(Risk(SubN_1), Risk(SubN_2), \ldots, Risk(SubN_i)) \quad (4)$$

In the AND and CAND nodes, the total risk value equals to the product of the joint probability of the sub-node events and the total consequences of the sub-node events (equation 5).

$$Risk(N) = P(SubN1 \cap SubN2 \cap \ldots \cap SubNi) \; x \\ C(SubN1 \cap SubN2 \cap \ldots \cap SubNi) \quad (5)$$

Where:

$$C(SubN_1 \cap SubN_2 \cap \ldots \cap SubN_i) = C(SubN_1) + C(SubN_2) + \cdots + C(SubN_i) \quad (6)$$

The joint probability of the sub-node events for independent attack series events equals to the product of the probabilities of each independent attack event (equation 7). On the other hand, the joint probability of the sub-node events for order-dependent attack series equals to the product of the probabilities of each attack event, in series, given the preceding events (equation 8).

$$P(SubN_1 \cap SubN_2 \cap \ldots \cap SubN_i) = P(SubN_1) x \; P(SubN_2) x \ldots x P(SubN_i) \quad (7)$$

$$P(SubN_1 \cap SubN_2 \cap \ldots \cap SubN_i) = \\ P(SubN_1) \; x \; (SubN_2|SubN_1) x \ldots x (SubN_i|SubN_{i-1} \ldots SubN_2 SubN_1) \quad (8)$$

4 Risk Analysis Approach: Step-by-Step

This section summarizes and presents the proposed risk analysis approach. It consists of two distinct processes: (a) risk identification and (b) risk estimation, each of which comprises a set of specific steps that are analysed bellow.

Risk Identification Process

The purpose of risk identification is twofold: (i) to determine what might happen causing potential loss, and (ii) to gain insight into how, where and why the loss occurs. To achieve this, both the business and the attacker's point-of-view should be taken into consideration. The risk identification process consists of the following five (5) steps:

Step 1: Asset Identification. In this step, anything that is important to the organization should be considered. This includes both primary assets (i.e., such as business processes/activities or information) and secondary (i.e., such as hardware, software, network, personnel, site and organization's structure). Assets' identification can be performed in various levels of details. However, the most appropriate is the one that provides sufficient information for the risk estimation process, which follows risk identification. However, since risk analysis is a recurrent procedure, the level of detail can be changed, accordingly, in further iterations of the risk analysis process.

Step 2: Threat Identification. In this step, anything that threatens assets and originates from deliberate threat-sources should be identified. These threats may arise either from inside or outside the organization. Threats should be identified as general as possible and elaborated further (i.e, going into a greater level of details), where appropriate. For every identified threat, possible threat-sources should be defined. Moreover, for each threat-source, a profile should be created giving weights to each attack attribute, using the threat-source profile matrix described in section 3.2.

Step 3: Existing Controls Identification. In this step, existing controls, if any, are identified in order to avoid unnecessary work in the next steps of the risk analysis process. According to ISO 27000, a control is the synonym of a countermeasure. Controls may reduce, minimize or even abolish the risk of a potential threat. Furthermore, in this step the efficiency of the existing controls should be verified. In many cases controls does not work as expected, creating new vulnerabilities, which should be treated either by replacing them or by implementing complementary controls.

Step 4: Vulnerability Identification. In this step, the vulnerabilities that may harm assets should be identified. Vulnerabilities may exist in an organization, processes and procedures, management routines, personnel, physical environment, information system configuration, hardware, software or even related external parties.

Step 5: Information Security Incident Identification and Identification of Corresponding Consequences. This step gets as input the identified assets, threats and vulnerabilities of the previous step and identifies the entire set of information security incidents, related to the identified threats. As mentioned above, information security incidents fall into three main categories: single attacks, independent attacks series events, and dependent attacks series events. Furthermore, the consequences that will occur by a security incident should be identified in terms of asset value, repair cost, reputational damage, operational damage and legal damage, as defined in section 3.1.

Risk Estimation Process

This process estimates, quantitatively, the risk of each threat using the tools and the mathematical formulas, described in sections 3.2 and 3.3, respectively.

Step 1: Assigning Values to Probability and Consequences Attributes. In this step specific values are assigned to each attribute related to the probability of occurrence and consequences of the identified attacks. In case of order-dependent attacks series, the attack should be examined as part of a sequence of events.

Step 2: Mapping Information Security Incidents with Threats. This step involves the construction of an attack forest. For each threat, a separate attack tree is constructed, as described in section 3.2. Extra nodes that represent intermediate system states or sub-threats should be added where necessary.

Step 3: Aggregating Risk using Attack Trees. In this step, the risk is aggregated from the leafs to the root of a tree, using the formulas described in 3.3.

5   A Simple Example

In this section, we provide a simple example where the proposed risk analysis approach is applied as a proof of concept, omitting the details of the system (such as assets, threats, vulnerabilities and attacks). After identifying the system's assets and the corresponding threats, the potential threat-source profiles should be determined. For the provided example, the following three attacker's profiles have been defined: (i) Professionals, (ii) Hackers/Crackers, and (iii) Script Kiddies (see Table 2). Using the threat-source profile matrix, weight values are assigned to each probability attribute, based on each attacker's expertise, motivation and resources.

It is assumed that the system under examination does not implement any security control. Moreover, it is assumed that after examining the system's vulnerabilities for a specific threat, three potential information security incidents have been identified: (1) a single attack incident, (2) an independent attacks series incident, and (3) a dependent attack series incident. Incident 1 consists of single attack A1. Incident 2 consists of attacks A2 and A3 which are two mutually independent events. Incident 3 consists of attacks A4, A5 and A6 which are three dependent events (i.e., A5 occurs under the condition that A4 have occurred and A6 occurs under the condition that both A4 and A5 have occurred). For all the attacks taking part in each identified incident, the values of attributes that are related to the probability of occurrence are assigned (see Table 3). Finally, it is assumed that the consequences of all the incidents are constant and equal to C.

Drawing the information security incidents to the single identified threat, we provide the following extended attack tree:

Theat 1
OR 1. Incident 1
    OR 1.1 Attack 1
    2. Incident 2
  AND 2.1 Attack 2
       2.2 Attack 3
    3. Incident 3
  CAND 3.1 Attack 4
       3.2 Attack 5
       3.2 Attack 6

Table 2. Threat-source Profile Matrix

	Professionals	Hackers/Crackers	Script Kiddies
Wcost	0.1	0.3	0.4
Wdetectability	0.6	0.4	0.2
Wdifficulty	0.3	0.3	0.4

Table 3. Assigned to each attack attribute values

	Incident 1	Incident 2		Incident 3		
	A1	A2	A3	A4	A5I A4	A6IA5A4
Cost	2	2	3	2	2	1
Detectability	3	1	4	2	1	1
Difficulty	4	3	1	1	1	1

Table 4. Attack occurrence probabilities

Incident 1	Incident 2		Incident 3		
P(A1)	P(A2)	P(A3)	P(A4)	P(A5I A4)	P(A6IA5A4)
0.30	0.55	0.70	0.65	0.95	1

Assuming now that we want to estimate the risk of a professional hacker realizing the threat under study. The probability of occurrence of one of the above mentioned attacks (i.e., incidents 1,2,3) by a professional hacker, according to the equation (2) and table 2, equals to:

$$P(Attack) = 0.1 \times U(cost) + 0.6 \times U(diff) + 0.3 \times U(detect)$$

By applying cost, difficulty and detectability values (see table 3) to the formula above, we get the results included in table 4:

Aggregating risk from the leafs to the root of the tree, using the equations (2), (7), (8), for each node of the tree, we get the following results:

$$P(Incident\ 1) = P(A1) = 0.30,$$
$$P(Incident\ 2) = P(A2)\ x\ P(A3) = 0.385,$$
$$P(Incident\ 3) = P(A4)\ x\ P(A5|A4)\ x\ PP(A6|A4A5) = 0.6175.$$

The risk of the root node (OR node), using the equation (4), equals to the maximum risk value of the sub-nodes, and thus:

$$Risk(Threat) = MAX\big(Risk(Incident\ 1), Risk(Incident\ 2), Risk(Incident\ 3)\big)$$
$$= MAX(0.30\ x\ C, 0.385\ x\ C, 0.385\ x\ C) = 0.6175\ x\ C$$

6   Conclusions and Future Work

In this work, a quantitative risk analysis approach for deliberate threats is proposed and analyzed. The conceptual and mathematical foundations of the approach, as well as the tools that facilitate the process of risk estimation are elaborated. The entities and attributes that take part in the risk analysis are defined and represented, graphically, using UML class diagrams. Moreover, the tool of threat-source profile matrix is introduced in order to get insights into who and how is more likely to attack to the system under examination. The specific steps of the proposed approach are defined and analyzed, in details, and all the necessary mathematical functions are explained. Finally, a simple example of the proposed approach is presented as a proof of concept.

This work sets the scene for a full quantitative risk analysis approach for deliberate threats. In contrast to the existing methods/approaches, it is fully ISO 27005 compatible and provides a suitable level of details for deliberate threats, taking into account both the attacker and business perspectives. It provides guidance into what should be measured and how should be used in order to estimate the risk of the identified threats, but it does not provide a way how to make these measurements. Although attributes such as the cost of an attack might be easy to be measured, attributes such as the difficulty of an attack or the reputational damage can be proved highly subjective. In future work, we plan to identify ways to measure all or part of these attributes independently of the analysts' subjectivity (i.e., different analysts will be able to reproduce the same results). Furthermore, it is planned to implement the proposed approach in a real system.

References

1. Shneier, B.: Attack Trees: Modeling security threats. Dr. Dobb's Journal (1999), http://www.schneier.com/paper-attacktrees-ddj-ft.html
2. Shneier, B.: Secrets & Lies: Digital Security in a Networked World. John Wiley & Sons, Chichester (2000)
3. International Organization for Standarization, ISO/IEC 27001, Information Technology – Security Techniques – Information Security Management systems – Requirements (2005)
4. International Organization for Standarization, ISO/IEC 27002, Information technology – Security techniques – Code of practice for information security management (2005)
5. International Organization for Standardization (ISO), ISO/IEC 27005: Information technology – Security techniques – Information security risk management (2008)
6. Stoneburner, G., Goguen, A., Feringa, A.: Risk Management Guide for Information Technology Systems. Recommendations of the National Institute of Standards and Technology, NIST (2002)
7. Computer Emergency Response Team (CERT), Carnegie Mellon University, Cert Statistics (Historical), http://www.cert.org/stats/
8. Moore, P.A., Ellison, J.R., Linger, C.R.: Attack Modeling for Information Security and Survivability. Carnegie Mellon University, Technical Note (2001)
9. International Organization for Standarization, ISO/IEC 27000, Information technology - Security techniques - Information security management systems - Overview and vocabulary (2009)
10. CRAMM User Guide, Version 5.0 & 5.1 (2005), http://www.cramm.com/
11. Zaobin, G., Jiufei, T., Ping, W., Vijay, V.: A Novel Security Risk Evaluation for Information Systems. In: Proceedings of the 2007 Japan-China Joint Workshop on Frontier of Computer Science and Technology, pp. 67–73 (2007)
12. Benini, M., Sicari, S.: Assessing the risk to intercept VoIP calls. Journal of Computer Networks 52(12), 2432–2446 (2008)
13. Object Management Group (OMG), Unified Modeling Language Specifications, http://www.omg.org/technology/documents/modeling_spec_catalog.htm#UML
14. The CORAS method, http://coras.sourceforge.net/
15. OCTAVE Information Security Risk Evaluation, http://www.cert.org/octave/

The EU FP6 Integrated Project IRRIIS on Dependent Critical Infrastructures
Summary and Conclusions

Rüdiger Klein

Fraunhofer IAIS, Schloss Birlinghoven, D-53754 Sankt Augustin
Ruediger.Klein@IAIS.Fraunhofer.de

Abstract. IRRIIS was an EU FP6 IST Integrated Project on "Integrated Risk Reduction of Information-based Infrastructure Systems". Whereas single Critical Infrastructures are well understood and managed today, dependencies and interdependencies between them are still a widely open issue within the same domain and across different domains. IRRIIS was focused on a comprehensive methodology, on integrated models and federated simulations of dependencies and interdependencies between Critical Infrastructures. The SimCIP system for federated simulation we developed and used in various cI use cases. An approach towards the communication between SCADA centers and risk estimation taking the situation in depending CIs into account will be presented here. Conclusions will be drawn, and challenges for future research in this area be identified.

Keywords: dependencies between Critical Infrastructures, modeling and simulation, communication between dependent CI, risk estimation.

1 Introduction

The following is a summary of the EU FP6 IST Integrated Project IRRIIS on "Integrated Risk Reduction of Information-based Infrastructure Systems" (see also [1]). IRRIIS started at 1st February, 2006 and ended after three and a half year in July 2009. Sixteen partners[1] from 10 European countries worked together in the challenging area of Critical Infrastructure Protection with a clear focus on dependencies and interdependencies.

Critical Infrastructures are of central importance for all European countries. There are a lot of new developments in this area resulting in fundamental changes on the technological, the organizational, the business, and the regulations level. They all result in growing dependencies between Critical Infrastructures within the same domain and across different domains.

The project IRRIIS is based on the idea of improved communication and information sharing between dependent Critical Infrastructures [9]. This is an important pre-requisite

---

[1] The partners were: Fraunhofer IAIS (D, coordinator), ACEA (I), AIS (Malta), Alcatel-Lucent (F), City Univ. London (UK), ENEA (I), ENST (F), ETHZ (Ch), Fraunhofer SIT (D), Grupo AIA (ES), IABG (D), RED (ES), Siemens (D), Telecom Italia (I), TNO (NL), and VTT (FI).

C. Xenakis and S. Wolthusen (Eds.): CRITIS 2010, LNCS 6712, pp. 26–42, 2011.

for dependency management of such Critical Infrastructures. It needs comprehensive analytical and methodological work in order to elaborate a deeper understanding of dependent Critical Infrastructures and their cumulative risk, it needs models and simulations for practical experiments and evaluations, and it needs a sophisticated concept of information sharing and risk evaluation. In order to achieve these goals IRRIIS has been based on three main objectives (see fig. 1):

- We determined private and public sector security and reliability requirements for Critical Infrastructures considering dependencies and interdependencies between them.

- We developed models and simulation techniques for the simulation of dependent and interdependent Critical Infrastructure in order to analyse their dependencies and to test and validate novel technologies to protect critical infrastructures against effects caused by interdependencies.

- We developed the Middleware Improved Technology (MIT) to facilitate communication within and between different critical infrastructures and to mitigate negative effects caused by interdependencies.

Critical Infrastructures are complex technical systems with various dependencies (for an overview, see for instance [2]). They have different characteristics in their behaviors and their risks [3, 6]. One of the main challenges of the IRRIIS project was to identify commonalities between such different systems enabling a common methodology, a common modeling and simulation approach, and common risk estimation and management techniques.

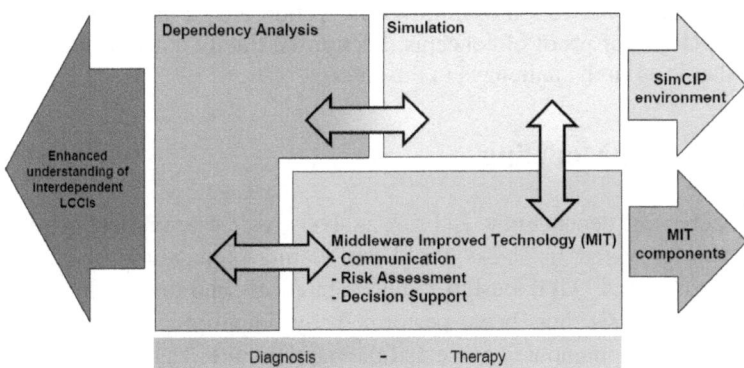

Fig. 1. Overview of IRRIIS with Dependency Analysis, Simulation, and MIT technology

As we will demonstrate within this report we developed methodologies for the analysis of Critical Infrastructures, modeling and simulation techniques, and ways to evaluate and manage risk in dependent Critical Infrastructures. These achievements are applicable to quite different types of CI. We focused our efforts on the two most important Critical Infrastructure types: electrical power grids and telecommunication networks, and on dependencies between them. Their services are essential for nearly every area in modern societies. This focus enables us to validate our approach in realistic use cases and scenarios. In parallel, we showed that our approach can be applied to other Critical Infrastructures as well.

The project follows a 'diagnosis – therapy' scheme and has three main areas of activities: Analysis and Research for 'diagnosis', the MIT system as 'therapy' and the simulation environment SimCIP for further 'diagnosis' and validation of the 'therapy'. All three areas are closely related to each other.

The paper is structured as follows: in Section 2 we summarize IRRIIS' results on analysis of dependencies in Critical Infrastructures and the conclusions drawn on modeling. In Section 3 we outline the IRRIIS Information Model as semantic top-level model for depending CIs which is built on the analysis and modeling conclusions of Section 2. The Preliminary Interdependency Analysis (PIA) methodology is outlined in Section 4 as a systematic approach towards light-weight dependency modeling and analysis. An important issue in dependency analysis of CIs is simulation outlines in Section 5. The behavior of such systems is too complex to be understood without simulations. Whereas today dedicated simulators exist for each CI they are too different for the various infrastructures to be used in simple integrated way. Federated simulation needs the IRRIIS Information Model as information backbone and a sophisticated federation architecture provided by the SimCIP agent based simulation platform. User interactions are of course an essential aspect in CI simulations, too. In Section 6 we outline the IRRIIS GUI, followed by a description of scenarios and experiments as methodology for dependency analysis in Section 7. Because dependent CIs need communication of their SCADA and control centers about their respective states the Middleware Improved Technology MIT was introduced in IRRIIS as communication platform between CIs. The main principles of MIT are introduced in Section 8, followed in section 9 by a brief outline of use cases built up in IRRIIS for proof of concepts. Section 10 finally contains the lessons learnt and formulates research challenges in this area.

2   Analysis and Modeling

Structure, behavior, dependency, and risk analysis were essential elements within our project. They provided the basis for the modeling, simulation, scenario building, experimentation, and MIT design, implementation, and evaluation activities. A detailed risk analysis has been performed by identifying possible threats and vulnerabilities. The potential damage and the incident rates have been estimated to get a detailed picture of the risk critical infrastructures are exposed to.

One of the main conclusions from IRRIIS is how the different aspects in Critical Infrastructure dependency analysis and understanding depend on each other. Methodology, data and models, scenarios, and simulations are based on each other and influence each other. One can not understand dependencies in CIs without realistic data and expressive models. One can not understand these models without complex simulations and without realistic scenarios.

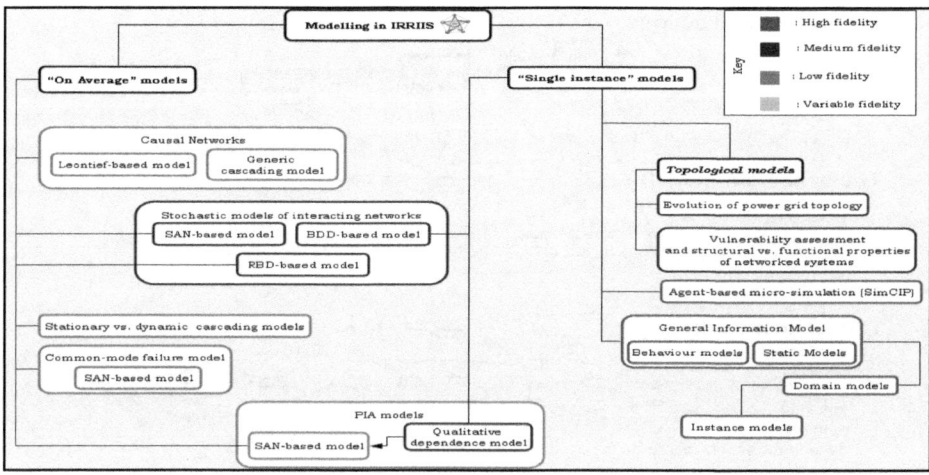

Fig. 2. The taxonomy of models of dependent Critical Infrastructures

This provides the basis for the "therapy" issue in IRRIIS: improved communication between Critical Infrastructures and risk estimation and decision support based on this information shared between dependent Critical Infrastructures.

A comprehensive compilation of information about different critical infrastructures has been collected and topology analyses have been performed. Vulnerabilities were identified from a topology point of view and strategies how to deal with these 'structural' vulnerabilities have been developed. A taxonomy of dependencies has been created and different models and approaches for dependency modeling of critical infrastructures have been developed.

Models and simulations are essential for the understanding of dependencies in Critical Infrastructures. Their structures and behaviors are too complex to be understood just on an analytical or empirical basis. Consequently, a main focus in our project was on the development of expressive and powerful models for critical infrastructures and their dependencies. These models provide the basis for simulation, diagnosis, and therapy.

IRRIIS investigated a couple of different modeling approaches. They are needed because no single model is able to capture the different relevant aspects. A taxonomy of models for Critical Infrastructures and their dependencies was elaborated (see fig. 2). It differentiates models according to various criteria: "on average" vs. "single instance" models, fine grained vs. abstract models, static vs. dynamic, etc.

3   The IRRIIS Information Model

We started with the Implementation-Service-Effect meta model (ISE) developed by Fraunhofer as a framework for the description of large critical infrastructures and their dependencies [4, 11]. Services have been shown to be a useful abstraction to dependencies between critical infrastructures. The loss of service is the main cause for

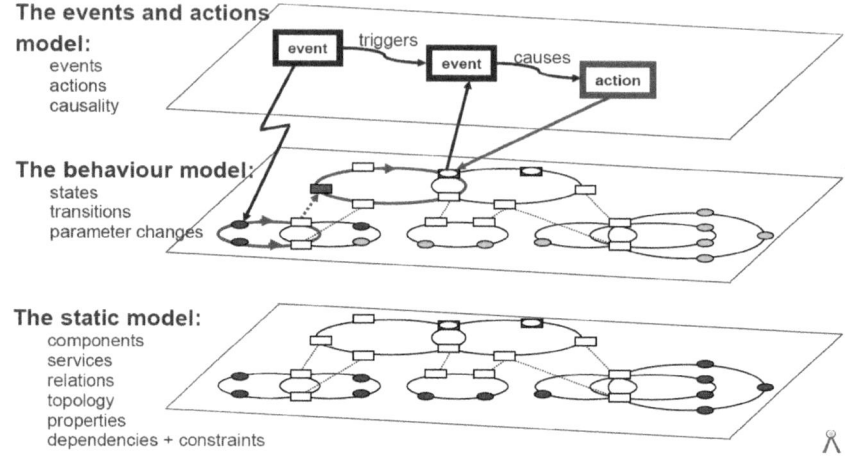

Fig. 3. The IRRIIS Information Model

failure propagation across different networks. Nevertheless, services are a complex function of Critical Infrastructures. Estimating if they are provided or lost frequently needs complex considerations, models, and simulations.

In order to be usable as a basis for realistic simulations and analysis, the original ISE model was further elaborated and extended into the *IRRIIS Information Model* [8]: a full fledged semantic model (an ontology [12, 13]) of *networks of networks* with systems and components, their behaviors, their services, of events and actions. Critical Infrastructures tend to be quite different – within the same domain and in particular between different domains. Consequently, the data models used by special purpose simulators suited for these domains tend to be quite different, too. Neither the power simulation model nor the telecommunication data model did have any notion of dependency and did provide any means to model them. The IRRIIS Information Model allows us to model dependencies of different kinds like physical, functional, control, and geo-spatial dependencies with all necessary granularity.

The IRRIIS Information Model has not necessarily to contain all particularities of network-specific information of a certain CI. This kind of information (like some physical parameters or material characteristics) can be left within the special-purpose models of each CI. The IRRIIS Information Model focuses on those information aspects of Large Critical Infrastructures which are essential for *dependency analysis* and risk estimation: the *states* of components, sub-systems, and services, how they *depend* on each other, and their relation to other Critical Infrastructures. This IRRIIS Information Model describes dependent Critical Infrastructures as a network of networks where each network comes with its own characteristic behaviors. State transitions are propagated through dependencies of different kinds within such a network of coupled state machines.

An important aspect in this kind of modeling (and simulation) is time. State transitions and their propagation along various dependencies have typically a temporal aspect, and events and actions perform in space and time. The time relations may have significant impact on the system behavior as a whole and on the influence on dependencies between Critical Infrastructures. Neither the native power data model nor the telecommunication data model did have a notion of time adequate for the description of temporal dependency aspects. This modeling gap was closed within the IRRIIS Information Model through appropriate model information.

The IRRIIS Information Model provides the basis for the SimCIP simulations (see below). It collects all dependency relevant information of CIs and can be considered as a generic ontology for dependent CI to be re-used in many similar cases.

4 Preliminary Interdependency Analysis (PIA)

In parallel, the Preliminary Interdependency Analysis (PIA) was developed in IRRIIS [7]. It provides a less detailed level of dependency modeling then the IRRIIS Information Model. PIA enables two different but related kinds of modeling:

- a qualitative dependency analysis enabling people easily to collect and structure different kinds of information about dependencies in CI, and
- a quantitative approach enabling abstract state space simulations using PIA on the Stochastic Activity Networks (SAN) tool Möbius [14].

Power grid specific aspects were integrated into Möbius' simulations for a more detailed analysis of system behavior, which in turn allowed for a study of the impact of the *level of abstraction* on the accuracy of modeling critical infrastructures.

In PIA Möbius simulations dependencies between the modelled elements were modelled at different levels of detail:

- as 'stochastic associations' which allow for rates of failure/repair of the modelled elements to be dependent on the state of other modelled element or of the environment;

- as deterministic tripping, e.g. of power elements in case of overloading or switching off telco elements in case of prolonged lack of power supply.

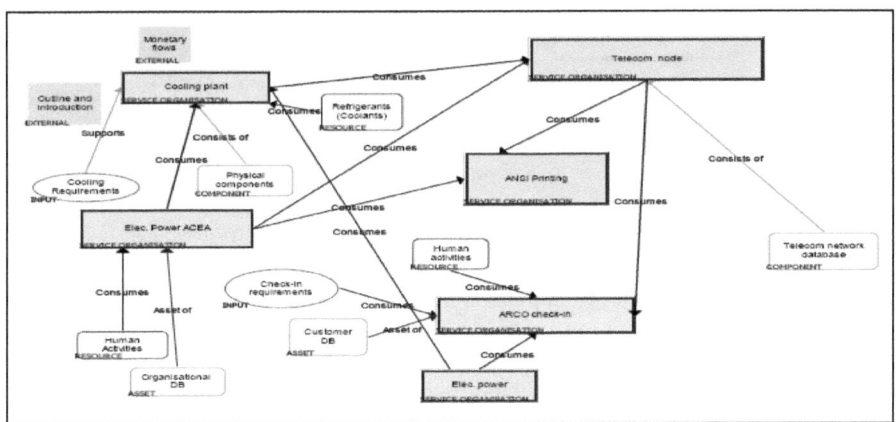

Fig. 4. The Preliminary Interdependency Analysis (PIA)

A range of studies with power-telco scenario (see below) was conducted in which a realistic parameterisation was applied with empirical data on rates of failure and repair of the modelled elements.

The quantitative PIA approach allows us to quantify the strength of the discovered dependencies and execute these models in the Möbius simulation tool. This approach allows us to investigate dependencies with stochastic methods 'on average' with different levels of abstraction so that the effect of the abstraction level on the accuracy of the model results could be studied.

5   Detailed Technical Federated Simulations

SimCIP is the central simulation tool of IRRIIS. It is based on a general-purpose, agent-based simulation kernel called LampSys developed by Fraunhofer IAIS. The model for SimCIP is based on the IRRIIS Information Model (see Section 3). This Information Model enables us to model the different complex Critical Infrastructures and their dependencies on a very detailed technical level as a *network of networks*. The SimCIP simulator allows us to simulate the behavior of this network of networks with the necessary precision and granularity.

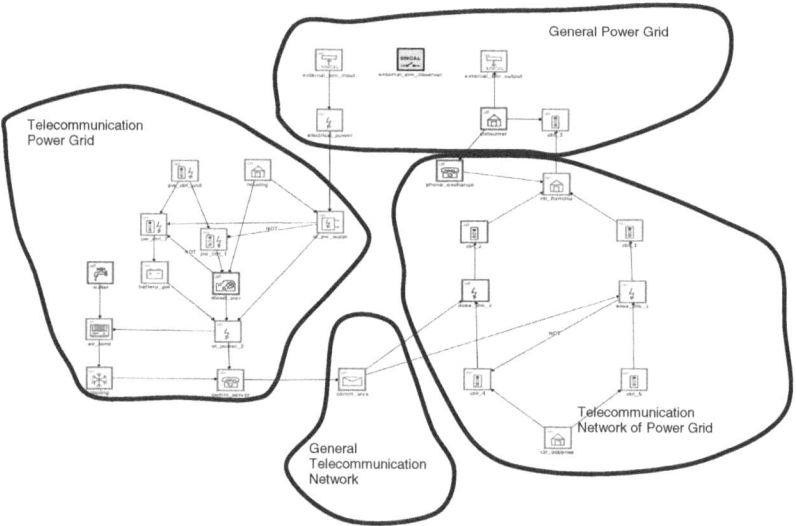

Fig. 5. Networks of networks for dependent Critical Infrastructures

SimCIP's main functionality is *dependency* simulation. The simulation models are built on the IRRIIS Information model as a network of coupled state machines with different states and dependencies. SimCIP uses LampSys' agent technology in order to assign a dedicated individual behavior to each network component. *Events and actions* can be modelled to simulate complete scenarios as state changes within networks. Dependencies between components are modelled as services and are used to propagate changes through this dependency network. Various scenarios can be modelled in a simulation consisting of event action chains. In this way SimCIP gives us a great flexibility for scenario creation and for experimentation.

Complex systems like Critical Infrastructures can show very complex behaviors. These behaviors are quite different between different CI. Power grids behave, of course, quite differently from telecommunication networks. We are able to integrate special purpose simulators (as for instance Siemens' PSS Sincal power grid simulator or the NS-2 system for telecommunication network simulations) in order to model and simulate such behaviors with the necessary *precision*. SimCIP is IRRIIS' top level federated simulation environment which integrates simulations from other tools. This allows us to simulate the different behaviors of different large complex technical systems with the necessary technical precision and to make use of these complex precise simulations for experiments and evaluations.

Consequently, the IRRIIS simulation approach is based on an integration of such special purpose simulators into the overall dependency simulation. This federated simulation approach is facilitated through SimCIP's generic simulation interface. It enables us to build bi-directional simulation interfaces to other special purpose simulators. The IRRIIS Information Model is used to provide the semantic mapping between the SimCIP model and the data model of the external simulator.

An important issue to be solved within IRRIIS' federated simulation approach was synchronization and control of federated simulation. Neither of the federated simulations has a notion of time – they focus on steady state simulations of their networks. On the other side, temporal aspects of system behavior play an important role in dependency analysis and management. SimCIP as federation platform was enabled to take the overall control and to synchronize the simulations of the federates. Time related aspects were dealt with in SimCIP through appropriate behaviors of all involved components.

The SimCIP simulation tool for fine grained technical simulations of networks of networks, and the PIA/Möbius system for quantitative Preliminary Interdependency Analysis are connected to each other and can exchange model and simulation information.

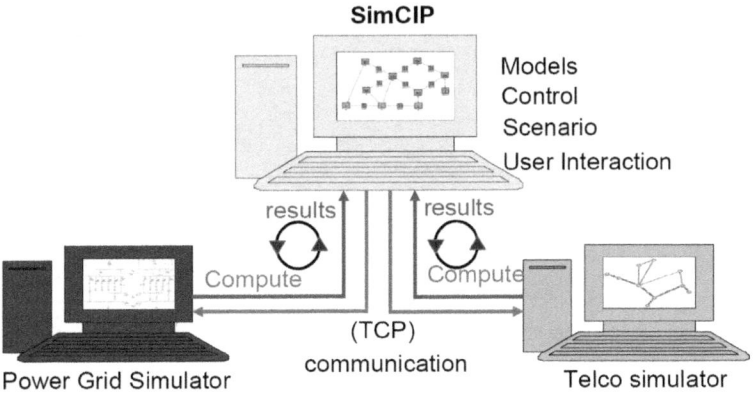

Fig. 6. Federated simulation with SimCIP

6 User Interactions

Critical Infrastructures possess dedicated control capabilities. SCADA or control centres are equipped with highly adapted systems and user interaction capabilities. Lots of information have to be presented in a way avoiding information overload of humans and allowing human decision makers to focus on the main control aspects. Highly adaptable and interactive Graphical User Interfaces are an essential prerequisite in order to enable humans to manage such complex situations.

SimCIP was built with such a sophisticated Graphical User Interface. It enables users to manage complex information in different case specific ways, and to make decisions about system control.

The component geo-positions, their dependencies, their states are shown in the left window. The upper right window shows descriptions of network components, and the lower right window their behaviors.

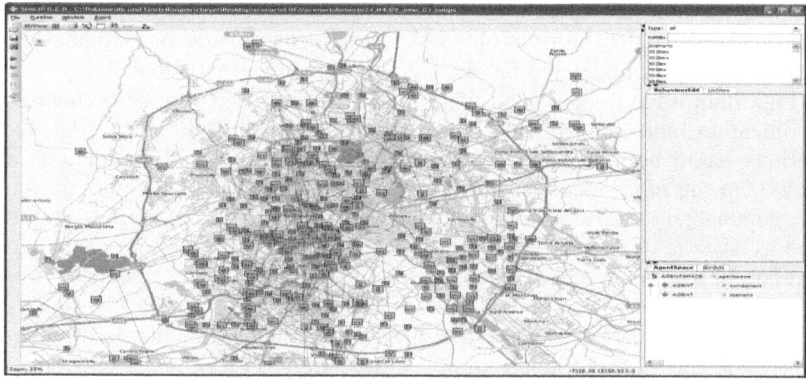

Fig. 7. The geographic view on Critical Infrastructures

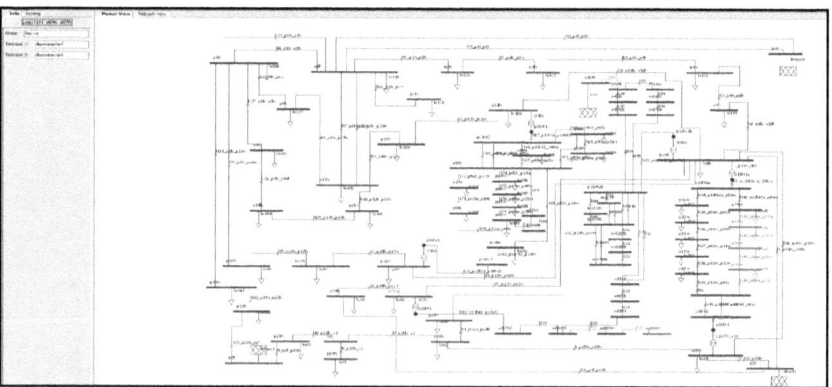

Fig. 8. The power view. It shows a schematic presentation of a power grid as used in power grid simulators. The different colors indicate the states of the components.

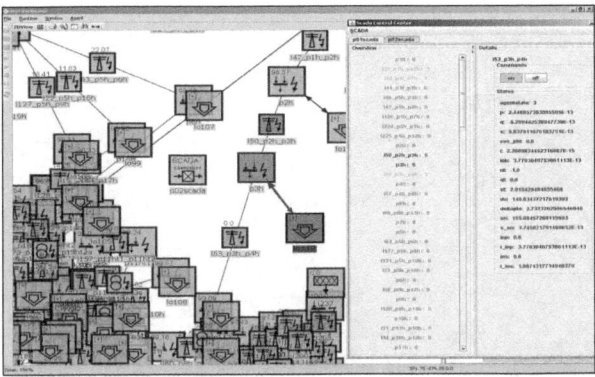

Fig. 9. The SCADA agent. It provides a user friendly information and user interaction capabilities enabling users to analyze dependencies between components, to investigate their states, and to trigger switching interactions changing component states.

An important aspect of SimCIP is the integration of the MIT middleware components enabling communication between different networks. The risk estimator is directly connected to SimCIP's simulation environment allowing users to make direct use of risk information from dependent Critical Infrastructures.

7 Scenarios and Experiments

The IRRIIS approach is based on scenarios. This is an essential element in our methodology. It enables us to investigate complex Critical Infrastructures and their dependencies in a systematic and realistic way. The complex structures of CI and of their behaviors imply complex relationships between failures in dependent Critical Infrastructures. The only way to manage this complexity is through adequate models and simulations of scenarios.

We focused our scenario efforts on the two most important Critical Infrastructure types [5]: power grids and telecommunication networks – and their mutual dependencies. Three different scenarios were created:

scenario					
File	Column				
Time		Agent	Path	Value	Comment
500	TP event 1	water	states/out		Water pressure -> Low
1000	TP event 2	diesel_pwr	states/out		Diesel -> Shutdown for maintenance
2000	P event 1	el_pw_suppl	states/out		Elec. power -> Down for flooding
4000	P event 2	consumer	states/out		Consumer -> Black-out due to short circuit
4000	TP event 3	water	states/out		Water pressure = 0
4500	PT event 1	phone_exchange	states/out		Difficult communicarion from consumers
9000	TP event 4	diesel_pwr	states/out		Diesel -> Start

Fig. 10. A SimCIP scenario as chain of events and actions on various network components

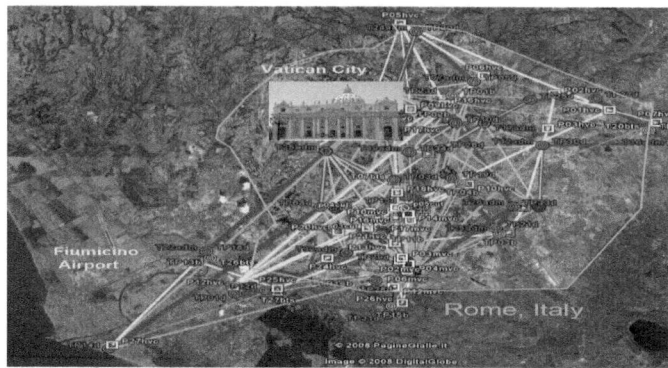

Fig. 11. The power and telco networks in the Rome scenario

The Rome Scenario:
The models of dependent electrical power and telecommunication critical infrastructures in Rome have been elaborated in full detail and prepared for simulation on SimCIP/Sincal. A network of four Critical Infrastructures (two from the power domain, two from telco) was formed and modeled in every necessary technical detail including the various dependencies between them.

The models of these four depending CI were simulated in PIA/Möbuis and in SimCIP. Detailed event action chains could be investigated and analysed. The propagation of failures within a network and across different networks was simulated and used for risk evaluation.

The "Rome flooding" scenario
A second scenario has been developed as the "Rome flooding" scenario. Based on the statement that flooding is one of the main risk factors in Rome it was analyzed, modeled, and simulated how a flooding could develop in the city of Rome, and how this flooding would affect the various Critical Infrastructures there. The flooding was estimated from assumption about a heavy rain weather scenario. This enables us to investigate which parts of the Critical Infrastructures in the city of Rome are affected by this flooding. The consequences of these effects were simulated using SimCIP's models of Critical Infrastructures. All redundancies and protections built into these infrastructures were taken into account. Various failure scenarios were considered and how these failures are propagated from one Critical Infrastructure to a depending one.

Next generation scenarios
Special emphasis was dedicated to the next generation power and telco scenarios. The structures and behaviors of power grids and telco networks will significantly change in the years ahead. New components like regenerative power generators will be added in power grids. A significant part of the electrical power will be generated in distributed networks of combined heat power plants. The distances between generation and consumption will grow due to off shore wind parks and increased power trading. The need for sophisticated information and communication technologies grows significantly for these next generation power grids. The use of smart metering and smart grids will additionally increase the need for advanced ICT as essential element in future power grids.

Fig. 12. The Rome flooding scenario

SimCIP's expressive and flexible modeling and simulation capabilities allowed us to run complex next generation scenarios for analysis and comprehensive risk estimation. The expressive modeling capabilities could be used to build different network types and structures and to run them in different scenarios.

8 Middleware Technology (MIT)

The middleware technology with the MIT Communicator and the Risk Estimator builds one of the core concepts of IRRIIS. The management of risk in dependent Critical Infrastructures needs the sharing of risk related information across organizational and technical boundaries of Critical Infrastructures. This is the role of the MIT Communicator. On the other hand, the shared information has to be processed for each Critical Infrastructure in a way appropriate for *cumulative* risk estimation. This is the function of the Risk Estimator (together with the TEFS information interface). It takes information from another CI into account to estimate the risk within the own network, and it provides risk estimations of the own network through the MIT Communicator to depending CIs.

Additionally, a holistic view on risk in dependent Critical Infrastructures can be supported by sophisticated decision support tools which capture the essence of knowledge on risk in such complex networks of networks. This is the idea behind the CRIPS decision support tool.

All MIT tools (MIT Communicator, Risk Estimator, the Incident Knowledge Analyser IKA, and CRIPS) have been implemented and evaluated. They provide the basis for information exchange between critical infrastructures, for risk estimation and decision support.

The MIT Communicator enables information exchange between CI. The information sharing is based on a common Risk Management Language (RML) - an XML variant of IRRIIS Information Models. Special attention has been paid to trust and security issues and the design of the communication.

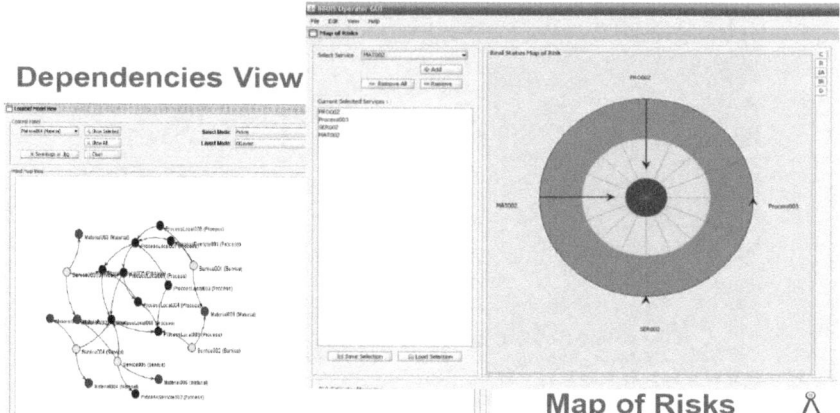

Fig. 13. The Risk Estimator

A key issue for the whole project was the integration of MIT technology and SimCIP simulation. The MIT components Risk Estimator (RE), the CRIPS decision support tool, and the Incident Knowledge Analyser (IKA) have been developed and implemented. Based on these implementations the evaluation of the MIT system in conjunction with the SimCIP simulator was performed in a series of experiments and systematic evaluations.

In parallel with the main effort on MIT, the IRRIIS partner CSR City University London developed the concept of PIA (see section 4) risk estimation and demonstrated the feasibility of the approach on a contrived example.

9   Use Cases

Our investigations revealed that there are a couple of typical use cases for IRRIIS' achievements:

1) Design optimization: Critical Infrastructure failures tend to be quite expensive. CI protection against failures can be expensive, too. It is far from easy to find the right balance. With IRRIIS' methodology, models, simulations, and MIT communication and risk estimation technology we will provide the means for such investigations.

2) Existing Critical Infrastructures are operated on the basis of complex rules and regulations. They try to minimize risk under all conceivable conditions. To some extend, these rules are implemented within the SCADA and control systems, to some other extend they are left with the human decision makers (a work share depending on many aspects). In the future, these rules and regulations will be even more complex. They have to take the management of dependencies into account.

3) Already today the operation of Critical Infrastructures is done with important support from ICT systems including complex special purpose analytics and simulations. If integrated into tomorrow's SCADA and control systems the

IRRIIS results will significantly improve this support of CI operation under the new more complex conditions.

4) Training is essential for all people involved in decision making in CI operation. The IRRIIS results enable more effective and efficient training for them.

10 Conclusions and Lessons Learnt

The following is a brief compilation of lessons learnt in IRRIIS and resulting challenges for future research in CIP.

10.1 Modeling and Simulation

In IRRIIS it became clear that without modeling and simulation the necessary comprehensive understanding of dependencies and the holistic risk approach can not be accomplished. Critical Infrastructures and their dependencies are too manifold and too complex to be understandable on a simpler way.

It was one of the challenges of the project to develop adequate models for Critical Infrastructures of different kinds and their dependencies. There is no "universal" modeling approach for all relevant issues. The different models developed in IRRIIS are applicable for investigations of different aspects. A taxonomy of models gave a first overview of relevant criteria and modeling approaches. This needs further elaboration in order to get a deeper understanding which models fulfill which needs and how they can be combined in necessary comprehensive investigations.

These modeling and simulation approaches need consolidation and extension. They must provide a stable and easy to use basis for complex investigations. Their combination – especially of detailed technical models and stochastic state space models – is a pre-requisite for the needed large scale simulations and holistic risk analysis. Federated simulation follows currently a kind of ad-hoc approach. There is no consolidated framework – neither conceptually nor on the implementation level - for the integration of different simulators. We need a solid ground for federated simulation.

The IRRIIS Information Model can be considered as a standard ontology of dependent Critical Infrastructures. It enables easy communication between dependent Critical Infrastructures. It should be further elaborated and prepared for standardization by an appropriate organization.

For the purpose of consolidation of modeling and simulation we have to consider four main isuues:

- Continued and extended research on complex and integrated models and on frameworks for federated simulations including sophisticated user interaction capabilities;

- Realistic (maybe anonymized) data and models to be provided by stakeholders including statistics about failures and risk;

- A more in-depth analysis of dependencies between CIs, including impact and consequences to other infrastructures, affected services and areas.

-   Easy access by researchers and stakeholders to models and simulations on an established platform (including an organizational framework for these activities). The proposed European Infrastructures Simulation and Analysis Centre EISAC [16] or a similar organizational structure should be established for these purposes.

10.2 User Interaction Capabilities

User Interaction is a key issue in such complex endeavors as dependencies of CIs. This is true in a research context and for real-world applications. The information to be processed is so complex that their adequate visualization and presentation to humans is essential. This can not be a static graphical presentation but a highly interactive and adaptive capability. IRRIIS invested a lot of efforts to build sophisticated Graphical User Interfaces which reflect the different needs of end users as well as of those responsible for model creation and simulations.

Many different kinds of information have to be presented: geo-spatial information, system structures, states, temporal developments, dependencies, numerical values, etc. They all are related to each other. Users should be able to adapt the GUI to their needs – in general to choose the kind of presentation which fits best to their needs and practices, and in concrete situations to the best way to get the information they need. The system should be able to "understand" in which way the user can manage a given situation and to present the information in an appropriate way. The user should be able to flexibly change between different graphical presentations and browsing relevant and related textual information and data.

The users must have the main control whenever feasible. They have to evaluate the situation and to decide what has to be done. They need support by the system in this process. Also in simulations the end user should be able to perform certain control actions. The so called SCADA agent within SimCIP was a first approach in this direction. It should be extended towards more sophisticated user interaction capabilities.

10.3 Scenarios

Scenarios are an essential element in Critical Infrastructure investigations. Things are too complex to be analyzed analytically or by other means. Scenarios allow us to capture typical aspects of Critical Infrastructures, their behaviors, and the influence of dependencies and control.

Scenario building is still far from being simple - neither on the conceptual level nor on the data level. We have a couple of complex issues to be dealt with:

-   Which aspects need consideration? What must the models look like in order to capture those parts of reality which have to be included for the analysis of a special issue?
-   How well do the data we can acquire reflect these needs?
-   Data come from different sources with different meaning, granularity, and assumptions. They need integration, consolidation, and validation.
-   They are not static but changing and need adaptation to changing scenarios.

10.4 Other Critical Infrastructure Domains

IRRIIS focused on the two most important domains [5]of Critical Infrastructures and their dependencies: power and telecommunication. Nevertheless, we always had in mind how our methodology, models, and tools can be used for other domains like transport, water, gas, etc.

First, our methodology and our modeling approaches are based on the assumption that there is a common ground for dependencies between Critical Infrastructures. The Preliminary Interdependency Analysis PIA enables dependency modeling and analysis independent from any concrete restrictions from the domain. Different types of dependencies can be established and analyzed for arbitrary domains. The Möbius tool enables us to run such dependency models independent from the concrete application domain using the general Stochastic Activity Networks formalism. We showed that the integration of special purpose procedures which reflect the concrete behavior of a specific Critical Infrastructure further improves the precision of the Möbius simulations.

10.5 Middleware Improved Technology

The IRRIIS Project developed and elaborated the concepts and the technology to support "information sharing" and "risk sharing" among different CI stakeholders. These concepts are now widely used in different FP7 and ERCIP Projects.

The information exchange enabled in IRRIIS by the MIT Communicator is focused onto information on the current status of CIs. The IRRIIS approach to communication enables us to abstract away those parts of the risk related information in a CI which is not understandable in a depending one, and which should not be disclosed by a stakeholder by its own business interests. In the future, extended variants of information exchange should be foreseen dealing with information about planned future states, probabilities of failure, and other more prospective assertions.

The Risk Estimator tool in IRRIIS is based on fuzzy rules. This is a quite simple approach which nevertheless enables us to show how information from other CIs can help to estimate the risk in a network. More elaborated risk analysis methods should be investigated in the future. They should be based on *integrated holistic* risk estimation of *depending* Critical Infrastructures. The joint state of all related CIs has to be considered and investigated systematically – including possible control actions.

A special challenge results from the role of communication networks for Critical Infrastructures. Today, in the power sector, the grid companies frequently operate their own, separate communication and control networks (which are sometimes using public telecommunication networks in addition or as back-up). Future Critical Infrastructures – for instance in the power sector, but also in transportation, logistics, and others) will much more rely on public communication networks. Smart grids in the power sector can not operate their own, independent communication networks – they will use common purpose communication infrastructures. Under these conditions the meaning of safe and secure communication networks will grow significantly. In parallel, it must be assured that even if communication is lost for a while in such a smart power grid the power services still can be provided. *Control under incomplete information* is a challenge for future research in this area. It is an essential pre-requisite for smart grids and will be supported by stakeholders active in this area.

References

[1] The IRRIIS European Integrated Project, http://www.irriis.org
[2] Pederson, P., et al.: Critical Infrastructure Interdependency Modeling: A Survey of U.S. and International Research, Technical Report, Idaho National Lab (August 2006)
[3] Kröger, W.: Reliability Engineering and System Safety. Reliability Engineering and System Safety 93, 1781–1787 (2008)
[4] Beyer, U., Flentge, F.: Towards a Holistic Metamodel for Systems of Critical Infrastructures. In: ECN CIIP NEWSLETTER (October/November 2006)
[5] Nieuwenhuijs, A.H., Luiijf, H.A.M., Klaver, M.H.A.: Modeling Critical Infrastructure Dependencies. In: Shenoi, S. (ed.) IFIP International Federation for Information Processing, Critical Infrastructure Protection. Springer, Boston (2008)
[6] Rinaldi, S., Peerenboom, J., Kelly, T.: Identifying, Understanding, and Analyzing Critical Infrastructure Interdependencies. IEEE Control Systems Magazine, 11–25 (December 2001)
[7] Bloomfield, R., et al.: Analysis of Critical Infrastructure dependence -An IRRIIS perspective. In: Klein, R. (ed.): Proc. IRRIIS Workshop at CRITIS 2008, Frascati, Italy (October 2008)
[8] Klein, R., Rome, E., Beyel, C., Linnemann, R., Reinhardt, W., Usov, A.: Information Modelling and Simulation in Large Interdependent Critical Infrastructures in IRRIIS. In: Setola, R., Geretshuber, S. (eds.) CRITIS 2008. LNCS, vol. 5508, pp. 36–47. Springer, Heidelberg (2009)
[9] Klein, R.: Information Modelling and Simulation in Large Dependent Critical Infrastructures – An Overview on the European Integrated Project IRRIIS. In: Setola, R., Geretshuber, S. (eds.) CRITIS 2008. LNCS, vol. 5508, pp. 131–143. Springer, Heidelberg (2009)
[10] Minichino, M., et al.: Tools and techniques for interdependency analysis. Deliverable D2.2.2, The IRRIIS Consortium (July 2007), http://www.irriis.org
[11] Flentge, F., Beyel, C., Rome, E.: Towards a standardised cross-sector information exchange on present risk factors. In: Lopez, J., Hämmerli, B.M. (eds.) CRITIS 2007. LNCS, vol. 5141, pp. 349–360. Springer, Heidelberg (2008)
[12] Staab, S., Studer, R. (eds.): Handbook on Ontologies. International Handbooks on Information Systems. Springer, Heidelberg (2004)
[13] Gruber, T.: Toward Principles for the Design of Ontologies. In: Proceedings of the International Workshop on Formal Ontology, Padova, Italy (March 1993)
[14] http://www.mobius.illinois.edu/
[15] Mies, C., Wolters, B., Steffens, T.: LAMPSys. In: KI Zeitschrift Schwerpunkt: Aktuelle Themen der KI, pp. 42–45 (2009)
[16] Rome, E., et al.: DIESIS. In: Proc. of the 2009 SISO European Simul. Interop. Workshop (ESIW 2009), San Diego, CA, USA, pp. 139–146 (2009) ISBN 1-56555-336-5

Towards Understanding Recurring Large Scale Power Outages: An Endogenous View of Inter-organizational Effects

Finn Olav Sveen[1,2], Josune Hernantes[3], Jose J. Gonzalez[2,4], and Eliot Rich[3,5]

[1] Prospectives Ltd Nuf, Postsvingen 5A, 3031 Drammen, Norway
[2] NISlab, Gjøvik University College, 2802 Gjøvik, Norway
[3] Tecnun (University of Navarra), Manuel de Lardizábal 13, 20018 San Sebastián, Spain
[4] University of Agder, Faculty of Engineering and Science, Department of ICT, Security and Quality in Organizations, 4898 GRIMSTAD, Norway
[5] University at Albany, School of Business, Department of Information Technology Management
finn.olav@prospective.no, jhernantes@tecnun.es,
jose.j.gonzalez@uia.no, e.rich@albany.edu

Abstract. In the last decade there has been a series of severe large scale power outages around the world. Deregulation and increasing interconnection among grids have left a complex topographical landscape of organizations and technology that spans traditional borders. Two examples are the 2003 outages in Italy and North America. Both these cases left more than fifty million people without power. As part of the European Programme for Critical Infrastructure Protection our team is considering how this integrated context affects the vulnerability of the power system. System dynamics modellers elicit fragmented domain expert knowledge using a group model building methodology. We present a qualitative version of the simulation model and discuss how the prevalence of long time delays, dynamic complexity and a tendency to view hazardous conditions as normal all contribute to long term crisis proneness. We argue that some common beliefs about crisis conditions actually are fallacies that must be overcome to avoid recurrent crises in the power generation and distribution sector.

Keywords: Critical Infrastructure, Power System, Crisis Management, System Dynamics, Group Model Building.

1 Introduction

In the last decade there have been several large scale power outages around the world. In 2003 alone outages in Italy and North America each left more than 50 million people without power [1, 2]. The consequences were serious, but thankfully such large outages are infrequent. Nevertheless, they represent a significant problem.

Large scale outages are easily considered as random independent events caused by unfortunate circumstances. Post-failure reviews have demonstrated that many of these apparently random events are the product of the way the system is organized, both

C. Xenakis and S. Wolthusen (Eds.): CRITIS 2010, LNCS 6712, pp. 43–54, 2011.
© Springer-Verlag Berlin Heidelberg 2011

technologically and administratively [1, 2]. Vulnerable conditions are the result of the accumulated effects of past decisions and actions. As such it should be possible to recognize and prevent them. Human psychology creates an important barrier which may prevent recognition. If some event, say a power outage, has not happened for a long time, we tend to reduce the attention given to that risk, which may in turn lead to inadequate allocation of time, financial and other resources to undertake prevention and mitigation. Therefore large scale outages, owing to their infrequency, may reoccur simply because we forget why they happened in the first place.

The complexity of the power system and its effects requires an approach that brings together technical and experiential knowledge over a wide range of areas. Many different organizations are involved in keeping the power grid in a reliable and stable functional state. In the last decades deregulation and increasing interconnection among grids have created a complex topographical landscape of organizations, governments and different technical solutions. Consequently, knowledge about the power system resides fragmented in the minds of many people, and little of that knowledge has been written down and unified in a holistic manner. We present the results of three exploratory workshops synthesized into a qualitative causal model. It is descriptive scaffolding upon which we will build future quantitative simulations.

The rest of the paper is organized as follows. Part 2, Problem, explains the problem of crisis preparedness and recurring crises in greater detail. Part 3, Hypothesis, a structural model of the experts' integrated perspective is presented. In Part 4, Analysis, some possible dynamic implications of the model are explored to set the stage for future research.

2 Problem

We rely on electricity to power our computers and machines so that we can work, and to heat our homes so that we can survive in winter. The ability to predict and avoid or minimize the impact of power outages is therefore vital. Power system events are rarely considered systemically or as the result of long-term factors. The relatively infrequent occurrences of large scale outages allows them to be framed as singular and extraordinary events, and analyzed as exceptions disconnected from normal operations. This implies that their causes of each outage are also independent and largely exogenous. Critical and extensive examination is performed only after the most severe outages occur, and limited to *a posterior* analysis. The event becomes the crisis and is subjected to scientific inquiry "..., as if in itself, the incomprehension it [the event] arouses justifies a crucial need for knowledge." [3]. The fascination with single major events obscures the inter- and extra-organizational processes that cause crisis proneness [3, 4].

Previous research has shown that crises often have long incubation times [5-7]. "A crisis do not just happen, it evolves" [8, p. 15]. Crisis precursors are either not detected or ignored, that is, not perceived as expressions of vulnerabilities in the system. If they had been detected as such, the system could have been improved and made less vulnerable. This is the basis of a very successful class of systems known as incident reporting systems. There is strong evidence that significant reductions in industrial accidents take place where these systems are implemented [9-11]. There are also indications that similarly structured systems can improve information security [12, 13], suggesting general applicability beyond the safety domain. See [14] for a general explanation of incident reporting systems.

When crises are treated as the result of exceptional and exogenously driven events, the value of implementing and maintaining incident reporting systems is not recognized, thereby allowing vulnerable conditions to persist until an accident or other severe event makes the vulnerabilities patent [4]. The vulnerabilities are allowed to accumulate because humans do not recognize them as such, but rather conditions within the system that do not affect normal operations; we become used to them and (overly) confident in our ability to manage the unusual. According to Roux-Dufort this is a form of ignorance [4]. In accordance with this "the ignorance mechanism" it is only after the eruption and review of the crisis event that the need to strengthen preventive measures and crisis management capabilities are recognized.

The massive scale of power systems creates additional problems of pro-active analysis. The 2006 outage which originated in Germany cascaded as far south as Morocco [15]. Power systems are interconnected but their regulatory and financial controls are subject to national and organizational boundaries, making vulnerability assessment complicated. A blackout across borders requires cooperation between the involved parties to prevent it. Lack of joint training between the Italian and Swiss operators was identified as an important factor in the 2003 Italian blackout [1].

The dependence of a society on its power infrastructure creates vulnerabilities from unrecognized dependencies. Chang et al.'s [16] analysis of the 1998 Canadian ice storm power outage showed, among other issues, that the extended loss of energy infrastructure led to oil supply problems as most gas stations were unable to use their electric pumps. Dorval Airport, a major facility serving Montreal, lost its power supply as well, and was unable to service flights.. Railways were shut down because signals and switches were no longer working. The Atwater and Des Baillets filtration plants had only 4-6 hours of clean water left. Patients stayed longer in hospitals to avoid returning to blacked out homes, tying up beds needed for new patients. In addition, patient care suffered as elevators were no longer operating.

The low frequency of severe power outages and the ignorance mechanism combine effects so that other priorities, principally economic ones, are given precedence over crisis prevention and preparation. The 2003 outages in North America and Italy were both caused by sagging power cables contacting vegetation [1, 2]. As heavily loaded cables heat up they expand and lengthen. As part of preventive maintenance the vegetation below the cables is trimmed to allow room for the cables to sag. This is expensive and time consuming, and both reports pointed to insufficient trimming.

Each of these factors – unrecognized technical and organizational dependencies, the ignorance mechanism, and de-emphasis on prevention activities – play a role in the problem of large scale power outages, but it is hard to point to a specific factor as the principal influence on success or failure. Rather we believe that the combination of independently benign weaknesses creates the platform for increased vulnerability. In the next section we describe a hypothetical structure that captures the problem of large scale crisis as the result of multiple endogenous factors that interact over time.

3 Hypothesis

When considering the state and stability of the power grid as a dynamic and accumulative process over time we move from an event-driven perspective to one that considers how decisions affect outcomes over time. For example, reducing maintenance expenditures may free income in the short term but increase the chance of a grid failure in the future. The effects of these decisions on those outside the power transmission firms may not be obvious. Creating a causal structure that captures some of these complexities helps illuminate these hidden effects.

To investigate the causal structure we executed three Group Model Building (GMB) workshops. GMB is a small-group focused methodology where experts provide insight which are captured in models for subsequent policy experimentation [17-19]. GMB is specifically designed to build System Dynamics (SD) models. SD is a modelling and computer simulation methodology which applies a holistic approach to systemic problems [20-22]. It focuses on identification of explicit endogenous causes of effects through feedback. SD investigates the problem's behaviour over time as a consequence of the system's causal structure, and is well suited for strategic problems. The model we present in this paper is qualitative, i.e., it has not been put into equations and simulated.

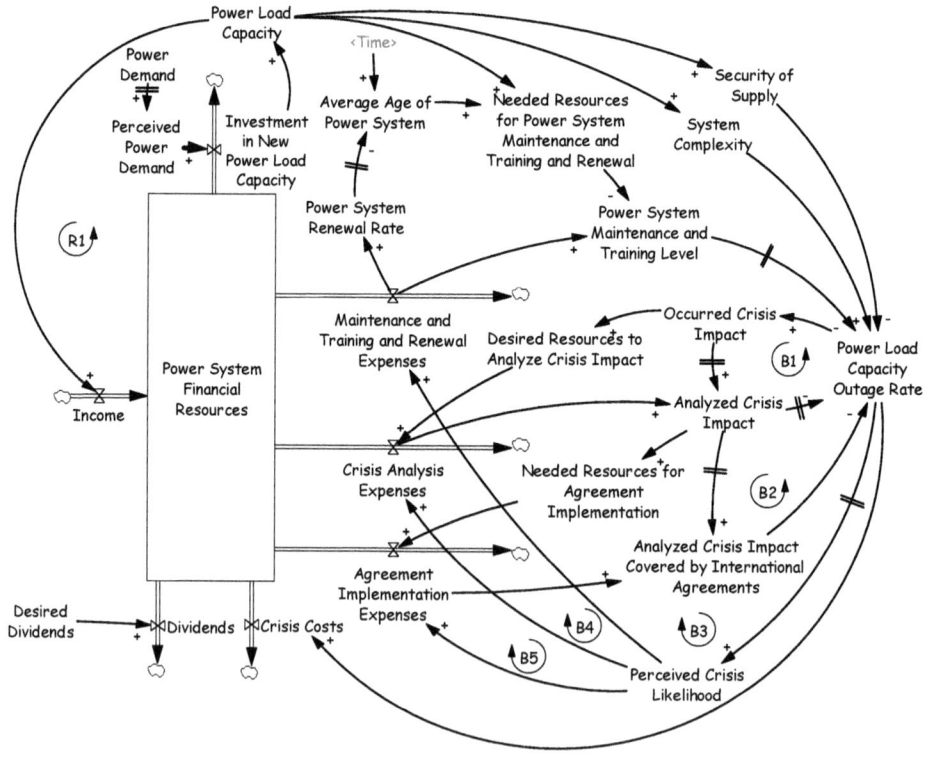

Fig. 1. Endogenous causal model of hypothesized system structure

For a full understanding of a system's dynamics simulation is needed. However, qualitative models are useful for describing the system structure and hypothesize potential dynamic effects. As such, they are a first step on the road to a full simulation model.

The causal model shown in Figure 1 embodies the problem factors described in the previous section, and carries elements of a working hypothesis about the cause of large outages, in other words, why organizations do not learn and set them self up for failure. Factors contributing to the problem are linked by explicit causal assumptions (arrows) and direction of effects (positive or negative). Parallel lines on an arrow indicate that there is an important delay between cause and effect. Loops in the model show how effects can reinforce (R) or balance (B) over time, driving the state of the system. See [22] for a complete definition of polarity and causality in SD.

Decomposition of the causal model shows how concerns and actions that span organizational and geographic boundaries are captured in the model. We first consider the various ways Transmission System Operators (TSOs), allocate their resources and then add the effects of outages and restoration, followed by the influences of size and integration. Understanding the intended effects of allocation decisions by the TSOs requires that short-term intentions be identified in isolation. When the results of these short-term decisions combine over time, the complexity of the system and inherent time delays can produce unexpected results, as we present later.

Grid Expansion. Our society is becoming increasingly more dependent on electric power and *Power Demand* is continuously increasing. The perception of this increase, denoted as *Perceived Power Demand*, determines how much power production and transmission capacity that needs to be invested in to maintain with demand. This is represented by the link from *Perceived Power Demand* to *Desired Power Load Capacity Investment. Investment in New Power Load Capacity* reduces *Power System Financial Resources* (Fig. 1, upper left). Investing in expanding the transmission network and generating capacity increases future income, which also increases available financial resources. This is a process that has the potential to reinforce itself, captured by loop R1. For this presentation we consider *Power System Financial Resources* as an average of an ongoing income stream, ignoring the accumulation of capital to finance major expansion. Investment in New Power Load Capacity causes *Power Load Capacity* increase which in turn allows for increase in *Security of Supply.*

Maintenance and Training. The power system, in this case the grid, requires ongoing maintenance. Additionally, personnel must be trained to operate the system and parts of it must be replaced with age, which cost money. This is represented by the link from *Power System Financial Resources* to the outflow *Maintenance and Training and Renewal Expenses* (Fig. 1, centre).

As time passes, the parts in the power system become older, as indicated by the link from *Time* to *Average Age of Power System.* An increase in this variable increases *Needed Resources for Power System Maintenance and Training and Renewal.* Old equipment is assumed to be more prone to failure therefore more maintenance intensive. Consequently, *Maintenance and Training and Renewal Expenses* also increase. More of this money spent on renewal, replacing old and problematic parts, decreases *Average Age of Power System.* (Fig. 1, top middle).

As resources are spent on maintenance and training, the number of outages are expected to decrease. *Maintenance and Training and Renewal Expenses* and *Needed Resources for Power System Maintenance and Training and Renewal* both affect Power *System Maintenance and Training Level.* If the needed amount is spent, the likelihood of power outages decreases, as shown by the link from *Power System Maintenance and Training Level* to *Power Load Capacity Outage Rate*.

Outages. Outages accrue significant costs for short-term mitigation and customer compensation. These drain the financial resources of the involved organizations, and is represented by the link from *Power Load Capacity Outage Rate* to *Crisis Costs*, which drains resources that would have otherwise been available (Fig 1, bottom). It also exerts pressure to adjust the allocation choices by the TSO on how its income should be spent, represented by the link from *Power Load Capacity Outage Rate* to *Perceived Crisis Likelihood*, which in turn influences allocation of resources.

When an outage has occurred there is pressure to identify and remediate the proximal cause, with effort and costs proportional to the size of the outage. Outages, represented by *Power Load Capacity Outage Rate,* give experiences that are present in an unanalyzed form, *Occurred Crisis Impact.* As resources are spent to examine it, it becomes *Analyzed Crisis Impact*, which helps reduce future outages, i.e., *Power Load Capacity Outage Rate.* The variables form a balancing loop, B1 (Fig. 1, right), which reduces available resources in the short-term. Analyzing past crises takes resources which have to be drawn from the resource pool, as do the decisions made for additional training, maintenance and capital replacement.

Effects of Internationalization. The modern power system is international. Each nation is a node in a much larger interconnected network. This increases supply security, as neighbouring countries can buffer the effects of unexpected production shortfalls. However, the high degree of interconnection also makes it easy for failures to propagate through the system [2]. Hence, it is necessary to make agreements and coordinate with neighbouring cross-border organizations, which also costs money. This is represented as *Agreement Implementation Expenses* (Fig. 1, middle bottom).

The agreements are expected to take into account lessons learned from past crises. These lessons, denoted by *Analyzed Crisis Impact*, must be implemented in the agreements (*Analyzed Crisis Impact Covered by International Agreements*) which in turn should reduce *Power Load Capacity Outage Rate* (Fig. 1, right).

Allocation Decision. As outlined at the beginning of this section, the supply of money is limited. The management of the individual organizations that make up the power system must decide how much to spend on each activity. This is influenced considerably by the perception of the likelihood of a crisis given the current level of maintenance and training, the age of the system, agreements in place, and previously occurred crises. If *Power Load Capacity Outage Rate* increases *Perceived Crisis Likelihood* will also increase since more outages are definite proof that current efforts are insufficient. Increased *Perceived Crisis Likelihood* therefore prompts an increase in *Maintenance and Training and Renewal Expenses, Crisis Analysis Expenses* and *Agreement Implementation Expenses*. This should over time reduce *Power Load Capacity Outage Rate*. This creates three more balancing loops B3, B4 and B5.

Other operating concerns. We have not included changes to the cost of power generation, fuel, or pollution regulatory effects in the model, as the focus of the workshops was crisis management rather than market performance and profitability. In addition, staff turnover and their effects on readiness were excluded from analysis.

In this section we have described the individual components which help determine how much money is spent on each activity and their influence on the likelihood of outages. Next we analyze how the different components work together dynamically.

4 Analysis

In this section we review the model qualitatively, considering possible outcomes from the interactions it contains. This review was validated and informed post-workshop by our expert panel. Our goal is to identify in the model structure the dynamic patterns provided by our experts. We report on these findings as a step towards a quantified and executable simulation model more useful for policy examination.

A first observation when analyzing the model in Figure 1 concerns the many time delays in the system. It takes time to replace old infrastructure, analyze crises, develop and implement agreements, and for maintenance and training to reach adequate levels.

Time delays are manageable as long as preventive actions receive continuous and balanced attention. Obviously, future investments cannot be ignored. Chronic transmission capacity shortage might arise. We assume that TSOs provide resources based on their perception of what is required for safe operation. But, experience does show that adequate levels are not always maintained. For example, the outages in Italy and North America in 2003 were both initially caused by insufficient trimming of vegetation under the power lines [1, 2].

The time delays affecting information and perception are a common mechanism by which imbalances occur. For example, insufficient maintenance of a well-designed network does not cause an immediate outage. It took the combination of high load and poor maintenance to trigger both 2003 crises. Similarly, lack of joint training was cited as an important contributor to the magnitude of the Italian outage. However, a similar event occurred a few days earlier without causing an outage, as a high load condition was handled correctly by the operator. A weakness existed in the system though it was not so severe as to always cause an outage. Similar events can have occurred many times before. Studies from other domains, such as safety, support such a notion [5-7]. It has been found that accidents are normally preceded by precursor events, and that the event: detectable precursor ratio can be as high as 1:10 [23, p. 24 and references therein]. Time delays as well as uncertain and inconsistent interpretation of information affect the outcomes of decisions.

Hence, insufficient attention to even well managed events may increases the probability that an outage will occur, but there may be a significant time delay between the forces that create the weakness and its consequences. The time delay between lower investment in prevention and maintenance and subsequent failures causes a form of short-time blindness, where short term economic pressures are more potent than concerns about potential outages.

While Figure 1 is relatively complex, it still remains a simplified abstraction of a highly-interlinked structure. One might consider the system presented in Figure 1 manageable if it pertained to one organization that is relatively small, but there are many organizations involved in each of the activities contained in the model. Diverse decision makers have different information and perceptions of the state of the system. This gives rise to potential differences in the quality of how each part of the system is managed. In particular, only big outages with major effects trigger substantial investigations and repercussions.

When a major outage occurs it disrupts both the technical and organizational network. Suddenly, the notion of additional vulnerability becomes real and not just a theoretic event. In this model *Perceived Crisis Likelihood* increases quickly, followed by a flurry of activities to investigate the event. Investigations are undertaken and reports issued, resulting in changes to regulations, training curricula and technical systems. Another example from outside the power sector is the ongoing changes to regulations following the US sub-prime mortgage crisis[1]. After this initial activity efforts to maintain, train, renew the system and enhance coordination between organizations might be increased for a time, the further away from the crisis the more likely it is that old practices re-emerge.

There are indications that systemic weaknesses are perceived "as business as usual" and necessary for the successful operation of power transmission systems. However, this may be a major fallacy. Schulman et al. [24] studied the activities in the control centre of a TSO in the United States. The TSO controls the grid "by developing and maintaining a repertoire of responses and options in the face of unpredictable or uncontrollable system instability produced either within the network (e.g., by generators acting in a strategic fashion) and from outside the network through its open system features (e.g., temperatures and climate change)." This unpredictability often caused unstable, high risk situations in which rules were bent or broken. One view is that rule bending in this situation is necessary because following them would have led to long delays in action, which would have caused outages. However, a different interpretation is that the way which the system is designed creates these unstable high risk situations, thus making it necessary with risky actions to "rescue" the situation. If the system is redesigned or improved, it may be possible to reduce or even eliminate the source of such high risk situations. On the other hand, as noted by Schulman et al. [24], it is almost impossible for the designers of a system to anticipate all weaknesses in advance, making some adaptive capability a necessity.

While a complete analysis requires a running model, we expect to expose several fallacies in managerial thinking that perpetuate crisis cycles. First, we hope to find that the belief that it is too expensive to anticipate problems before they occur is mistaken. Following this mindset the crisis has to happen first, with damage done and major costs incurred. This includes not only the costs of repairing equipment, but also temporary relief actions such as distributing diesel generators for temporary use in affected areas, and the cost of post-crisis claims by customers who may have suffered economic losses and are seeking to get them covered. Some countries now require power companies to pay compensation to not only businesses, but also normal households in the event of a power outage [25].

The second fallacy is the belief that a low frequency of severe outages means they are unlikely to occur. Low frequency is an expression of low probability which does not mean that the event cannot occur, but that it could happen tomorrow or in ten years, particularly if the unit of analysis is the individual organization. Europe has experienced several large scale outages, but only one occurred in Italy. For each organization the total experience base from actual large scale outages remain low, but the network integration extends their impact.

The third fallacy is the widespread belief that the crisis reveals most or all the weaknesses in the system. The amount of lessons that can be learned from a single crisis is limited. A single crisis is only the expression of a few systemic vulnerabilities. It is unlikely that those vulnerabilities are the cause of all outages. For example, the 2006 European wide outage was caused by a ship crashing into a power line not by vegetation. Thus, if there is no system in place to detect, report and investigate potential weaknesses before an outage occurs, we will always be waiting for the next major outage. One of the explanations for the success that many safety incident reporting systems, such as those used in the air transportation industry, have achieved is that they provide a much greater basis for learning [14, 23].

A final fallacy is the perceived need to reduce operational costs after a major crisis. A severe outage carries with it many costs. It is conceivable the recovery and restitution of losses from the crisis puts the affected organizations in such a state that decreasing costs is perceived as mandatory, thereby reducing available resources for activities that prevent future crises. An extreme example of this from outside the electric power industry is the Westray mine disaster in Canada [26]. Accidents caused downtime, and thus lost productivity. Since the mine was struggling economically, there was high pressure to increase productivity. This was only possible by taking safety shortcuts. In time the degraded safety led to more accidents, which caused more lost productivity and even higher pressure to increase it, resulting in even more safety shortcuts being taken. This vicious circle ultimately caused a major explosion which cost many lives. Cooke's analysis supports the notion that had safety been prioritized, then the productivity lost by maintaining high safety levels would have been less than the productivity lost due to the accidents. Thus, the negative economic effects of a crisis may divert resources needed for subsequent corrective actions.

It is beyond this paper to provide a detailed analysis of the economics of the power generation and distribution sector, but it is likely that time delays, the difficulty of accurately perceiving the likelihood of infrequent crises, and the ignorance mechanism make it difficult to accurately perceive what the correct level of investment in crisis preparation and prevention activities is. The perceived utility of further investments may be very different from the real utility of it.

The above analysis supports the notion that major power outages are going to reoccur. However, experience from other domains, principally safety, indicates that it is possible to create systems to in advance detect weaknesses that may later cause crises. If they are known and recognized as weaknesses they can be removed and at the very least, protected against. The question is how to achieve that?

5   Policy and Implementation

It is not the objective of this paper to analyze in detail the policy implications, but we can conclude from the analysis that some sort of system is needed to counteract the short term economic pressures. One possibility for raising awareness is distributing information on weaknesses and outages. While outages are seldom for individual parts of the grid, they are common for the grid as a whole.

A possible solution is centres for information sharing and coordination. An example of such centres come from the information security domain in the United States where they have established Information Sharing and Analysis Centres (ISACS) for different industrial sectors at the encouragement of the US Government [27]. Existing organizations such as ENTSOE[2] may be able to fill some of this role. A question to consider is whether participation should be encouraged, that is voluntary, or required, or a combination. A purely voluntary model might make it subject to the same short term economic pressures as described in the previous section.

It is also unlikely that a central information sharing and analysis centre will work if the participating organizations do not have adequate corresponding local systems. It is likely that an attempt at establishing a European wide system for vulnerability detection must be supported by legislation at both the European and national level.

Implementation of such a solution is likely to be an arduous effort, given the many involved states and organizations and the complexity of the problem. There are many accounts of the difficulty of implementing near-accident/vulnerability reporting systems even in single organizations [10, 28].

This short and incomplete analysis of policy and its implementation is a first step to address the complexity of achieving a uniform solution across the European power system.

6 Conclusion

We have presented the outcome of two Group Model Building workshops performed with participating experts on the power system and crisis management. The examination has been from a high level strategic viewpoint and we have avoided technical details. The analysis indicates that long time delays in the system, combined with an ignorance of crisis causing weaknesses are a principal cause of long term crisis proneness. Our work is still in progress. We are currently building a simulation model to further examine the behavioural implications of the model structure presented in this paper. We are also working on extending the analysis beyond the power system itself to the effect on other critical infrastructures and society in general. Our goal is to be able to simulate the system as it is today to allow crisis managers to simulate outages with different severity, and test policies in order to deliver recommendations to mitigate damage and improve recovery for future crises..

The model presented here embodies a problem which has both high combinatorial and dynamic complexity. Validation is therefore not a trivial task and is still ongoing. To determine whether the model is useful we are consulting literature, the experts attending our workshops and other data sources. When the simulation model is developed comparison of its behaviour with statistics, when they are available, provide another check. However, in many cases statistics are not available and expert judgment must substitute.

Acknowledgments

We would like to acknowledge the support of the Directorate-General of Justice, Freedom and Security of the European Commission which through the programme for "Prevention, Preparedness and Consequence Management of Terrorism and other Security related risks" has financially supported our project SEMPOC (www.sempoc.eu, agreement no JLS/2008/CIPS/024), in which the three GMB workshops s took place. We also thank the experts who participated in our workshops.

---

[2] ENTSOE is an association of 42 TSOs from 32 countries in Europe.
   http://www.entsoe.eu/

References

1. CRE and AEEG, Report on the events of September 28th, culminating in the separation of the Italian power system from the other UCTE networks. CRE & AEEG (2003)
2. Force, U.-C.P.S.O.T., Final Report on the August 14, Blackout in the United States and Canada: Causes and Recommendations, US Department of Energy & Canada Ministry of Natural Resources (2003)
3. Roux-Dufort, C.: Is Crisis Management (Only) a Management of Exceptions. Journal of Contingencies and Crisis Management 15(2), 106–114 (2007)
4. Roux-Dufort, C.: The Devil Lies in the Details! How Crises Build up Withing Organizations. Journal of Contingencies and Crisis Management 17(1), 5–11 (2009)
5. Turner, B.: The Organizational and Inter-organizational Development of Disasters. Administrative Science Quarterly 21(3), 378–397 (1976)
6. Turner, B.: Man-Made Disasters. Wykeham Publications, London (1978)
7. Vaughan, D.: Autonomy, Interdependence and Social Control: NASA and the Space Shuttle Challenger. Administrative Science Quarterly 35(2), 225–257 (1990)
8. Coombs, W.T.: Ongoing Crisis Communication: Planning, Managing and Responding, 2nd edn. Sage, Los Angeles (2007)
9. Jones, S., Kirchsteiger, C., Bjerke, W.: The Importance of Near Miss Reporting to Further Improve Safety Performance. Journal of Loss Prevention in the Process Industries 12(1), 59–67 (1999)
10. Nielsen, K.J., Carstensen, O., Rasmussen, K.: The Prevention of Occupational Injuries in Two Industrial Plants Using an Incident Reporting Scheme. Journal of Safety Research 37(5), 479–486 (2006)
11. Phimister, J.R., et al.: Near-Miss Incident Management in the Chemical Process Industry. Risk Analysis 23(3), 445–459 (2003)
12. Sveen, F.O.: The Dynamics of Incident Reporting Systems: From Safety to Security. In: Department of Industrial Management, p. 438. San Sebastian, Tecnun (University of Navarra) (2009)
13. Sveen, F.O., Sarriegi, J.M., Gonzalez, J.J.C.: Incident Response and User Awareness. In: Mjølsnes, S.F. (ed.) NISK2009 - Norsk Informasjonssikkerhetskonferanse, pp. 13–26. apir Akademisk Forlag, Trondheim (2009)
14. Sveen, F.O., Rich, E., Jager, M.: Overcoming Organizational Challenges to Secure Knowledge Management. Information Systems Frontiers 9(5), 481–492 (2007)
15. ERGEG, ERGEG Final Report: The lessons to be learned from the large disturbance in the European Power System in the 4th of November 2006. In: European Regulators' Group for Electricity and Gas (2007)
16. Chang, S.E., et al.: Infrastructure failure interdependencies in extreme events: power outage consequences in the 1998 Ice Storm. Natural Disasters 41, 337–358 (2007)
17. Andersen, D.F., Richardson, G.P.: Scripts for Group Model Building. System Dynamics Review 13(2), 107–129 (1997)
18. Richardson, G.P., Andersen, D.F.: Teamwork in Group Model Building. System Dynamics Review 11(2), 113–137 (1995)
19. Vennix, J.A.M.: Group Model Building: Facilitating team learning using System Dynamics. John Wiley and Sons, Chichester (1996)
20. Forrester, J.W.: Industrial Dynamics. Productivity Press, Cambridge (1961)
21. Richardson, G.P., Pugh III, A.L.: Introduction to System Dynamics Modeling with DYNAMO. Productivity Press, Cambridge (1981)

22. Sterman, J.D.: Business Dynamics: Systems Thinking and Modeling for a Complex World. Irwin McGraw-Hill, Boston (2000)
23. Johnson, C.: Failure in Safety-Critical Systems: A Handbook of Incident and Accident Reporting. Glasgow University Press, Glasgow (2003)
24. Schulman, P., et al.: High Reliability and the Management of Critical Infrastructures. Journal of Contingencies and Crisis Management 12(1), 14–28 (2004)
25. Palm, J.: Emergency Management in the Swedish Electricity Grid from a Household Perspective. Journal of Contingencies and Crisis Management 17(1), 55–63 (2009)
26. Cooke, D.L.: A System Dynamics analysis of the Westray mine disaster. System Dynamics Review 19, 139–166 (2003)
27. Gal-Or, E., Ghose, A.: The Economic Incentives for Sharing Security Information. Information Systems Research 16(2), 186–208 (2005)
28. Cooke, D.L., Rohleder, T.R.: Learning from Incidents: from Normal Accidents to High Reliability. System Dynamics Review 22(3), 213–239 (2006)

Early Warning System for Cascading Effect Control in Energy Control Systems

Cristina Alcaraz, Angel Balastegui, and Javier Lopez

Computer Science Department - University of Malaga,
29071 - Malaga, Spain
{alcaraz,balaguesti,jlm}@lcc.uma.es

Abstract. A way of controlling a cascading effect caused by a failure or a threat in a critical system is using intelligent mechanisms capable of predicting anomalous behaviours and also capable of reacting against them in advance. These mechanisms are known as Early Warning Systems (EWSs) and this will be precisely the main topic of this paper. More specifically, we present in this paper an EWS design based on a Wireless Sensor Network (using the ISA100.11a standard) that constantly supervises the application context. This EWS is also based on forensic techniques to provide dynamic learning capacities. As a result, this new approach will aid to provide a reliable control of incidences by offering a dynamic alarm management system, identification of the most suitable field operator to attend an alarm, reporting of causes and responsible operators, and learning from new anomalous situations.

Keywords: Early Warning System, Wireless Sensor Network, Forensic Techniques, Energy Control Systems, SCADA Systems, Cascading Effect.

1 Introduction

In recent years, electrical energy industry, scientific community and governments are becoming interested in bringing new energy distribution strategies, since these services are fundamental for our economy and social well-being [1]. To be more precise, the most of our critical infrastructures (e.g. transportation systems or communication systems) are highly dependent on electrical energy services to efficiently work and provide their respective services. In other words, a failure (cause) in an energy substation could involve a harmful *cascading effect* (effect) in the business continuity [2]. For this reason, these systems have to trust in other specialized systems, known as SCADA (Supervisory Control and Data Acquisition) systems.

A SCADA system is a complex and distributed system composed of communication networks using a wide range of technologies for control in real-time. These technologies allow human operators to keep a global view of the real state of the critical infrastructure and its application context. However, this technological use involves a new challenge give that these control systems are more and more dependent on communication systems to supervise remote substations localized at different and distant geographical localizations. A failure in the satellite/microwave communication could result in a lack of monitoring, meaning important consequences in energy distribution. Then, it is clear

C. Xenakis and S. Wolthusen (Eds.): CRITIS 2010, LNCS 6712, pp. 55–66, 2011.

that different stakeholders are joining efforts to try to solve some security issues related to communication and technology systems.

So far, some security aspects have already been considered by the literature. Among them, identification and authorization, security policies, control access policies, communication network protection and information systems protection. All of these security areas make use of different security mechanisms (such as firewalls, Demilitarized Zones (DMZs), Intrusion Detection Systems (IDS), Virtual Private Networks (VPNs), etc.), cryptographic primitives, standards and recommendations (such as ANSI/ISA-99 [3]). However, there are other security mechanisms that are not yet properly used by the Industry, such as for example EWSs. These systems could add new security functionalities by offering control of anomalous events. Thus, it is possible to previously predict a failure or a threat, and react against it. Therefore, these mechanisms could aid to control significant anomalies which could trigger a possible cascading effect. Precisely, the purpose of this paper is to design an EWS based on a WSN and on forensic techniques to offer: (i) a constant control of anomalous events, (ii) a timely response and (iii) capacity for learning of future anomalous events. As a result, the system will be able to face new situations without requiring a manual procedure to update its knowledge.

The paper is organized as follows. Section 2 presents the SCADA architecture and an alternative technology for industrial control. Section 3 highlights our contribution (specifically in Section 3.2) and justifies its importance in industrial systems through a use case presented in Section 3.3. Finally, Section 4 concludes the paper and outlines the future work.

2 SCADA System and Control Technologies

Any activity and event executed in an electrical energy system must be properly controlled. To this end, these systems have to trust other specific systems to manage, control and supervise such activities, ensuring performance and reliability in energy distribution. These control systems are known as SCADA systems.

2.1 SCADA Network Architecture

A SCADA system is based on three types of sub-networks (see Figure 1): (i) the central network, (ii) remote substations composed of Remote Unit Terminals (RTUs) and (iii) the corporative network. The operations carried out in the central network are related to the control and management of the critical infrastructure. Such operations are managed through specific operator consoles or human-machine interfaces (HMIs), which allow operators to read specific physical parameters (e.g. electrical signals, temperature, etc.) or alarms received from RTUs, or even transmit certain commands to specific field devices located in remote substations. The operations carried out in the corporative network are directly related to the general supervision of the system whose accesses to databases and servers (installed in the central network) are rather restricted.

This network architecture is complex and heterogeneous (see Figure 1), where new and old technologies have to coexist in a same environment of control. To be more precise, a SCADA system, belonging to the third generation or *Networked* generation, includes in its network design both serial and TCP/IP communication in order to break

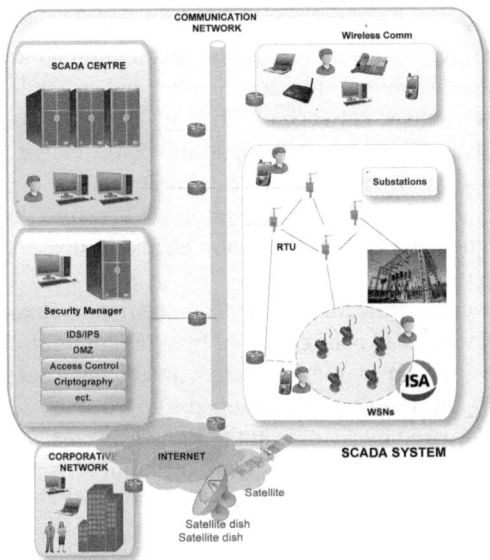

Fig. 1. A SCADA Network Architecture

with the isolation concept of the previous generations (i.e. *Monolithic* and *Distributed*) [4]. Furthermore, TCP/IP connections make possible monitoring in real-time, peer-to-peer communication from anywhere at any time, multiple sessions, concurrency, maintenance, redundancy, security services and connectivity.

Likewise, all these technical advances are also used in remote substations, where RTUs are able to provide a hierarchical and an inter-RTU communication (i.e., interconnectivity among RTUs) under TCP/IP, as well as wired and wireless communication interfaces, Web services, management and forwarding to other remote points. Due to these advances, RTUs might work as data concentrators (to store large data streams) and/or as remote access controllers (to autonomously and remotely reconfigure/recover parts of the system). Lastly, migration to TCP/IP also meant the standardization and implementation of new SCADA protocols capable of understanding TCP/IP connections. Currently, there are several IP-based SCADA protocols, such as Modbus/TCP, DNP3, IEC-104 and ICCP/TASE2. The three first ones are used for automation, whereas ICCP is specific for inter-communication between telemetry control systems.

Special attention should be paid to wireless industrial sensor networks since this is nowadays one of the most demanded wireless control technologies by the Industry. In fact, they are considered as an optional control technology (see Section 2.2) for monitoring since it can offer the same functionalities as an RTU but to a low installation and maintenance cost. This new alternative and its communication constitute an essential part of the contribution of this paper (see Section 3.2).

2.2   WSN, An Alternative for the Control

A WSN is basically composed of resource-constrained devices, known as sensor nodes. They are autonomous devices capable of sensing information from their surroundings (such as high/low temperature or strong fluctuations in power lines), as well as being capable of processing data streams and communicating with other network nodes. Sensor nodes are also self-configurable, self-healing and smart devices. Precisely, self-configurability allows a sensor network to adapt its topology in order to react against failures, whereas self-healing provides capabilities for facing unexpected network events. Moreover, sensor nodes are able to collaborate among them in order to achieve a common goal (e.g. control of energy generators). Therefore, this technology can be useful in monitoring and surveillance applications, and in inaccessible applications for the human-being (e.g. electrical posts).

Regarding the network architecture, WSNs can be deployed and distributed following a flat, hierarchical or hybrid configuration. In a flat configuration, all the nodes can participate in both the decision-making processes and the internal protocols. In contrast, in a hierarchical configuration they are grouped into clusters where all the organizational decisions are addressed by a single entity known as *cluster head* [5]. This node is also in charge of aggregating data streams from different sensor sources for increasing the accuracy of the observed parameters.

As previously commented, this technology is currently considered as one of the most demanded wireless technologies by the control Industry, since it guarantees the same control services as a RTU but to a low installation and maintenance cost [6]. More explicitly, these control services are: on-demand query, detection/tracking capacity of anomalous situations, generation of alarms, and reporting of any life-threatening situation. In addition, there are some examples within the literature that show its useful features for critical systems, since they are also considered as a suitable tool for their protection [7]. Moreover, several wireless industrial communication standards have been recently defined for WSNs, such as ZigBee PRO [8], WirelessHART [9] and ISA100.11a [10]. As a special note, it is important to highlight that this paper is mainly focused on ISA100.11a, since it is an extended version of WirelessHART and it improves some of its services [6].

ISA100.11a allows both mesh and star topologies using: (i) sensor nodes, (ii) routers, (iii) gateways (one or several) to establish redundant connection with the SCADA centre, (iv) backbone routers to provide connectivity to other networks, and (v) two special managers: a system manager and a security manager. The system manager is in charge of allocating resources and providing communication, whereas the security manager affords key management services. Moreover, ISA100.11a is based on the IEEE 802.15.4-2006 standard, which specifies the physical (PHY) and Media Access Control layer (MAC) layers for Wireless Personal Area Networks (WPANs), providing it with security mechanisms based on AES-128 bits, Message Authentication Codes (MAC) and an Access Control List (ACL) to authenticate any received message. Furthermore, this standard guarantees an adaptive frequency hopping method and a blacklisting method, synchronization, redundant paths, diagnostic mechanisms, low duty cycle, frequent key update, firmware update in all the devices, compatibility with IPv6 and the 6LowPAN standard, as well as alarm and priority management. Specially, this priority management depends on four subcategories (a device diagnostic, a communication diagnostic, a security alert and a process alarm) and on five priority levels (urgent, high, medium, low and journal). Information from sensors is accessed and managed by objects, such as for example DMAP (Device Management Application Process) and ARMO (Alert Reporting Management) objects. To be more precise, the ARMO class is included within the DMAP class where their objects are able to manage, configure, supervise and request parameters belonging to sensor nodes.

3   Early Warning Systems on the Critical System Protection

A SCADA centre is the main system in charge of managing any data stream received from remote substations. So far, its security basically depends on security policies, access control mechanisms, security applications and specialized mechanisms whose basis is supported by patterns and rules that are capable of identifying anomalous behaviours or events[1], like IDSs. However, all of these security mechanisms do not provide enough resources to predict anomalous events and to previously react against them, such as an EWS could offer us.

3.1   Preventing and Controlling a Cascading Effect

Some examples in real life have shown the importance of protecting these types of critical systems. For example, in 2003, numerous blackouts occurred in United States and Canada, and even in Europe because of various failures found in the information and communication technologies systems (ICTs) [11]. In 2009, a U.S. electrical grid was penetrated by Chinese and Russian intruders resulting in the disruption of the system [12]. In the same year, Brazil and Paraguay suffered a serious blackout during four days due to a failure in Itaipu Dam [13]. Furthermore, the U.S. Department of Energy's Idaho laboratory documented a cyber-attack performed on an energy generator that was shaken violently before going into total meltdown [14]. The idea consisted of showing that many of our critical infrastructures are subject almost to the same vulnerabilities. If this attack had been carried out on a real electrical energy plant, the results could have been devastating for society and economy, whose effect would correspond to a cascading effect. [2]. Due to this, some actions plans and European initiatives have already been proposed [15], as well as approaches based on EWSs [16] to prevent anomalous situations.

Basically, an EWS consists of integrated techniques with capability for providing an advanced monitoring. In other words, this system is able to offer, on the one hand, an analysis and intelligent interpretation of readings obtained from sensors distributed in remote substations. On the other hand, it has the decision-making capacity for avoiding or reducing the propagation of a possible effect originated by an anomalous event [17]. For example, if a threat/failure appears in a substation, it is not enough to detect it and subsequently correct it. The success of an EWS depends on the ability to anticipate the events that could lead to major problems. This way of predicting events could help us face a situation that may disrupt the performance and business continuity of our system or systems because of the strong relationship of interdependence among them.

---

[1] It is important to know the difference between an event and a failure/threat. An anomalous event can be considered as an array of suspected actions. In contrast, a failure or a (either logical or physical attack) threat can be considered as an event sequence related to an anomalous behaviour pattern (or rule).

In any EWS there are four main components: (i) a *detection component*, based on information received from sensors capable of predicting a possible threat, (ii) a *reaction component*, (iii) an *information recollection component* to store evidences, and (v) an *alarm management component*. The reaction component includes a process of decision-making whose determination will depend on the type of threat, criticality of the affected environment, interaction with other involved elements, associated risk and relationship between damage and cost. All of these components have to be working during the three following phases [18]: (1) before a threat/failure (an EWS must anticipate and warn that a set of suspected actions have been registered), (2) during an attack/failure (an EWS must avoid that an effect starts to propagate itself, using for example any isolation technique of nodes, components, networks or connectivity among systems) and (3) after a successful attack/failure (an EWS must control the propagation of a threat towards other systems).

Our contribution goes a step further. The approach proposed in this paper is based not only on components previously mentioned but also on forensic techniques as a special support that aids to understand, at first level, the causes of an incidence and to learn from it. To this end, our forensic component has to include a set of processes capable of analyzing the evidences that took place before and during a fact, in addition to applying learning techniques to automatically update the knowledge of the system with new behaviour patterns. Lastly, it is important to highlight that although this approach has been exclusively focused on energy control systems, it can be equally applied in other critical systems (see Section 3.3).

3.2   Early Warning System Based on Forensic Techniques

This section presents our approach of an EWS based on the ISA100.11a standard, which defines a set of parameters, services and connections among network components [10]. In our case, sensor nodes are grouped into clusters and deployed close to controlled critical infrastructure, i.e. close to electric energy generators (see Figure 2). This network follows a hierarchical structure to allow a more detailed control in different areas, facilitating a better localization of anomalies. For example, if a failure happens in a determined point of the infrastructure, it is possible to attend it by knowing a priori the affected area belonging to a specific cluster.

Due to the functionality of each cluster head, it is possible to filter readings (e.g. temperature, voltage) and check alarms generated by sensors at a first level. The result must be retransmitted to a special node (i.e., a gateway), which includes all the logical of the approach (see the Figure 2). As already mentioned, ISA100.11a allows network configurations based on gateways with enough resources to interpret and translate SCADA commands (e.g. step up input voltage) to a protocol that the sensor nodes can understand, and vice versa. Moreover, the EWS design could be implemented in several gateways, one of them working as a primary node and the rest in standby. Note that this aspect is out of the scope of this paper, but we believe that it should be considered for a future work.

Our EWS design is based on two main components: (i) an *EWS component* and (ii) a *forensic component*. Both collaborating with each other in order to share information. From an abstract point of view, the EWS component will be in charge of analyzing and

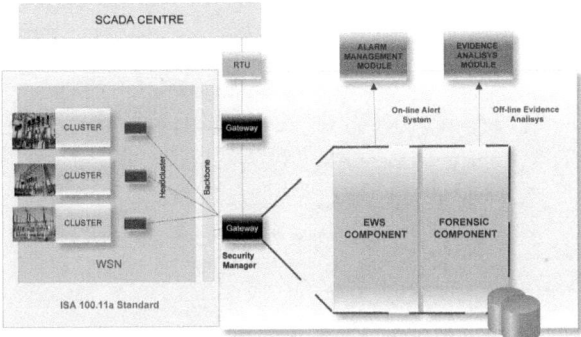

Fig. 2. An Early Warning System based on WSNs and Forensic Tecniques

managing event streams received from cluster heads in *on-line* mode [19]. In particular, this type of management involves analyzing, prioritizing and alerting the closest field operator through an alarm that facilitates a timely response.

Likewise, the EWS component has to activate the forensic component in order to inform the SCADA centre about the causes of a fact and its origin, specifying the evidences happened. However, its functionality does not finish here. The forensic component has to be able to learn from this fact, as well as generating a new pattern/rule if a specific event is not associated to a determined pattern. To this end, it will be necessary to analyze a set of factors (e.g. past evidences, sensitive parameters, context conditions, criticality of affected area, impact and risk, etc.) and/or use specialized techniques, some of which will be discussed below. The procedure finishes when the new pattern is stored for a future use. Due to the complexity of this last component, it has to work in *off-line* mode (i.e., it is only activated when an anomalous event is detected), avoiding that the overall performance of the system becomes degraded. Lastly, both modes allow the system to manage properly any type of event given that the EWS component and the Forensic component always deliver such events to the SCADA center.

EWS component. Figure 3 shows how the system is able to receive any event flow and how the system is able to filter and normalize such information to be managed later by the rest of modules. The idea is to combine and represent different event inputs in a same generic format under a semantic abstraction. This abstraction facilitates obtaining a general description of the entities and elements involved with their respective ontological links. The final representation has to be analyzed and compared using a knowledge source based on anomalous behaviour patterns or rules.

However, how can we establish the difference between a normal behaviour or an anomalous behaviour in our critical environment [19,20]? To answer this question, it is necessary to identify a priori a set of anomalous events within this particular critical scenario, such as a circuit break, stresses, strong fluctuations, high voltage in a power line, structural changes in the environment, etc. However, these are not the only events to be taken into account within a control industry. Nowadays, it is important to consider those events related to ICTs since today's industry is more and more dependent on them for the control. Hence, an event can be also found at any level of the TCP/IP

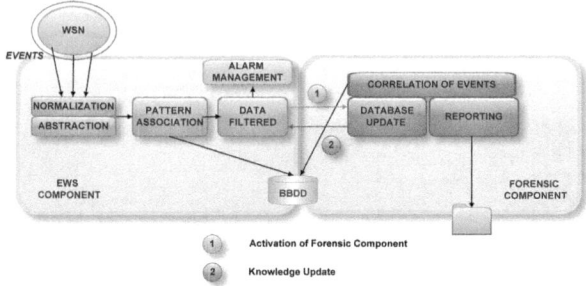

Fig. 3. Internal Structure of the EWS based on WSNs and Forensic Techniques

standard, i.e. from the physical level to the application level. For instance, an anomalous event may come as disturbances in IP packets (e.g. IEC-104 commands), changes in nodes synchronization processes, changes in network initialization processes or alterations in key negotiation processes. It would be also interesting to analyze the state of communication channel, the functionality of nodes (dead or alive nodes), addressing, I/O interfaces, routing and interconnection among nodes. Furthermore, some security weaknesses, vulnerabilities, threats and intruders corresponding to specific industrial standards, among them the ISA100.11a standard, have already been analyzed in [6].

Four situations may arise in our critical context: (i) *false positive*, if the analyzed event is innocuous, but it is classified as a threat (failure/intrusion); (ii) *true positive*, if the analyzed event is properly classified as a threat (failure/intrusion); *false negative*, if the analyzed event is a threat (failure/intrusion) but it is classified as normal/innocuous; and *true negative*, if the analyzed event is correctly classified as normal/innocuous. This fact means that our approach has to be configured with some existing anomaly-based detection technique (e.g. Bayesian networks, Markov models, fuzzy logic, etc. [21]) to ensure a low false negative rate. Note that a low false positive rate would also be ideal, but a low false positive rate in a CI is not really a problem, since any type of suspect threat/failure must be managed. The problem emerges when anomalous events really appear in the system and they are not properly detected.

The next step of this component would be to analyze what type of information to include in an alarm (such as the identification of the affected node, the localization of the affected area/line, the event, etc.) and locate the closest field operator in the area. To this end, the alarm manager must configure in its system an intelligent mechanism with a support to estimate the suitable field operator to efficiently respond to a determined incidence, such as the Automated Adaptive Response Manager based on reputation proposed in [22]. Finally, and equally, it is important to provide the forensic component with enough information to carry out its activities.

Forensic component. This component, configured in parallel to the EWS component, is based on forensic techniques. A traditional forensic technique is composed of four essential phases [23]: (i) information recollection, (ii) relevant information extraction, (iii) information analysis and (iv) reporting. Note that the two first phases were already carried out by the EWS component through a filtered and an abstract representation of an event sequence received from sensors. On the contrary, the two last phases have to be contemplated by this component to correlate and trace such an event sequence, which will likely lead to an incidence.

A way of correlating and tracing events could be to include a unique ID to each system process, such as Goel et.al. described in [20]. Thus, it is possible to efficiently trace accesses registers, services and resources, as well as commands and alarms signalled. Another solution could be to represent the event sequence and their links through a Markov graph on a time line [24]. However, none of them establishes a relationship between an event/process and a responsible member in the system. For this reason, the operator's ID must be also required for the detection along with an identity database to efficiently carry out this new purpose. As a result, the system will be able to estimate the real causes of an incidence along with the responsible operator/s. Last but not least, in case where an event (or an event sequence) is not related to a pattern, the system will have to activate the *pattern generation* module to update our knowledge source (i.e., the pattern database) of our design (see Figure 3), using for example data-mining [25].

3.3   Use Case and Discussion

In order to understand with more detail the functionality of our approach, the discussion will mainly be focused on analyzing a Denial of Service (DoS) attack in a specific cluster head corresponding to an energy substation. It is clear that the intruder's goal is basically to isolate an essential part of the control. Nevertheless, our system can face this situation, since the gateway has to constantly receive information from the environment. If a cluster head stopped sending messages during a long time, then the gateway detects an anomalous behaviour in the network and it starts to check the node state and its availability (i.e., dead or alive node) using DMAP objects. If the node does not respond, then the EWS component determines that something happened in that network area.

Consequently, the EWS component also starts to analyze the application context using information of neighbour nodes (i.e. using DMAP objects to receive such information from them) and anomaly-based patterns. Obviously, in this situation, the first patterns to analyze should be those related to the availability (e.g. flooding, black hole attack, wormhole attack, etc.) to provide a quick response. When an intrusion is detected in the system, the alarm management module has to generate an ISA100.11a alert (using ARMO objects) with high priority in order to guarantee assistance in the isolated area. The information to transmit has to include, at least, the affected area localization, the compromised node and the type of event. Note that if such alarm is not attended in a determined time $t1$, a new alarm will have to be sent with an urgent priority to ensure response in a time $t2$, where $t1 > t2$. This time limitation makes the system react quickly, and thus to recover the control before a serious problem appears definitively in the non-controlled and unattended area.

In parallel, the forensic component has to determine the main causes and the operator's ID, analyzing commands, active services, registers, unauthorized accesses, etc. Some of these attacks were recently analyzed in [6], where type of intruder (i.e., insider and/or outsider), original causes and countermeasures were identified. Taking advantage of this analysis, we can previously initialize the system with information from attacks and provide the SCADA centre with information to identify intruders and some countermeasures. For example, and according to this, if a black hole attack (not retransmit messages to the next hop) was launched, then we can ensure that a selective forwarding attack previously took place by a malicious insider with enough permission to access the energy substation. All of this information must be immediately sent to the SCADA centre. Lastly, it is worth mentioning that this component does not require updating the database, since the attack was properly detected by the EWS component. Otherwise, a learning technique/model should have been applied, such as for instance a Markov model or data-mining. Nonetheless, this is still an unexplored research area, since the context is highly-critical and it requires a constant performance and reliability of the learning.

Finally, the expected results from the approach in critical scenarios are as follows:

1. Supervision in areas to offer a timely response and control of a possible cascading effect.
2. Safety and Security: Safety in the control of cascading effect and its repercussion in our society and economy. This control is based on a detection mechanism under the use of a persistent and smart alarm manager. This manager is capable of reaching the most suitable field operator (which is equipped with mobile devices) to attend a determined incidence. With respect to security, the system is able to identify a responsible operator since an event is associated to an operator's ID, in addition to learning how to face future situations through forensic techniques.
3. Performance: The approach is included in a high-resource gateway (or several) to work in parallel with other elements of the system. It is important to highlight that part of this logic runs in off-line mode.
4. Adaptability. This approach can equally work in an ISA100.11a network, a ZigBee PRO network and a WirelessHART network, since all of them keep certain topological, structural and functional characteristics. Moreover, as this approach is based on a specific and recognized standard, it can also work in any type of application context (e.g. a transportation system, oil/water distribution systems...).
5. Auditing and maintenance. The system could improve its auditing and maintenance procedures given that the the system is able to keep the operator's ID and explain the causes of an incident.

4   Conclusions and Future Work

This paper presents a design of an Early Warning System used to control anomalous behaviours and events registered in electrical energy substations. The approach is based on Wireless Sensor Networks under the ISA100.11a standard and on forensic techniques. More specifically, WSNs allow supervising the controlled critical infrastructure whereas the forensic techniques ensure an updated knowledge. The idea is to anticipate anomalous event sequences, react against them on time and dynamically learn from new anomalous situations. As a result, the proposed design tries to solve one of the security issues still unexplored in critical systems, i.e. the control of the cascading effect.

The approach is based on two main components whose main goals are: (i) to detect an anomaly, (ii) to efficiently manage an alarm, (iii) to identify the most suitable field operator to attend it, (iv) to analyze causes and responsible members, and (v) to automatically learn from this anomaly. This latter point helps the system not to require a manual process to update its own knowledge source. The functionality of this approach has been also discussed by using a specific scenario as a use case. Lastly, this paper has also opened new research areas to explore, such as intelligent alarm management systems, dynamic localization mechanisms, and design of both detection models and forensic techniques for highly-critical applications, which require a quick and reliable response.

For the future, we intend to implement the proposed design in order to show its feasibility in a real and critical context, in addition to researching how to directly include all the logic of this approach within sensor nodes. However, this will depend on the computational capabilities and resources offered by sensor nodes, which are still constrained. Likewise, a security analysis of the approach will have to be performed to evaluate its integrity against existing and future vulnerabilities, threats and failures.

Acknowledgments

This work has been partially supported by the projects: PROTECT-IC (TSI-020302-2009-10), ARES (CSD2007-00004) and SPRINT (TIN2009-09237), being the last one also co-funded by FEDER. The first author has been funded by the Spanish FPI Research Programme. The authors would like to thank M. Carmen Fernandez-Gago her constructive comments and valuable suggestions.

References

1. NIST, Smart Grid Cyber Security Strategy and Requirements, The Smart Grid Interoperability Panel-Cyber Security Working Group, Draft NISTIR 7628, U.S. Department of Commerce (2010)
2. Peerenboom, J., Fishe, R.: Analyzing Cross-Sector Interdependencies. In: IEEE Computer Society, HICSS, pp. 112–119. IEEE Computer Society, Los Alamitos (2007)
3. ANSI/ISA-99.02.01-2009 standard, Security for Industrial Automation and Control Systems Part 2: Establishing an Industrial Automation and Control Systems Security Program (2009)
4. Mcclanahan, R.: SCADA and IP, Is Network Convergence Really Here? IEEE Industry Applications (2003)
5. Lopez, J., Roman, R., Alcaraz, C.: Analysis of Security Threats, Requirements, Technologies and Standards in Wireless Sensor Network. In: Foundations of Security Analysis and Design V. LNCS, vol. 5705, pp. 289–338. Springer, Heidelberg (2009)
6. Alcaraz, C., Lopez, J.: A Security Analysis for Wireless Sensor Mesh Networks in Highly Critical Systems. IEEE Transactions on Systems, Man, and Cybernetics, Part C: Applications and Reviews PP(99), 1–10 (2010)
7. Roman, R., Alcaraz, C., Lopez, J.: The role of Wireless Sensor Networks in the area of Critical Information Infrastructure Protection. Information Security Technical Report 12(1), 24–31 (2007)
8. ZigBee Alliance, http://www.zigbee.org/ (accessed on May 2010)
9. WirelessHART, http://WirelessHART.hartcomm.org/, HART Communication Foundation, (accessed on February 2010)

10. ISA100.11a, ISA-100.11a-2009. Wireless systems for Industrial Automation: Process Control and Related Applications, ISA. The International Society of Automation (2009)
11. Bialek, J.: Critical Interrelations between ICT and Electricity System. In: Electricity Security in the Cyber Age: Managing the Increasing Dependence of the Electricity Infrastructure on ICT (NGInfra), Utrecht, The Netherlands (2009)
12. Electricity Grid in U.S. Penetrated By Spies, The WallStreet Journal News registered on (April 2009), http://online.wsj.com/article/SB123914805204099085.html
13. Power Failure Blacks Out Much of Brazil, Paraguay, The WallStreet Journal News registered on (November 2009), http://en.wikipedia.org/wiki/Itaipu
14. Salmon, D., Zeller, M., Guzman, A., Mynam, V., Donolo, M.: Mitigating the Aurora Vulnerability With Existing Technology. Schweitzer Engineering Laboratories, Inc. (2007)
15. Critical Infrastructure Warning Information Network, EPCIP, http://europa.eu/legislation_summaries/justice_freedom_security/fight_against_terrorism/l33260_en.htm, (accessed on July 2010)
16. Apel, M., Biskup, J., Flegel, U., Meier, M.: Towards early warning systems – challenges, technologies and architecture. In: Rome, E., Bloomfield, R. (eds.) CRITIS 2009. LNCS, vol. 6027, pp. 151–164. Springer, Heidelberg (2010)
17. Walter, K., Nash, E.: Coupling Wireless Sensor Networks and the Sensor Observation Service - Bridging the Interoperability Gap. In: 12th Agile International Conference on Geographic Information Science (2009)
18. Bastke, S., Deml, M., Schmidt, S.: Internet Early Warning Systems. Overview and Architecture (December 2009)
19. Technologies and Techniques for Early Warning Systems to Monitor and Evaluate Drinking Water Quality: A State-of-the-Art Revie, Office of Research and Development National Homeland Security Research centre. EPA, United States Environmental Protection Agency (August 2005)
20. Goel, A., Shea, M., Ahuja, S., Feng, W., Mailer, D., Walpole, J.: Forensix: A Robust, High-Performance Reconstruction System (2009)
21. Garcia, P., Diaz, J., Macia, G., Vazquez, E.: Anomaly-based network intrusion detection: Techniques, systems and challenges. Computers & Security Journal 28(1-2), 18–28 (2009)
22. Alcaraz, C., Agudo, I., Fernandez-Gago, C., Roman, R., Fernandez, G., Lopez, J.: Adaptive Dispatching of Incidences Based on Reputation for SCADA Systems. In: Fischer-Hübner, S., Lambrinoudakis, C., Pernul, G. (eds.) TrustBus 2009. LNCS, vol. 5695, pp. 86–94. Springer, Heidelberg (2009)
23. NIST, Guide to Integrating Forensic Techniques into Incident Response, National Institute of Standards and Technology (2006)
24. Syr, B.K.: Integrating intrusion alert information to aid forensic explanation: An analytical intrusion detection framework for distributive IDS. In: Information Fusion, Elsevier, Amsterdam (2009)
25. Zanero, S., Savaresi, S.: Unsupervised learning techniques for an intrusion detection system. In: SAC 2004: Proceedings of the 2004 ACM Symposium on Applied Computing, pp. 412–419 (2004)

Emergency Response with Proactive Crowd-Sourcing Reverse-111

Anu Vaidyanathan

Computer Engineering Department,
Indian Institute of Technology,
Nangal Road, Ropar, India
anu@iitrpr.ac.in

Abstract. In this paper, we demonstrate the use of Reverse-111, a *proactive crowd sourcing system* which takes into account the fact that several users might be co-located with an emergency and can be contacted by an Emergency Response Centre (ERC), to provide relevant and useful information pertaining to an emergency situation. We have co-developed a variety of first responder agents who can participate within a response simulation wherein participation is solicited from local citizens in a crowd. Cell-phone records are used to identify the location of callers on the ground and choose people close to an emergency scene in order to obtain information about the emergency and issue early warnings about changing resource requirements.

Keywords: emergency response, early-warning systems, crowd sourcing, cell-phone caller record, first-responder simulation.

1 Introduction

The Reverse 111 tool extends the RimSim Response architecture [1] that has been developed as a visual analytics project, which enables ERCs to plan and train for potential emergencies and crises that might arise in their area of responsibility. This architecture was built primarily to enable the notion of synchrony amongst the various administrative units, in responding to an emergency. The Emergency Response Centre personnel are required to manage situations on a day-to-day basis and participating in a variety of drills prepares them for scenarios that are unforeseen. Within Reverse-111, various situations can be simulated including bio-weapon attacks, tsunamis and earthquakes. Several bodies including the National Incident Management System (NIMS) provides first responders with guidelines for activities to train personnel in. A lack of real-time data and an increase in complexity when it comes to distributed management provides a sizeable challenge in this area.

We develop a tool for New Zealand, which simulates disasters at various intervals and various geographic locations, that are potentially tied to different administrative domains and we present our initial findings from interacting with multiple agent simulation sessions. Our tool introduces the location of citizens as a layer in our visualization, as identified by per call measurement data (PCMD), obtained from a leading cell-phone provider within New Zealand. PCMD is a feature-rich data-set

C. Xenakis and S. Wolthusen (Eds.): CRITIS 2010, LNCS 6712, pp. 67–80, 2011.

recoding several aspects on a cell-phone call such as the identifier pertaining to individual phones, service type, number dialed, call length, signal quality, timing from pilots, sector in which the call was placed, the call result, the reason why the call ended etc. By using an anonymized trace and the attributes pertaining to the caller's location, we identify one or more citizens on the ground that are co-located with the emergency being simulated. As we simulate emergencies and their respective resources, used to mitigate the emergency by moving the resource in the direction of the emergency (incident), the ERC obtains real-time information from callers and is able to change the resource requirements or access-paths by means of a feedback loop, as if in conversation with a caller who is providing information as the emergency unfolds. In this case, co-located citizens are proactively sourced to obtain early warnings about the changing parameters, relating to an incident. The most famous example where this could be applied is a post-mortem analysis of Hurricane Katrina, where the biggest requirement for the evacuees was ice, which is not an intuitive resource that first responders carry with them.

In the first part of our evaluation, we propose the use of three different agents, greedy, round-robin and lottery that implement response heuristics and communications strategies to enable a successful community response to crisis. In the second part of our evaluation, we introduce two more agents (also referred to as schedulers), the local and local-plus, which are designed to contrast resource to incident matching strategies, in order to discern which of the greedy, lottery and round-robin schedulers perform the best, while encoding crowd-sourced information as a fixed delay in the simulator. Section 2 outlines the basic system for proactive crowd sourcing within reverse-111, section 3 introduces the resource schedulers in detail, section 4 talks about the visualization interface that we have used and section 5 presents the performance evaluation in terms of throughput and latency of the various schedulers.

2   Reverse 111 – Proactive Crowd Sourcing

Reverse 111 proposes *co-locating users with emergencies and obtaining information from them* about the emergency. Older proposals for emergency management have overlooked developing a step-wise and methodical consideration of the phases within an emergency situation, shown in Fig. 1.

Keeping this modular design goal in mind, we present a solution to enable various administrative domains, varying *scales* of emergencies and *proactive* real-time information gathering to respond better to situations. Current implementations of emergency situations [2,3,4,5] are not dynamic enough to take into account real-time

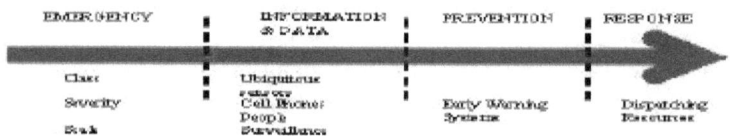

Fig. 1. Phases in an emergency

information (which is essentially a resource, in the abstract sense) that might be made available to the emergency responders, by contacting users on the ground. By delineating a resource-scheduling strategy into different *schedulers* or *agents* we demonstrate the utility of evaluating various response mechanisms, which will contribute to our overall understanding of how well systems perform, in times of crisis. Our system further incorporates live caller data from PCMD records within New Zealand, which is the country within which our system is run.

2.1 System Overview

Reverse 111 extends RimSim Response in the design, implementation and evaluation of computer-mediated agents by adding agent-driven communication services and agent-driven dynamic visualization interactions into our software. The central communications server, relational database services and machine algorithm components did not need to change to support our experiments. We further added a layer to the system, comprised of cell phone calls in the area, which enables us to identify users co-located with the emergency. The overall system is shown in Fig. 2.

Traces were collected from a leading telephone service provider's CDMA network, where a Per Call Measurement Data (PCMD) feature is present. PCMD provides access to key network information for every 3G1x (voice, SMS or data) call that is placed via the network. PCMD records provide an unprecedented, unobtrusive view of customer behavior and end-user performance, collected live from ubiquitous and pervasive mobile sensors, cell phones. In order to obtain a geographical view of information pertaining to the network, a geo-location algorithm was used to extract location information from PCMD. CDMA has a unique timing and hand-off system, which make the data very fine-grained. By utilizing maximum likelihood methods in the geo-location algorithm, triangulation estimates are refined to the highest probability location. Field calibration has a per-call median error of ~140meters, averaged over all call locations wherein increased accuracy results from the user placing the call when closest to cell sites. The main data-set used in this study was collected from the Wellington on the date of an All-Blacks rugby game to understand how traffic varies on important or event-oriented days of the year. Further, data was collected on a Friday and a Sunday, wherein the number of calls on a Friday is orders of magnitude larger than those placed on Sunday on the dates of March 27th, 2009 and March 29th, 2009, in Wellington. Analysis of the traces was carried out by incorporating the data sets into the system.

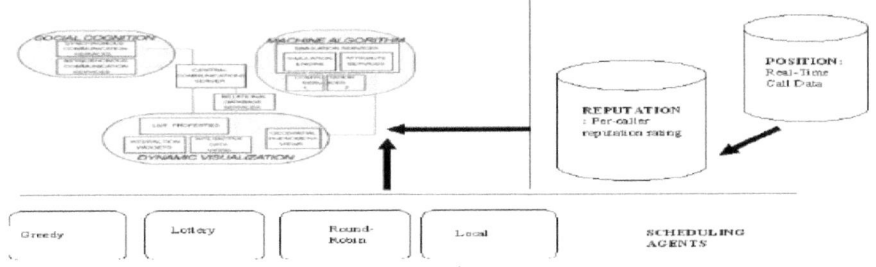

Fig. 2. System Overview including agents

PCMD traces are collected from three switches in Auckland (AK), Christchurch (CH) and Wellington (WN), in order to analyze user patterns in these big urban centers. The data is accumulated at a file server and transferred there via FTP. This is then sent to a data-loader with our custom software, which parses the raw PCMD to scan for characteristics of interest. The data-loader contains means to load the data into custom databases, run queries on the data and means to interact with the data and feed it to a visualization interface. Standard maps of New Zealand in general and the three urban centers in particular are also stored in the data-loader, in order to map the location of calls and track them through the lifetime of the call. Fig. 3 shows how the data is collected from three different switches and sent to an FTP server, where it is temporarily stored before being passed

2.2   System Architecture

Fig. 3 shows the overall system architecture of Reverse 111. The system has several modular entities that act in conjunction to simulate emergencies, resource-requirements of the emergency events, resource locations, path attributes considered while routing a resource to the requesting event, schedulers that are used to evaluate various metrics including the ease of incorporating real-time information from users o-located with those emergencies, the ease of transcending administrative domains when responding to an emergency and the ease of path re-computation given that in a crisis situation the initial assumptions about the environment are not valid if the situation changes (for example, in the case of an earthquake, the roads might not be functional along the line of the fault and may vary in time as follow-on quakes happen or other constraints present themselves). We discuss the main entities of our system below with working examples:

EVENTS. These refer to emergencies that are occurring in an area, that are represented in our system by means of icons appearing at certain latitude, longitude combinations over a geographic area. The icons chosen for these represent the resource requirements for these events. There are four different types of resources an event could need, and this is indicated by different colors. Figure 4 shows the iconic depiction of an event in our system.

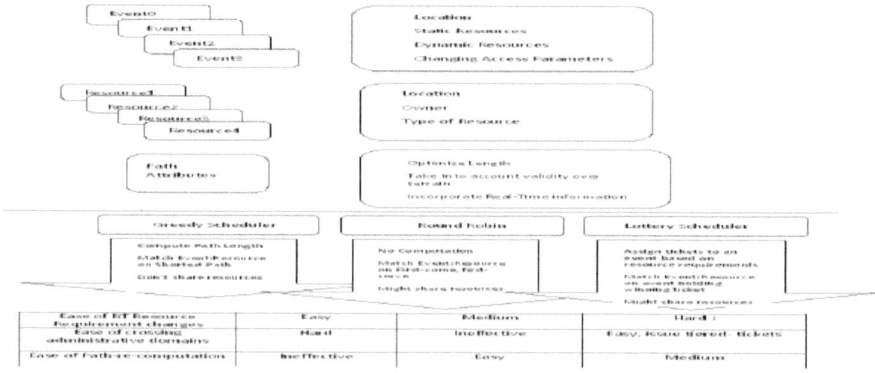

Fig. 3. Overall System Architecture

Fig. 4. Event Depiction. FIGURE 4. Resource Depiction. Physical resources are static and decision-making resources are more dynamic in our system.

The attributes associated with each event are outlined below:

i.   *Event Location* refers to the actual physical location of the event;

ii.   *Event Static Resource Requirements* describes the static resource requirements that are assigned upon the creation of every event;

iii. *Event Dynamic Resource Requirements* describe the changing nature of an event with the progress of time. While we borrow from the RimSim Response depiction, we extend an event's resource requirements to be more *dynamic*. In the original RimSim Response, an event is static in its resource requirements and this is not a realistic depiction of any emergency, where the needs are constantly changing over time. Additionally, the objective of Reverse 111 is not training (as was the case with RimSim Response), rather it is to make a case for obtaining better information from citizens or cell-phone users that are co-located with an emergency. Therefore, our system needs to model an emergency event more realistically in order to support end-to-end evaluation;

iv.   *Event Changing Access Parameters* describes how the areas surrounding an event might change over time, given that our initial assumptions about an emergency may not be valid as time goes on.

RESOURCES. These refer to the resources that are applied in order to ameliorate the emergencies. Examples include various state services and every resource has a number of attributes detailed below

i.   *Resource Location* refers to the geographical location of a resource. For example, a fire-truck might be at a fire-station when the emergency event occurs or might be returning to its home-base and therefore at a different location at the absolute time-stamp when it's required.

ii.   *Resource State* indicates whether the resource is stationary or is in motion towards the event of interest.

iii. *Resource Owner* refers to which administrative domain owns the resource. These could include state bodies such as the fire-department, police, and military can also be extended to include *commercial* emergency responders, which motivates our lottery-scheduler to evaluate a heterogeneity in such resource ownership.

iv.   *Resource Type* refers to whether the resource is a static resource (such as the ones described before) or a more dynamic resource, such as a user providing images of the façade of the building that has fallen down. The latter is more information than an actual physical resource and can be used for decision making. This is separate from the physical resources but an integral component of Reverse 111. Fig. 4 shows the types of resource used in Reverse 111.

PATH ATTRIBUTES. These refer to the set of allowable paths over the map, while trying to get the physical resources to the emergency event.

  i.   *Path Length* Our system assigns path-length depending on the distance of the resource from the emergency event. In the case where our system evaluates various scheduling policies, these path lengths may be pre-computed, based on requirements.

  ii. *Path re-construction based on live information* This is based on re-constructing the path (including length and validity) based on live information provided by co-located callers. Fig. 5 shows the valid regions being marked in our system such that the ocean is marked invalid on a resource-path towards the event. The green lines mark the administrative and legal geographic boundaries within which the simulation might be run and the pink lines denote the Ashley and Rakaia gorges, which cannot be traversed (and are marked off as fences in our system).

  iii. *Path Length* Our system assigns path-length depending on the distance of the resource from the emergency event. In the case where our system evaluates various scheduling policies, these path lengths may be pre-computed, based on requirements.

  iv. *Path Validity* a valid assumption during the occurrence of a crisis is that all roads are not equal and all paths may not be open for the resource to take, in order to get to the event. For example, a bridge might have collapsed or an area might be too flooded to navigate. In these cases, the path validity is computed as a function of (valid_flag, time_slot) wherein the valid_flag indicates whether or not a path is valid and the time_slot indicates how *long* the flag contains robust information.

  v.   *Path re-construction based on live information* This is based on re-constructing the path (including length and validity) based on live information provided by co-located callers.

Fig. 5. Valid Regions The valid paths that a resource can traverse to get to an event are based on demarcated areas, such that the resource is not trying to cross the sea, while trying to reach an event on the other side of the administrative or geographic divide

3   Resource Schedulers

In order to simulate which emergencies are dealt with first, within a response scenario, a number of agent services to the dynamic visualization component of RimSim Response. The three different schedulers we designed include the *greedy* [7,8] scheduler, the *lottery* [6] scheduler and the *round-robin* scheduler. The performance of these schedulers are compared and contrasted in the coming sections, for reference. We also add another service called the *oracle player* that controls the progress of the system, to run an entire scenario of multiple incidents occurring and being responded to, and run these schedulers in turn, in order to understand the differences in the optimality of various approaches to solving the same problem. We propose augmenting the schedulers with live call data, obtained from understanding a callers *location* and *reputation* and informing the schedulers decision dynamically with the incoming information. Three parameters differentiate agents from one another including their policy on sharing resources with neighboring jurisdictions, their strategy for determining which active unresolved incident should be attended to next, and their strategy for determining which available resource to assign the targeted incident. Since administrative boundaries exist in real-life, the performance of these agents mirrors how a real first-responder might think. In the case of a *greedy* scheduler, the attitude being simulated is one of the mayor of Christchurch always solving his or her local incidents first with their resources and never sharing anything. In the case of a *round robin* scheduler, it mirrors solving incidents one after another, in their order of appearance, without considering the class, severity or scale of the emergency such that all incidents are given equal priority. In the case of a *lottery* scheduler, this could mirror a commercial emergency responder that has to await their turn at state-based resources (hence the casting of a lottery by the oracle, in our case representing the state) before arriving to solve the incident. In the second part o the evaluation, we introduce two more schedulers, local and local-plus and demonstrate crowd-sourcing as a fixed delay based on some input from one or more co-located citizens on the ground.

3.1   Greedy Scheduler

The greedy scheduler allocates resources to incidents based on the greediest approach that of pre-computing resource distance, storing the shortest path and allocating resources to events based on which resources are closest, even if the events are serviced out of order in terms of arrival time.

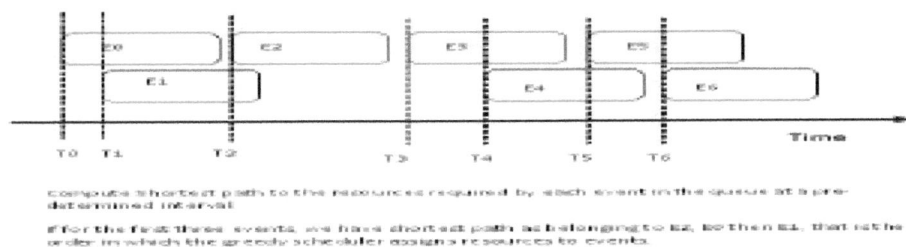

Fig. 6. Greedy Scheduler This scheduler pre-computes the shortest path of resources to events and assigns resources based on the closes event

Figure 6 shows a greedy scheduler wherein the system sees the arrival of emergency events E0, E1, E2,E3,E4,E5 and E6 at time T0, T1, T2, T3, T4, T5 and T6. The scheduler then pre-computes the shortest path of the resources required by each event, the pre-computation happening at a set time-interval, such that in case event E2's resources are the closest to it, followed by E0's resources and then E1's resources, that is the order in which resources are dispatched to events. This scheduler is also administratively greedy in that it does not share its resources across administrative domains. In case an event's resource requirements change dynamically, it is easy to incorporate this change within the greedy scheduler as there is a pre-computation of shortest path of resources to events and this is dynamic in nature. In case the administrative domains need to be transcended (assume a resource is right at the border of two counties wherein the event the resource is closest to is not in the greedy scheduler's administrative domain, rather the one next-door) this scheduler will not perform well as it doesn't share resources. In case the path needs to be re-computed, this scheduler is again ineffective as the pre-computation of shortest path will undergo several extra steps to calculate the new shortest path and cannot use cached values.

3.2 Lottery Scheduler

In case an emergency event has to be handled by one or more commercial service providers, there might be contention for the critical resources (such as fire-trucks etc.) that are not essentially in the private service provider's domain of resources. In this case, events could get *starved* of resources if they wait for the authorities to make up their minds as to who to dispatch next. To handle this scenario, we propose a lottery scheduler [2], which borrows ideas from the Mach Kernel, to implement *proportional fair-share scheduling* and adapt the same to Emergency Management.

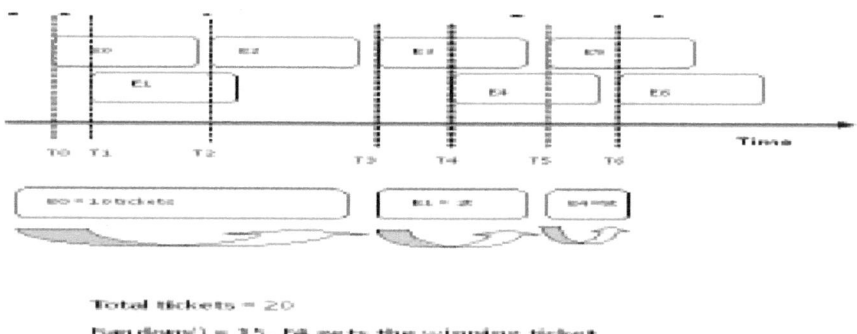

Fig. 7. Lottery Scheduler This scheduler pre-computes the shortest path of resources to events and assigns resources based on the closes event

Figure 7 shows a lottery scheduler wherein the system sees the arrival of emergency events E0, E1, E2,E3,E4,E5 and E6 at time T0, T1, T2, T3, T4, T5 and T6. This scheduler uses the concept of currencies to denominate tickets to each of the events. Each currency (resource-type) is *funded* by tickets at a certain exchange rate (i.e., a military-truck might be more expensive to dispatch than a fire-truck). Every event is assigned tickets from a pre-set pool of tickets depending on their resource requirements. A random-number generator picks the winning ticket and the list of events is traversed until the event holding the winning ticket-number is found. This method avoids starvation amongst the various events and also designates tickets based on resource requirements therefore giving every event a fair chance at obtaining the resources they need. Since the tickets are assigned before hand, in case an events resource requirements change in real time, this will affect the performance of the scheduler as it has to recomputed tickets on the fly, which makes the subsequent steps of casting the lottery through the random-number generator and then finding the winner stall, until the requirements are re-calculated. Crossing administrative domains with this scheduler is easy as tickets can be tiered or valued differently based on the notion of different *currencies* for different resources. In case the path needs to be re-computed, this scheduler's performance will not be affected that much as the only event affected will be the current event and the others can have their paths re-assigned in the background, while the current set of events are being handled.

3.3 Round-Robin Scheduler

Figure 8 shows a round-robin scheduler wherein the system sees the arrival of emergency events E0, E1, E2,E3,E4,E5 and E6 at time T0, T1, T2, T3, T4, T5 and T6. This scheduler uses a first-come, first-served policy wherein the order of appearance of events determines which event is allocated resources.

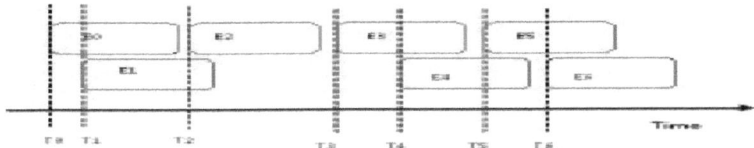

Fig. 8. Round Robin Scheduler This scheduler is the most primitive of all three

4   Visualization Interface

In this section we briefly present the visualization interface, which was built to simulate emergencies in New Zealand. We focus our discussion to the South Island for purposes of example and this tool is built to incorporate really any region in the world. There are three steps in the visualization, *setup and initialization*, which allows the user to set the administrative boundaries and invalid paths on the map, *visualizing events* which occur on the map, depending on the type of the emergency, *visualizing resources* which are placed at certain locations and are of four primitive fixed types (red, blue, green, yellow) for purposes of this example and *visualizing co-located callers* that provide dynamic, real-time information about the emergency.

Figure 9 shows the system setup phase of this visualization tool. Parameters that are initialized during setup include setting administrative domains, shown in pink on the panel on the left-hand side and setting invalid paths, shown in green such that the ocean, the gorges (Ashley, Rakaia, etc.) are not valid paths for resources to travel through while getting to the event.

Fig. 9. System Setup Several parameters are initialized in this step including setting the administrative domains (shown in pink), setting invalid paths (shown in green), and setting boundaries for each domain (shown in yellow)

Fig. 10. Proactive crowd-sourcing for emergency response using caller records in an emergency simulation to identify co-located citizens who are contacted for information about changing resource requirements for an emergency incident or changing access parameters for a resource en-route an incident

Further, the system sets the boundaries for each administrative domain to solve events in. In this example, the global domain is the outermost yellow-line enclosed area on the panel on the right hand side. Each of the smaller yellow-line enclosed regions correspond to the administrative regions of Christchurch, Ashburton, Oxford and Rangiora. Figure 10 shows the visualization of an event (depicted by the diamond shaped object with resource requirements, in this case, this incident needs one blue resource, zero red resources, zero yellow resources and three green resources). The resources themselves are shown by means of circular objects (in this case, we have only shown the red resources). The transparent grey-line depicts the path that a resource is taking towards an incident The light-blue dots show co-located citizens, identified as being there by their caller record (PCMD) and can change the resource requirement of the incident or the path that the resource takes to reach the incident. For example, a caller could say that an access bridge has been erected over the Rakaia gorge and that this path is now traversable, as shown in Fig. 10. The visualization sub-system further allows the ERC to view tower-level statistics to further assist them in identifying which citizen to contact, at the time of an emergency. Fig 11 shows a second level of detail, wherein the emergency manager is accessing the statistics of one of the towers, in terms of aggregate usage.

In this case, the tower in question has the ID 14. Some of the information that is made available to the engineer include the time at which that information is being accessed (9:10am), the number of calls placed in that particular tower (322), within that, the number of calls pertaining to SMS transmissions (123), toll calls (10) and dropped calls (45). The number of unique users (13) that the tower has seen in the time the data was collected and aggregated, which is done in 60 minute samples. The aggregate number of RLP bytes transmitted (10454) and the number of paging requests greater than 3 (5), which might indicate the onset of a security violation at that tower. The tool has the ability to depict user-mobility, which can be visualized by the ERC, who may wish to find out how users are moving across the various cities. In our tool, the trajectory of the user is mapped and animated, using various colours corresponding to the speed (shown in light green lines in Fig 11) at which the user is travelling between cell-phone towers.

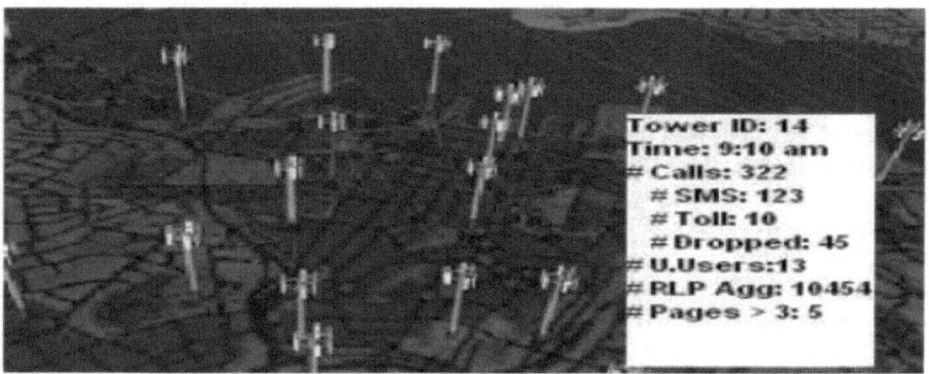

Fig. 11. Tower-level statistics and user-mobility

5   Evaluation

In this section we present our preliminary evaluation results for throughput and latency of the three different schedulers. In our set-up an incident occurs every 4 seconds and the greedy and lottery schedulers perform their pre-computation simultaneously with incident arrival, thus there is no lead time. We present our results over 600 incidents that are occurring in the South Island of New Zealand, at random locations.

Figure 12 plots the average latency between the event occurring and having its resource-requirements satisfied. We note that the greedy approach out-performs the round robin and lottery schedulers by quite a bit up to 200 incidents, at this point, the three approaches seem to perform equally. This is followed by the greedy scheduler out-performing the round-robin and the lottery schedulers at a steady rate. At the heaviest event load, the greedy scheduler is closer in performance to the lottery but both out perform the round robin approach by quite a bit. The round robin scheduler

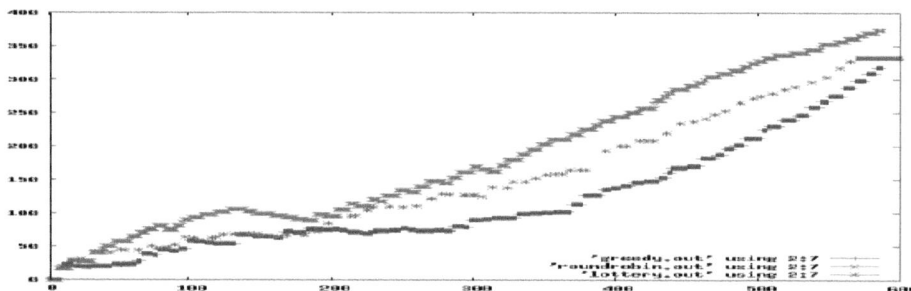

Fig. 12. Scheduler Latency The x-axis shows the number of incidents that are occurring and the y-axis shows the average latency in the scheduler assigning resources to events

is the most primitive approach to resource scheduling. This does not take into account the proximity of the resources to the events or the resource requirements of individual events. The lottery scheduler is proportional fair-share but involves allocating and de-allocating resources to events as the winning ticket changes. For a small number of incidents, the lottery scheduler performs comparably to the greedy approach, at one point even doing better (180 incidents), however the greedy approach scales better.

Figure 13 plots the average throughput of each of the three schedulers. We note that the greedy approach out-performs the round robin and lottery schedulers by quite a bit up to 100 incidents. Beyond this, the throughput (number of events handled by each scheduler within a certain time interval) deteriorates as the number of events increase with the greedy scheduler outperforming the lottery scheduler and the round-robin scheduler, in that order. This result is best explained as the round robin scheduler has to wait till the event the resources are currently serving, free up, before they are re-assigned to other events. In the case of the greedy approach, pre-computing the shortest path also takes into account the final position of the resource (i.e., if the resource moves to handle and event, that position is its final position) and therefore when the shortest path is re-computed once that resource is free, it is still the shortest path to the next event it will service. The throughput of the three approaches gradually converge as the number of incidents increase demonstrating the need to evaluate these proposals at different granularities of event occurrence.

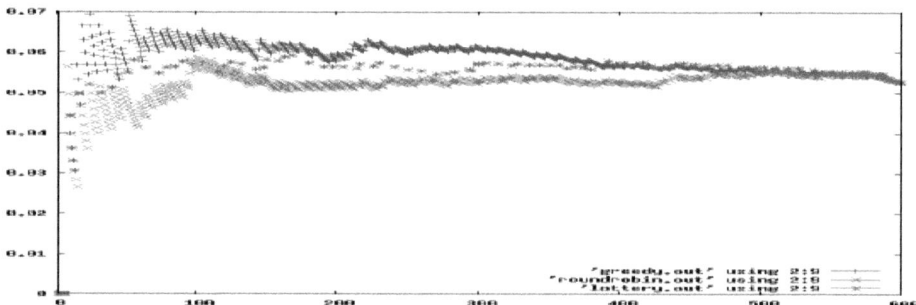

Fig. 13. Scheduler Throughput The x-axis shows the number of incidents that are occurring and the y-axis shows the average throughput in the scheduler assigning resources to events

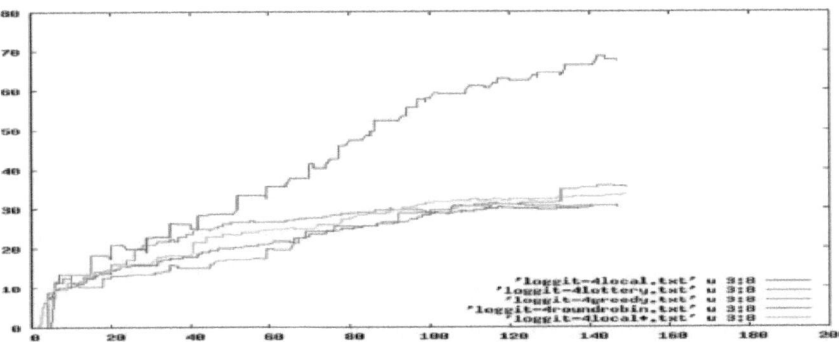

Fig. 14. Proactive Crowd-Sourced Scheduler Latency The x-axis shows the number of incidents that are occurring and the y-axis shows the average latency in the scheduler assigning resources to events

5.1 Evaluation of Proactive Crowd-Sourcing

We look at two additional schedulers, Local and Local-Plus in the second part of our evaluation. The Local scheduler uses the first-fit policy for resource to incident matching, rendering its latency the worst of all. Local-Plus uses the first-fit policy as well but is not an entirely greedy scheduler in that once its incidents are resolved, it helps other jurisdictions and it performs slightly better than lottery for up to 100 incidents after which its performance gets much worse than all three, as shown in Fig 14. In the second part of our evaluation, we encode feedback from the crowd as part of our system and this is depicted as a fixed delay in the resource getting to the incident.

We see that the performance of all schedulers converges much quicker than the latencies shown in Fig 12 because o proactive crowd-sourcing improving the information available to the ERC and thereby assisting in better emergency response.

6 Related Work

The Pacific Rim Visualization and Analytics Center coordinated at the University of Washington, known as the PARVAC to other regional centers, has been working on developing improved shared artifacts for communicating during community-wide first response activities. Acknowledging the magnitude of the cognitive load involved in maintaining situation awareness for effective first responder behavior they have studied successful distributed cognition methods for embedding mission-critical knowledge in shared visualization tools. Their primary focus has been on the embodied mind model that suggests humans need a wide arrange of external thinking tools in order to embody an internal model for effective action. In order to share situation awareness, they have explored the emerging model for augmented cognition – a model that looks to improve social cognition between humans given solid shared artifacts and associated computation support.

7 Conclusions and Future Work

In this work, we introduce different types of schedulers to assign resources to emergencies, each scheduler differing in the policy it adapts to resolve contention or pick emergencies from a list of emergencies. One of the main reasons to understand how various scheduling policies perform is that several actors need to co-operate in order to mitigate emergencies. These actors include, but are not limited to, various first-responder units, citizens groups, emergency care providers etc. When there is a multitude of administrative domains to be traversed both in policy and with respect to resources, understanding the performance of schedulers gives us some insight into how these various actors might end up co-operating and performing in real situations. For example, the lottery scheduler could well be applied to the case where several first-responder units have resources to offer and differing numbers of resources. In order to determine which responder is allowed to assign their resources to an emergency, some authoritative source (in our case, the oracle player) might have to cast a lottery ticket to the responder. Thus, our schedulers try to mirror real-time discrepancies in the number of actors and resources they offer to the emergency situation and try to evaluate the performance of the same. We notice that proactive crowd-sourcing leads to quicker convergence.

References

1. Campbell, B., Schroder, K.: Training for emergency response with RimSim:Response! In: Proceedings for the Defense, Security, and Sensing Conference, Orlando, FL (2009)
2. Filippoupolitis, A., Hey, L., Loukas, G., Gelenbe, E., Timotheou, S.: Emergency response simulation using wireless sensor networks. In: Ambi-Sys 2008: Proceedings of the 1st International Conference on Ambient Media and Systems, ICST, Brussels, Belgium, Belgium, ICST (2008)
3. Walker, D.M., Jenckes, T.A.: Emergency monitoring, assessment and response system for diablo canyon nuclear power plant. IEEE Transaction on Nuclear Science
4. Chitumalla, P., Harris, D., Thuraisingham, B., Khan, L.: Emergency response applications: Dynamic plume modeling and real-time routing. IEEE Internet Computing 12(1), 38–44 (2008)
5. Basu, S.N.: Fermi 2 emergency response information system. IEEE Transactions on Energy Conversion EC-1(2), 16–22 (1986)
6. Waldspurger, C.A.: Lottery and Stride Scheduling: Flexible Proportional-Share Resource Management, Ph.D. dissertation, Massachusetts Institute of Technology (September 1995)
7. Mansour, Y., Patt-Shamir, B.: Greedy Packet Scheduling on Shortest Paths. Journal of Algorithms (1991)
8. Ruiz, R., Stützle, T.: A simple and effective iterated greedy algorithm for the permutation flow-shop scheduling problem. European Journal of Operational Research (2006)

Anonymity and Privacy in Distributed Early Warning Systems

Martin Brunner, Hans Hofinger, Christopher Roblee,
Peter Schoo, and Sascha Todt

Fraunhofer Institute for Secure Information Technology SIT,
Parkring 4, 85748 Garching n. Munich, Germany
firstname.lastname@sit.fraunhofer.de
http://www.sit.fraunhofer.de

Abstract. As the Internet continues to emerge as a critical information infrastructure, IT early warning systems (IT-EWS) have taken on
greater importance in protecting both its endpoints and the infrastructure itself. Although it is generally accepted that open sharing of cyber
data and warnings between the independent (but mutually vulnerable)
endpoints promotes broader situational awareness, such openness introduces new privacy challenges. In this paper, we present a high-level model
for security information sharing between autonomous operators on the
Internet that enables meaningful collaboration while addressing the en-
during privacy and infrastructure needs of those individual collaborators.
Our concept for a collaborative and decentralised IT-EWS is based on
a novel combination of existing techniques, including peer-to-peer networking and Traceable Anonymous Certificates. We concentrate on the
security and confidentiality of the data exchange platform rather than of
the data itself, a separate area of research.

Keywords: Early Warning Systems, Secure Information Sharing, Privacy, Anonymity, Critical Information Infrastructure Protection.

1 Introduction

Today's enterprises, organisations, governments, and private end users depend
heavily on information and communication technologies. Their disruption-free
operation is crucial to guaranteeing quality and continuity of each sector's respective service, ranging from energy supply to health care to the operation of
the information infrastructures themselves. Whereas, historically most disruptions to these sectors were due to localised operational failures, the increasing
connectivity of their IT infrastructure has rendered them more vulnerable to
both directed and undirected remote cyber attacks [6].

IT Early Warning (IT-EW) is evolving into an increasingly important topic,
and the need for IT Early Warning Systems (IT-EWS) generally understood
among political, economics and security experts alike [5]. The ultimate goal of
an IT-EWS is to inform IT systems operators as early as possible about security-
related incidents or indicators that may affect their assets and allow them to

C. Xenakis and S. Wolthusen (Eds.): CRITIS 2010, LNCS 6712, pp. 81–92, 2011.

take appropriate countermeasures to mitigate or avert the impact of the observed phenomena. This primary objective of IT-EW requires local information to be collected and aggregated from different locations on the Internet to form global situational views and facilitate appropriate responses [1]. Such collaborative information exchanges should help identify trends, especially with regard to the distribution of undirected malware (e.g., worms), that might otherwise be obscured within the noise of network traffic at the local level. The prospect of enhanced sharing and mutual, decentralised analysis of cyber threat data introduces new challenges for anonymity, privacy and efficient data exchange. The community lacks a viable solution to enable such collaboration while adequately addressing the privacy and infrastructure needs of individual collaborators.

Our conceptual solution addresses these issues by combining different techniques to fulfill the requirements of privacy and anonymity in a decentralised, distributed, and collaborative IT-EWS. Guaranteeing suitable privacy levels for participants is a pervasive challenge in early warning systems [2]. This primarily entails *participant anonymity* (non-disclosure of identifiable information), which in turns requires obfuscating both transmitted data (*data anonymity*) and the transmission process itself (*originator anonymity*). Participation in the collaborative EWS scheme should also be authorised by independent third parties or by the participants themselves.

Our approach to these challenges combines established techniques used in other fields (namely Traceable Anonymous Certificates [20] and GNUnet [4]) in the application domain of protecting the Internet's endpoints and the Internet as critical information infrastructure.

The remainder of this paper is organised as follows. In Section 2, we briefly discuss related work in the area of collaborative early warning with special regard to anonymity and privacy issues, distinguishing between centralised and distributed approaches. Section 3 presents our distributed, collaborative, privacy-preserving early warning approach in more detail. Since the scope of this paper is more conceptual, we focus on describing the application domain, the design goal, and the trust model rather than providing considerable technical detail. Thus, we depict the implementation components at a high level, provide a sketch for a network layout and outline some use cases. In Section 4, benefits and limitations of our approach are discussed by describing the assumptions and design decisions made within the novel combination of existing technologies. Consequently, we also provide an outlook on future work. Finally, Section 5 summarises our conclusions achieved so far.

2   Related Work

Several approaches address the challenges of distribution and collaboration in early warning frameworks. As different administrative domains have varying privacy and infrastructure needs, most contemporary solutions make significant performance, privacy and utility trade-offs appropriate for their anticipated operating environments and users.

2.1 International Activities

The Messaging Standard for Sharing Security Information (MS3i) and National & European Information Sharing & Alerting System (NEISAS) projects, both funded by the European Union, aim to develop a framework for trusted critical infrastructure information sharing. MS3i focused on surveying current information sharing projects and related standards, and defining a trust model and requirements for such a framework [17]. The NEISAS project [18] builds on the MS3i project findings to advance the development of the ISO/IEC 27010 standard. While MS3i ended in 2009, the NEISAS project was in the platform design phase at the time of writing, and hence no detailed design description was publicly available. In contrast to the MS3i findings, our concept focuses on the component technologies proposed for the implementation of a decentralised, distributed and resilient information sharing network.

2.2 Collaborative Centralised Approaches

The aggregation and correlation of data collected at different sites can help confirm whether local trends and threats exist on a broader scale and to identify other threats that would not have been classified as such on the basis of local data alone.

CarmentiS

In CarmentiS, members of the German CERT association and the German Federal Office for Information Security (BSI) provide a collaborative network of different administrative domains (i.e., data providers). Sensor data is sanitised through pseudonymisation techniques such as CryptoPan [10]. The input is transferred to an early warning central control where cross-site analysis is performed (in part) manually. Certificates assure integrity and confidentiality as well as authenticity and non-repudiation of the transmitted data. Access to the results is restricted [12].

ANL Federated Model for Cyber Security

The Federated Model for Cyber Security [21] is a framework developed by the Argonne National Laboratory for trusted collaborators to share warnings about Internet threats. It is a centralised approach in which threat signatures are collected at the participants' sites and submitted to a central repository accessible by the collaborators. Privacy is ensured by the originator encrypting each alert file only for the trusted participants that they would like to share their data with. By construction, the Federated Model offers end-to-end data privacy through asymmetric encryption, but no originator anonymity.

2.3 Distributed and Collaborative Approaches

The vulnerability of centralised approaches to disruptions can be reduced by mirroring central repositories [21], or by constructing a distributed service to avoid single points of failure.

Worminator and Whirlpool

Locasto et al. [15] propose a collaborative distributed intrusion detection system (IDS) that offers privacy-preservation, decentralisation and efficient alert exchange across administrative domains. The authors address several practical challenges of any collaborative IDS solution, such as timeliness, data explosion, single points of failure, and private information exchange across administrative domains. Their approach does not provide anonymous communication (i.e., originator anonymity) as alerts are sent directly by their originator, allowing peers to glean potentially sensitive information about each other when they share information in common (e.g., both vulnerable to the same exploit). This can lead to asymmetrical sharing relationships between peers, in which only the alert recipient learns (through unilateral comparison) of its commonalities with its sender and becomes an information sink.

DOMINO

The Distributed Overlay for Monitoring InterNet Outbreaks (DOMINO) [24] is an overlay network for distributed network intrusion detection. It enables collaboration among heterogeneous nodes that can join and non-obtrusively leave the network. The network, whose entire communication is encrypted by public-key cryptography, is stretched out via axis nodes that gather information from satellite nodes. The axis nodes communicate among each other and maintain local and global views of attack activity using an extended version of IDMEF [8]. Raw alerts from the satellite nodes are aggregated before being sent to the axis nodes. Once transmitted, the satellite does not appear to have control over the distribution of its input.

3   A Distributed Collaborative Privacy-Preserving Approach

The envisioned collaborative IT-EWS is based on decentralisation and sharing of actionable security information across administrative domains. The reluctance of organisations to share network threat data collected inside their administrative domains is addressed initially by the concepts of *data* and *originator anonymity* as well as *membership anonymity*, described below.

3.1   Design Goals

Although a centralised collaborative system is efficient with regard to data traffic and computational resources for data analysis, its disadvantage is its dependency on a central instance. Transferring the analytic duty cycle from the central instance to each node of the collaborators clearly does not minimise computational effort; neither does the mutual exchange of data among the participants minimise the necessary network traffic. However, it enables participants to conduct analysis locally and independently from a central instance, leading to a higher degree of autonomy and resilience. If a participant decides to share information, it will in turn receive data collected by another participant that can be analysed locally within the context of its own data. To authenticate participants and counter attacks against the IT-EWS itself (e.g., by distributing falsified alerts), members should register through a trusted service (perhaps served by a trusted third party).

If group membership information is itself deemed sensitive by its participants and must remain hidden, a collaborative IT-EWS should offer *membership anonymity* in addition to *originator anonymity* (anonymity of the transmission process itself). Membership anonymity serves participants who require stronger protection against inference attacks and therefore wish to hide their membership status from other participants. Inference attacks occur when third parties reasonably infer a participant's identity from partially-attributable traces in its messages, such as network traffic volumes, domains queried, and IP exposure. Inference attacks are much more tractable with a limited candidate pool of known participants, and can potentially leak sensitive information about the originator of anonymised messages [13]. For total membership anonymity, each participant must naturally provide its own additional layer of indirection (e.g., anonymous proxy, onion routing) between their node and the federation, as peers could otherwise map participant IP addresses to identities.

Conversely, prospective participants might only be willing to join federations composed of known trustworthy organisations. For example, a large enterprise participant may only wish to share data with similarly-sized organisations or consume data from organisations that it considers reputable (e.g., CERTs). In this case, membership lists would need to be disclosed beforehand for review. Although we consider membership disclosure the more advantageous strategy, the solution should support either operating mode while maximising originator anonymity. An adequate data sanitisation regime to maximally avoid inference analysis is the responsibility of each participant in both scenarios.

As known from file-sharing networks, the resulting structure should additionally offer the opportunity to apply accounting models for different parties' "behaviour" and willingness to share knowledge, as realised for example in GNUnet in the context of file-sharing [4].

3.2 Component Technologies

The Related Work section described existing collaborative solutions that we find promising but do not address all of our early warning objectives, such as anonymous communication [15], as some of these features were likely deemed less important in their anticipated environments. In this section, we propose a combination of existing technologies and protocols to satisfy the requirements and objectives of a more scalable and collaborative IT-EWS.

The GNUnet peer-to-peer routing scheme, as discussed below, could help resolve the issue of anonymous communication between collaborators. GNUnet could be used as an overlay network through which other IT-EWS approaches (such as that of Locasto et al.) communicate. The natural trade-off for such an overlay is an increase in network communication and latency.

GNUnet

GNUnet is a secure, completely decentralised peer-to-peer (P2P) networking framework. Its core API provides applications with authenticated, confidential, anonymous and censorship-resistant communication over a P2P network. While GNUnet was designed to facilitate any decentralised application, it has mostly been used for file sharing [4]. GNUnet can be used to anonymise senders through GAP, its protocol for anonymous data transfer [3]. Section 3.3 summarises how GNUnet or other P2P protocols may be used for decentralised, anonymous communication. The advantage of GNUnet is that it does not rely on external or centralised nodes to relay messages, and integrates GAP for originator anonymity. P2P protocols lack connection anonymisation as long as they don't provide corresponding measures such as onion routing. Onion routing services like TOR, however, depend on external servers run by third parties to initialise the indirection process [23]. GNUnet also provides an excess-based economic model for resource allocation to reward contributing peers, optimally resulting in equilibria between data fed into the IT-EWS and additional information acquired.

PKI Using Traceable Anonymous Certificates

A Public Key Infrastructure (PKI) can be deployed to achieve integrity, authentication and confidentiality, thereby maintaining compatibility with existing standards and formats, such as X.509 certificates [11] and common certificate requests (i.e., PKCS10 [19]). To furthermore guarantee (the PKI-contradictive concept of) privacy to the participants, we propose the application of Traceable Anonymous Certificates (TAC) [20], which offer the issuance of certificates containing a pseudonym. The architecture separates the involved authorities as follows: (i) the Blind Issuer (BI) verifies private key ownership and (ii) the Anonymity Issuer (AI) validates the certificate contents. In an anonymous certificate (end entity, EE) the holder's true identity is not present in the subject field.

The AI has knowledge of the certificate issued to the user, but no knowledge of the user's true identity ("anonymity"). It performs the common functions of a Certificate Authority (CA). In contrast, the BI knows the user's true identity, but has no knowledge of the certificate issued to that user and acts as a Registration Authority (RA). The BI and AI pair appears as a single CA to the outside world (i.e., represented by a single CA certificate). However, only if AI and BI collude can they map the TAC to the corresponding user's true identity ("traceability"). Whether or not a participant's true identity needs to be revealed is defined by the organisational rules agreed on by the participants.

Section 3.3 describes at a high level how TACs can be used within an IT-EWS P2P network to enforce originator anonymity.

3.3 Integration and Use Cases

We now demonstrate the envisioned sharing network and its functionality through simple use cases. Figures 1 and 2 present generic operational scenarios for our IT-EWS communication framework concept using P2P routing and

Traceable Anonymous Certificates [20]. There are two modes of IT-EWS information exchange: (i) broadcast requests for information on locally observed phenomena (e.g., unusual scanning, mysterious e-mail attachment), and (ii) broadcasts of potentially interesting information or warnings to the entire federation (e.g., signatures of locally-confirmed attacks, suspicious IP addresses). Our model provides anonymity to participants in both communication modes, whether they be requesters, responders, or broadcast senders.

Network Layout

Figure 1 depicts an example heterogeneous pool of participants logically connected via a private or overlay network such as GNUnet. The system comprises nodes through which information is circulated and which can perform analysis tasks. The exchange of collected data between participants enables improved data analysis through data comparisons, and facilitates timely dissemination of security-related warnings.

Use Case: Joining the IT-EWS

Figure 1 shows the process of adding a new participant to the IT-EWS federation network. Initially, the federation consists of four participants (P), which communicate anonymously through an indirect P2P routing protocol, such as GNUnet. The example prospective participants illustrate the envisioned system's support for diverse member types and sizes (e.g., private home user to large multinational corporation). Formation of independent, sector-specific federations (e.g., government, finance, CERT, security vendor) would also be supported.

The applicant, *Large Company*, initiates the process by requesting authorisation from one or more current participants, or from the trusted third party when membership anonymity is required. When requested directly from the participants, they must determine whether or not to accept the interested party through a collective agreement strategy, such as anonymous voting.

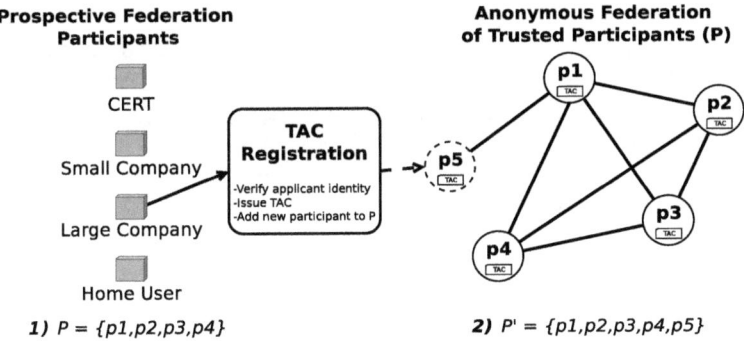

Fig. 1. Example use case with prospective participant (*Large Company*) granted membership to the IT-EWS federation network by the TAC registration authority, and assigned node identifier p5

Alternatively, current participants can invite new prospective participants to join. If the invitee wishes to remain entirely anonymous (i.e., membership anonymity), it could simply refuse the invitation. In both cases, the prospective participant must pass the PKI/TAC registration process, during which its identity is verified, and assigned a Traceable Anonymous Certificate (TAC) through standard TAC issuance procedures [20].

As depicted in Fig. 1, once the applicant's eligibility is verified, it is issued a TAC, assigned the node identifier p5, and provided a list of participant IP addresses to initiate the P2P bootstrapping process. The list of participant names, P, is not distributed if membership anonymity is enforced. After bootstrapping, other participants confirm p5's authorisation to participate by verifying its TAC. Participant p5 can now communicate confidentially and anonymously with all other federation participants.

Use Case: Anonymous Data Exchange

Figure 2 shows a simple anonymous data exchange between two participants in the IT-EWS network, p5 (the initiator) and p2 (the responder). In this scenario p5 initiates the communication by issuing a query, query_5, into the network through an entry node selected from the initial list of participants it received upon joining the federation, in this case p1.

At this point, p5 knows only its own query and that it was sent through entry node p1. Participant p1 only knows that it received a query, query_?, that was either initiated or indirected by p5. The query's origin remains hidden as it is routed through the network, en route to a participant capable and willing to respond. Participant p2 eventually receives the anonymous query and crafts a reply, reply_2. As the responder, p2 only knows the query and that it was initiated or indirected by p3. The reply is then returned anonymously to the initiator along a (perhaps identical) indirect path. Neither the intermediate hops

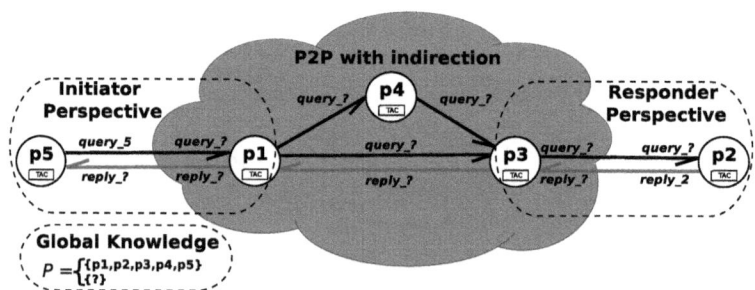

Fig. 2. Use case of anonymous query-response communication between participants p2 and p5. Node p5's query (query_5) is propagated anonymously throughout the IT-EWS federation network as query_? until it reaches p2, which issues an anonymous response by way of p3 and p1. When membership anonymity is enforced, the list of participant identities is not known (P={?}). Query and response sources remain anonymous.

(p3, p1) nor the initiator (p5) are able to identify the originator of the reply, assuring originator anonymity. Participants may also know the membership of the federation, P, if membership anonymity is unenforced. The anonymity of the actual query and response data remains the responsibility of the initiator and responder, respectively.

In the case of a single broadcast event, data would propagate from the initiator throughout the network in the form of *unsolicited* replies (i.e., not in response to a query).

4   Discussion and Future Work

To fully address the privacy and anonymity requirements of modern operators, a collaborative early warning system should obscure data origins, both within shared data and throughout the data exchange process. While data obfuscation is the responsibility of the contributor, the exchange should be handled transparently by the data sharing protocol and infrastructure. The protocol should also provide features like traffic encryption and network resilience.

Although there are many advantages to adopting a P2P infrastructure, it raises scalability and efficiency issues that need to be investigated in the context of IT-EW. This requires an adequate balance between increased network traffic and originator anonymity. Addressing this and further topics is part of the necessary future work related to this concept.

4.1   Reputation Tracking

As with any anonymous P2P system, establishing trust in the quality of received data is a major challenge. Without knowing the originator's true identity, message reliability cannot be qualified based on the source's prior reputation, competence, or authority. In our application, consumers may wish to weigh messages based on both preexisting and evolving trust in the originator. Neither of these is feasible with full anonymity, but the latter can be partially solved by pseudonymity, in which the source's true identity is replaced by a pseudonym [17,16]. In the proposed design participants' node identifiers or TACs, as shown in Fig. 1, could serve as pseudonyms to tag the data. Unfortunately, pseudonymity increases the risk of inference attacks when pseudonyms persist long-term, especially if membership anonymity is unenforced. To avoid profiling and maximise anonymity, participants would need to regularly update their node identifiers and TACs. Overall confidence in message quality may be improved by disclosing and independently verifying membership lists, as discussed in section 3.1 (i.e., no membership anonymity). In this configuration, prospective participants can simply decide to join a federation based on their trust in its current members. Ultimately, participants must choose whether or not to sacrifice some of their anonymity for access to better reputation data. This trade-off is a well-established and ongoing research challenge [9,16].

4.2   Role of a Trusted Third Party

To control participation in a collaborative early warning system and maintain anonymous communication, the community can agree on a central trusted third party (TTP) responsible for admitting new participants. To avoid the need of a TTP, such a service could also be implemented by the participants themselves, as mentioned earlier. To distribute responsibility and control of the service, required resources could be provided or created collaboratively (e.g., key pairs using threshold signature schemes like those described in [22]). Establishing a PKI to issue and handle anonymous certificates is one possibility to manage integrity, authentication and confidentiality of the communication routes. Combined with an anonymous P2P protocol, it does not require a central instance for data exchange, increasing the independence of the participants and resilience of the network.

4.3   Data Analysis

The predominant challenge so far has been the sharing of data without revealing its origin to other participants in the IT-EWS. To enable analysis of this data, the anonymous P2P network can be supplemented by techniques from the field of Secure Multi-party Computation (SMC). These primarily address the issue of jointly processing data distributed among different parties without revealing the data to the other parties.

In 2009 Burkhart et al. presented SEPIA [7], a library of protocols for event correlation and network traffic analysis, and proposed its application to network security. Due to its computational and bandwidth overhead, the applicability of SMC techniques in large scale applications has been questioned by Lincoln et al. [14]; however, in the thoroughly investigated example of 25 peers [7] its application appears to be feasible. Future work will involve researching the applicability and performance impact of SMC (including its use for anonymous voting as proposed in section 3.3) in the context of decentralised IT-EW.

4.4   Practical Implementation of the Concept

The proposed concept and future extensions will be evaluated in a prototype deployment. We will evaluate the degree to which the P2P network structure improves this testbed's resilience to simulated attacks and failures. The testbed will also be used for a comprehensive security analysis of the individual components proposed, as well as the their full integration. After a positive evaluation of our initial prototype, we will solicit participation for a real-world pilot deployment.

5   Conclusion

We consider a robust, secure and confidential information sharing network as essential to a practical IT-EWS. We believe that combining aspects of many existing early warning approaches would enable more effective security collaboration between disparate and independent organisations connected to the Internet, and offer a significant contribution to the field of critical information infrastructure protection. In this paper, we proposed a concept based on a novel combination of existing technologies and introduced several underlying challenges for the development of a distributed, privacy-preserving, collaborative early warning system. Our approach combines features of a PKI using TACs and anonymous P2P networking using GNUnet and GAP.

Establishing trustworthiness through authentication, integrity and confidentiality (realised by a PKI) is well-known from other domains and best-practices. TACs offer the advantages of a PKI while preserving anonymity between participants. GNUnet enables the confidential and anonymous communication within a distributed environment.

Each of the proposed technologies has proven itself capable of fulfilling the described needs and is well-established in its corresponding application domain. Since the technologies complement each other, we do not expect the fusion to negatively impact their quality; whether the resulting overhead negatively affects the overall system's sustainability needs to be validated.

Several topics addressed in this paper (e.g., use of SMC) still require further research, practical evaluation and validation. Future work will show, in the form of a prototype implementation and necessary security reviews, how the novel fusion of techniques presented fulfills the demands of privacy-preserving, collaborative IT-EW.

References

1. Apel, M., Biskup, J., Flegel, U., Meier, M.: Early Warning System on a National Level - Project AMSEL. In: Proceedings of the International Workshop on Internet Early Warning and Network Intelligence, EWNI (2010)
2. Bagheri, E., Ghorbani, A.A.: The State of the Art in Critical Infrastructure Protection: a Framework for Convergence. International Journal of Critical Infrastructures 4(3) (2008)
3. Bennett, K., Grothoff, C.: GAP – Practical Anonymous Networking. In: Dingledine, R. (ed.) PET 2003. LNCS, vol. 2760, pp. 141–160. Springer, Heidelberg (2003)
4. Bennett, K., Grothoff, C., Horozov, T., Patrascu, I., Stef, T.: GNUnet - A truly anonymous networking infrastructure. Tech. rep., In: Proc. Privacy Enhancing Technologies Workshop, PET (2002)
5. Brunner, E., Suter, M.: International CIIP Handbook 2008/2009. In: CRN Handbooks, vol. 4, Center for Security Studies, ETH Zurich (2008)
6. Bundesministerium für Inneres: CIP Implementation Plan of the National Plan for Information Infrastructure Protection (2005), http://www.bmi.bund.de/cae/servlet/contentblob/994784/publicationFile/63256/kritis.pdf
7. Burkhart, M., Strasser, M., Dimitropoulos, X.: SEPIA: Security through Private Information Aggregation. Tech. rep., Computer Engineering and Networks Laboratory, ETH Zurich, Switzerland (2009)
8. Debar, H., Curry, D., Feinstein, B.: The Intrusion Detection Message Exchange Format (IDMEF). RFC 4765 (Experimental) (March 2007)
9. Dingledine, R., Mathewson, N., Syverson, P.: Reputation in P2P Anonymity Systems. In: Workshop on Economics of Peer-to-Peer Systems (2003)

10. Fan, J., Xu, J., Ammar, M.H., Moon, S.B.: Prefix-preserving IP address anonymization: measurement-based security evaluation and a new cryptography-based scheme. Comput. Netw. 46, 253–272 (2004)
11. ITU-T: Information technology - Open Systems Interconnection - The Directory: Public-key and Attribute Certificate Frameworks X.509 (March 2000)
12. Kossakowski, K., Sander, J., Grobauer, B., Mehlau, J.I.: A German Early Warning Information System - Challenges and Approaches. In: Presentation at 18th Annual FIRST Conference (June 2006)
13. Li, C., Shirani-Mehr, H., Yang, X.: Protecting Individual Information Against Inference Attacks in Data Publishing. In: Kotagiri, R., Radha Krishna, P., Mohania, M., Nantajeewarawat, E. (eds.) DASFAA 2007. LNCS, vol. 4443, pp. 422–433. Springer, Heidelberg (2007)
14. Lincoln, P., Porras, P.: Privacy-preserving Sharing and Correlation of Security Alerts. In: USENIX Security Symposium, pp. 239–254 (2004)
15. Locasto, M., Parekh, J., Misra, V., Stolfo, S.: Collaborative Distributed Intrusion Detection. Tech. rep., Columbia University (2004)
16. Marti, S., Garcia-Molina, H.: Taxonomy of Trust: Categorizing P2P Reputation Systems. Computer Networks Management in Peer-to-Peer Systems 50(4), 472–484 (2006)
17. Messaging Standard for Sharing Security Information (MS3i): JLS/2007/EPCIP/007 - Project Report (June 2009),
    https://www.neisas.eu/wp-content/uploads/2010/01/MS3i_main_Report_v3.0.pdf
18. National & European Information Sharing & Alerting System: NEISAS, https://www.neisas.eu/
19. Nystrom, M., Kaliski, B.: PKCS #10: Certification Request Syntax Specification Version 1.7. RFC 2936 (November 2000)
20. Park, S., Park, H., Won, Y., Lee, J., Kent, S.: Traceable Anonymous Certificate. RFC 5636 (Experimental) (August 2009)
21. Pinkerton, S.: A Federated Model For Cyber Security. In: Cyberspace Research Workshop, Shreveport, LA (November 2007)
22. Tang, S.: Simple Threshold RSA Signature Scheme Based on Simple Secret Sharing. In: Hao, Y., Liu, J., Wang, Y.-P., Cheung, Y.-m., Yin, H., Jiao, L., Ma, J., Jiao, Y.-C. (eds.) CIS 2005. LNCS (LNAI), vol. 3802, pp. 186–191. Springer, Heidelberg (2005)
23. The TOR project: TOR: Anonymity Online, http://www.torproject.org/
24. Yegneswaran, V., Barford, P., Jha, S.: Global Intrusion Detection in the DOMINO Overlay System. In: NDSS (2004)

A Formal Adversary Capability Model for SCADA Environments

Thomas Richard McEvoy[2] and Stephen D. Wolthusen[1,2,*]

[1] Norwegian Information Security Laboratory,
Department of Computer Science,
Gjøvik University College, Norway
[2] Information Security Group,
Department of Mathematics,
Royal Holloway, University of London, UK
{T.R.McEvoy,stephen.wolthusen}@rhul.ac.uk

Abstract. Conventional adversary models used in the analysis of cryptographic protocols such as the Dolev-Yao model and variants rely on a simple communication model in which an adversary fully participates in network communication. In the case of control (supervisory control and data acquisition, SCADA) systems, this set of assumptions can lead to undesirable results as constraints on communication affect both defender and adversary capabilities. These include a restricted topology for message passing and real-time processing constraints resulting in message prioritisation. We therefore propose an alternative adversary model explicitly capturing these constraints. We use a π-calculus variant to reason about priorities and constraints on messages (names) and explicitly model multiple adversarial *agents* rather than a single omnipotent adversary so as to capture synchronisation and communication effects. As an example of the model's capabilities, we derive targets for intrusion detection based on constraints on adversary action resulting from adversary-agent communication capabilities.

1 Introduction

Conventional adversary capability models, such as the Dolev-Yao model [6] assume an open network environment in which all principals participate equally in communication [1]. This assumption breaks down in DCS and SCADA where networks are segmented and real time processing dominates. As a result, an adversary *must* control multiple *agent* processes to subvert a SCADA network. Only then can production values be manipulated whilst disguising outcomes or other attacks successfully undertaken.

We propose a model based on a *pi*-calculus variant. The utility of this type of model in this context lies in proof of security properties [3, 1, 10]. Our primary interest is intrusion detection. We show that constraints on adversary action – such

---

* Corresponding author.

C. Xenakis and S. Wolthusen (Eds.): CRITIS 2010, LNCS 6712, pp. 93–103, 2011.

as message loss and latency – may lead *under certain conditions* to anomalous control readings, *even where such readings are falsified.*This is determined by process *context* and our model can be used to develop and test context based methods of detection. These properties may also be formally proved, at a later stage, by the addition of "lifting rules" [3].

Section 2 defines our variant calculus. Section 3 models infrastructure and communication within a SCADA network. Section 4 defines adversary capabilities.Section 5 shows how limitations in adversary capabilities increase the probability of detection. Section 6 describes related work and motivates the choice of adversary capability model. We conclude and discuss future work in section 7.

2 π-Calculus Variant

We use a π-calculus variant for our model. The capabilities of our π-calculus are

$$\pi ::= \bar{x}y_{p,r} \mid x(z_{p,r}) \mid \tau \mid f(\overrightarrow{z}) \rightarrow \bar{x}w, w, \nu w \mid \lambda \mid [x = y]\pi$$

which are *send* with priority and routing, *receive* with priority and routing, *unobserved* action, a *name generating* function, *message drop, replication* and *conditional* capability, respectively. $\overrightarrow{z}$ is used for a vector of names where required. The conventional processes of the basic π-calculus are retained, with one exception:

$$P ::= M \mid P|P' \mid \nu z \, P \mid !P$$
$$M ::= \mathbf{0} \mid \pi.P \mid M + M'$$

where P is a process which may be a *summation, concurrent,* a *new process* with (restricted) names, or *replication*. M is a summation which may be *null,* a *capability guarding a process* or a *choice* between two alternatives (see Sangiorgi et al. [10] for details, the exception being that the alternatives are retained for processing (*alternate sequencing*); here, we concentrate mainly on added features or assumptions).

The name generating function can be thought of as a process which returns a name whose value depends on the names used to generate it. The *message drop* λ expresses this potential for all or part of a process and may be made channel explicit.

We use a term re-writing system (TRS) to demonstrate that loss and name generation capabilities are conservative extensions of the π-calculus. In a TRS, if a notational term can be re-written as a basic term, using a set of finite reductions, not necessarily confluent, without introducing new terms, then the notation is a conservative extension of the algebraic system which may be employed freely without arbitrarily altering outcomes. We use the syntax $\alpha \rightarrow_{\equiv} \beta$ to re-write a term α as basic term β. Assuming that $\overrightarrow{z}$ is a sequence of names which have been received, we obtain a conservative extension of the π-calculus for the salient features by:

$$f(\overrightarrow{z}) \to \bar{x}u, u, \nu w \to_{\equiv} \tau \bar{x}u.\mathbf{0}$$
$$\lambda \to_{\equiv} \mathbf{0}$$

Further, though we omit the details, the use of prioritization and routing can be re-written as basic (if lengthy) pi-calculus terms by the simple expedient of imposing an order over the use of channels and conditional use of channels i.e. send x on y, if z, where the condition z is sent as a precursor to x.

3   Model of a SCADA Network

We assume that a (simple) SCADA environment consists of a set of processes P – partitioned hierarchically into supervisor processes S, one or more generations of communication processes M and control loops consisting of controllers C, sensors R and actuators A. The set of names $N = \{W, X, Y, Z\}$ are names of channels which are (roughly) indexed to show assignments. We use the notation νX to indicate $\nu x_1, x_2, \ldots, x_n$. U is the set of names for commands and data values.

$$\begin{aligned}
P := \nu \, WXYZU \; (!S_1| &\ldots |!S_i \\
|!M_{1,1}| &\ldots |!M_{i,j} \\
|!C_{1,1,1}| &\ldots |!C_{i,j,k} \\
|!A_{1,1,1}| &\ldots |!A_{i,j,k} \\
|!R_{1,1,1}| &\ldots |!R_{i,j,k})
\end{aligned} \tag{1}$$

We map channel names to processes as follows:

$$S \to W, X \qquad M \to W, X, Y \qquad C \to W, Y, Z \qquad A, R \to Z$$

In general, channels X, Y, Z process SCADA data and commands in U and W is used for network supervision and interprocess requests such as routing. All names are free (i.e. unique in the scope of the system, but we assume that each process only has access to a limited set of named channels and that name assignments are stable. We assume some redundancy in processes and channels. Message addressing achieved by two features, *channel selection* and *channel assignment*. The former implies that we may request a data item be sent by a particular channel. The notation $\bar{x}a_w$ sends a by x and requests forwarding by w. The latter means that a process will only accept data for processing from an assigned set of channels and messages to other channels are forwarded.

A SCADA system requires processes to meet both hard and soft real time process targets, but must also deal with latency arising from external communications. To represent this, messages are prioritized to represent the effects of real-time as opposed to best-effort processing. Process statements are hence exhausted in order of priority.

We use the notation $\bar{x}a_p$ where p is message priority. Low values attract the highest priority. Where values are not stated, priorities are defaulted to the lowest value. Hence, given a choice $\bar{x}a_1 + \bar{y}a_2$ we hold that $\bar{x}a_1$ is sent first. If we have $\bar{x}a_1|\bar{y}a_2$ again a_1 is sent first. Similarly, for $x(a_1) + y(a_2)$, $x(a_1)$ is received first and equivalently for $x(a_1)|y(a_2)$. If priorities are equal then outcomes are non- determined. We can use prioritisation in conjunction with routing, e.g., $\bar{x}a_{1,w}$ requests name a be sent at priority 1 by channel w. We may also omit this information, if clear from context.

4   Agent-Based Adversary Capabilities

We describe an agent-based adversary capability model. For simplicity, we define processes by their salient capabilities during the discussion. Hence, all processes are defined by $!(\sum_i \pi_i.P + U|V_1|\ldots|V_n)$ where $\sum_i \pi_i$ is the set of capabilities under consideration and U and V_i are non-salient capabilities (and are normally omitted).

We assume by τ that all processes may route, store, retrieve, create, prioritise and manipulate messages and determine choices between alternative actions [1].

4.1   Adversary Communication with SCADA Processes

We motivate model selection by a discussion of adversary participation in SCADA network communication. In essence, an adversary is forced to employ *agents* as direct communication is not possible owing to topology constraints.

We assume a set of channels W_I which are network entry points. We call W_I the *initial attack surface* of P. Taking account of latency, adversary communication is defined to be at a lower priority than internal SCADA communication. We define the adversary after Mao et al. [1]:

$$\Omega := (\sum_{w_i, w_i \in W_I} \bar{w}_i a_r.\mathbf{0} + \sum_{w_i \in W_I} w_i(a).\mathbf{0} + \tau.\mathbf{0} + \lambda.\mathbf{0}|!\Omega) \qquad (2)$$

Hence the adversary may communicate by channel $w_i \in W_I$ with a messenger M_i. We define a messenger process as:

$$M := \bar{x}_i a_1.\mathbf{0} + x_i(a_{1,y}).\mathbf{0}$$
$$\bar{y}_i a_1.\mathbf{0} + y_i(a_{1,x}).\mathbf{0}$$
$$\bar{w}_i a.\mathbf{0} + w_i(a).\mathbf{0} + \lambda_{w_i}.\mathbf{0}|!M \qquad (3)$$

where a is any name.

In contrast with a Dolev-Yao adversary [1, 6], the adversary is not the source and sink of all network communication. The adversary may only communicate by request and all communication with the network is at the lowest priority and subject to loss. Consider the following interaction between a supervisor, a communication process and an adversary, where we assume the messenger has been requested to send data to the adversary[1]:

---

[1] For simplicity, we ignore channel indices unless necessary from this point on.

$$P := (\bar{x}u_{1,y}.\mathbf{0}||!S)|$$
$$(x(a_1).\mathbf{0} + \bar{y}a_1.\mathbf{0} + \bar{w}a.\mathbf{0}||!M)|$$
$$(x(a_1).\mathbf{0}||!C)|$$
$$(w(a).\mathbf{0} + \lambda_w.\mathbf{0}||!\Omega) \tag{4}$$

By reduction we obtain –

$$P := (\bar{w}u.\mathbf{0}||!M||!S||!C|(w(u).\mathbf{0} + \lambda.\mathbf{0}||!\Omega) \tag{5}$$

which shows that the adversary will always receive information on supervisory commands last or not at all. Similar results will be obtained for control data or for any message by the adversary to a process M intended for a supervisor or control function.

Making the working assumption that protocols requiring freshness are robust in a real-time system, it follows that any process in a SCADA system can distinguish a manipulated message m' on these grounds. Hence the adversary is forced to use agents to maintain message freshness in order to subvert the network.

4.2   Agent Recruitment

We assume that all processes will contain exploitable security weaknesses and may be subverted. We consider a process in abstract and show how it may be recruited by an adversary. Let Q be any automated process in $S \cup M \cup C$ and let m be any malicious message then by the *subversion assumption* we have –

$$Q := ((\sum_i \pi_i.\mathbf{0}||!Q) + R + (w(m)[x = m]\tau.\nu\overrightarrow{z}.Q'||!Q')) \tag{6}$$

where Q' is a malicious version of Q. Hence, from an initial attack surface, an adversary may develop a *secondary attack surface*, defined by the neighborhood of its agents. We limit the extent of subversion by τ allowing the adversary only a limited number of subversion attempts, where R is the capability to resist attack. The ability to re-write a process also implies the potential to alter its capabilities.

4.3   Covert Communication

It is desirable for an adversary to use covert channels. By extruding the scope of a restricted name, an adversary may create a set of covert channels C. This capability is modelled by –

$$S := (f(M_i) \rightarrow \nu c_i.\bar{w}_i c_i.\mathbf{0}||!\Omega)|(w_i(c_i).\mathbf{0} + \bar{z}u.\mathbf{0} + z(u).\mathbf{0}||!M_i')$$
$$\rightarrow !\Omega|(\bar{c}_i u.\mathbf{0} + c_i(u).\mathbf{0}||!M_i') \tag{7}$$

We assume this capability may be exercised transitively. Covert channels are assumed to suffer from message loss and latency.

4.4   Message Interception and Manipulation

A malicious agent will have the capability on behalf of an adversary to intercept messages and send results to the adversary. An agent may also manipulate
message content. Because an adversary may not act directly (cf. section 4.1), he
must embed the functionality to alter messages within agents:

$$M' := (x(a_{1,y}).f(i) \rightarrow a'.\mathbf{0} + \bar{y}a'_1.\mathbf{0}$$
$$+ (y(a_{1,x}).f(a) \rightarrow a'.\mathbf{0} + \bar{x}a'_1.\mathbf{0}|!M') \tag{8}$$

For example, if we define a controller process as in eq. 9, we see that an agent
may manipulate the parameters k and p to malicious versions k' and p' which
are respectively the gain and set point parameters of a controller process so as
to affect the outcome of the signal.

$$C := z(s_0).f(s, p', k') \rightarrow \bar{z}e_0.\mathbf{0} + y(k_1).\mathbf{0} + y(p_1).\mathbf{0}|!C \tag{9}$$

Conversely, adversaries can manipulate the data presented to supervisor functions, either providing inaction or else poor decision making. In either case, the
effects will be deleterious. It is also possible to directly subvert these processes
but it is sufficient to subvert communication agents in the network to achieve the
same goal. We assume the volume of communication and process capacity are
constrained, so any agent functionality is relatively simplistic, e.g., we would not
expect to encounter the use of real-time numerical simulation software, but we
could reasonably expect the adversary to use a linear approximation of control
system behavior between two limits such as might be provided by a second order
Taylor series[2]. Hence, under normal conditions, agents should be able to mimick
control system responses to supervisor instructions to conceal their presence.

4.5   Denial of Service

An adversary may carry out an internal denial of service attack. Clearly, where
enough agents are recruited, dropping messages may be sufficient to create denial
of service conditions. More subtlely, an adversary with fewer agents which are
arbitrarily dispersed may use these to send messages to each other, utilising
all available channels leading to resource exhaustion. Let P_I and Q_I be sets of
processes which are agents. Let $P_I = Q_I$ on receive and let $P_I = Q_I \setminus P_i$ and
$Q_I = P_I \setminus P_i$ on send. We obtain using routing requests

$$P_I := \overrightarrow{\bar{w}u_{Q_I}}.\overrightarrow{\bar{x}u_{Q_I}}.\overrightarrow{\bar{y}u_{Q_I}}.\overrightarrow{w(u_{P_I})}.\overrightarrow{x(u_{P_I})}.\overrightarrow{y(u_{P_I})}.\mathbf{0}|!P_I$$
$$Q_I := \overrightarrow{w(u_{Q_I})}.\overrightarrow{x(u_{Q_I})}.\overrightarrow{y(u_{Q_I})}.\overrightarrow{\bar{w}u_{P_I}}.\overrightarrow{\bar{x}u_{P_I}}.\overrightarrow{\bar{y}u_{P_I}}.\mathbf{0}|!P_I \tag{10}$$

Let there be n agents and p processes. We assume at most $p - k$ channels per
process. Hence the total number of channels is $p(p-k)/2$ assuming bi-directional
channels. We define $m = \frac{p-1}{p-k}$ to be the ratio of total potential channels to actual

---

[2] In fact, this sort of approximation is exactly of the order of that used by control
system engineers in SCADA systems.

channels and claim that if $mn \geq p/2$ then all channels are exhausted. This is shown for all k (and using $k = 1$) by

$$\frac{p-1}{p-k}n(p-k) \geq \frac{p(p-k)}{2} \Leftrightarrow n(p-1) > \frac{p(p-k)}{2} \tag{11}$$

I.e. ignoring the contribution of normal network traffic, based on the "pigeonhole" principle, each agent only has to set and maintain in motion $\lceil m \rceil$ messages such that $mn = p/2$, although by choice, so as to implicate all processes, to overwhelm the network.

5   Model Utility: Discussion and Example

To show the utility of our model, we use of the concept of *context-based intrusion detection* [11] to investigate security properties relating to intrusion detection. Let Q be any process, then $Q := \nu \overrightarrow{z}(\sum_i s_i(u).\mathbf{0} + \sum_i \bar{s}_i u.\mathbf{0})|!Q$ where s and u are any name and $i \in \mathbb{N}_+$. Let $\langle U \rangle$ be the set of names received by Q and $\bar{U}$ be the set of names received by Q. Let $U := \langle U \rangle \cup \bar{U}$. Moreover, let P and Q be two processes. We write $P \cong Q$ if and only if for some distance function ϕ the distance between U_P and U_Q is insignificant for some threshold T_ϵ. We write $\phi[(U_P \cup U_Q) - (U_P \cap U_Q)] \subseteq \epsilon$ where $\epsilon := \emptyset \cup \delta$. We say that P and Q are equivalent[3], because given approximately the same inputs they produce approximately the same outputs. We say approximately because to deal with real-world systems, we must allow for natural variation. Hence, if we create a context $[\cdot]$ by removing P from a system and replace the hole left by Q - retaining U - the system will behave virtually identically.

On the other hand, if we hold for two processes P and Q that $P \cong Q$ and $\phi[(U_P \cup U_Q) - (U_P \cap U_Q)] \nsubseteq \epsilon$ for some threshold T_ϵ, then we consider this to be a detection event. Hence, we treat P as a model for Q and conversely. Without loss of generality, P may be a simulation of Q. P and Q may be concurrent, weakly bijective processes, which share related or identical causes. P and Q may also be dependent processes where events in P cause events in Q and we can map the outputs of P which are the inputs of Q to the outputs of Q and so apply ϕ to their analysis. The key observation is that contextual comparison will highlight significant differences *where none should exist*. We use our model to predict the appearance of broken contexts, hence potential detection events. As an example, we consider the manipulation of data acquisition and command dispersion defined in section 4.4. We assume the results of real analysis are available to us.

Let P be a SCADA system which controls a system $F(\overrightarrow{u})$ (we naturally treat physical systems as functions over names) which has two modes of operation which require different set points. Such systems are not uncommon. For example, [7] is a realistic example of a plant-wide production system with various modes of operation. We treat these modes, for simplicity, as limits and label these α, β, γ. Let $\overrightarrow{u}$ be the set point, gain parameters and signal of $F(\overrightarrow{u})$. We assume that the

---

[3] We note that process equivalence is not well-researched for hybrid systems [3].

adversary has available two continuous functions for approximating the behavior of $F(\overrightarrow{u})$ – see section 4.4 – which are $f(\overrightarrow{u}) \approx F|_\alpha^\beta(\overrightarrow{u})$ and $g(\overrightarrow{u}) \approx F|_\beta^\gamma(\overrightarrow{u})$ and that for any $\overrightarrow{u}$ $f(\overrightarrow{u}) \neq F|_\beta^\gamma(\overrightarrow{u})$ and $g(\overrightarrow{u}) \neq F|_\alpha^\beta(\overrightarrow{u})$. In the interest of brevity we use $F(u) := F|_\alpha^\beta(\overrightarrow{u})$ and $F(v) := F|_\beta^\gamma(\overrightarrow{u})$. Let P be such that a supervisor function S issues the command to change modes by sending a new name for the set point such that $F(u) \rightarrow F(v)$. We show that the adversary is faced with a paradox, if seeking to avoid detection. Let p be a set point. Let i be an instruction and let u be a data reading. All communications with the adversary are by convert channel c. Initially, starting in mode $F(u)$, we define our processes by

$$
\begin{aligned}
S :=& \bar{x}p_1.\mathbf{0} + x(u_1).\mathbf{0}|!S \\
M' :=& x(u_1).f(u,d) \rightarrow u'.\mathbf{0} + y(i_1).f(i,d) \rightarrow i'_1.\mathbf{0} \\
& + \bar{x}i'_1.\mathbf{0} + \bar{y}u'_1.\mathbf{0} + \bar{c}z.\mathbf{0} + c(z).\mathbf{0}|!M \\
C :=& z(s_0).h(s,p',k) \rightarrow \bar{z}e_0.\bar{y}e_1.\mathbf{0} + y(p_1).\mathbf{0}|!C \\
\Omega :=& \bar{c}s.\mathbf{0} + c(s).\mathbf{0} + \tau + \lambda|!\Omega
\end{aligned}
\tag{12}
$$

We now outline the reduction of this model, assuming the adversary will replace the embedded function f by g when notified of the change $F(u) \rightarrow F(v)$ and demonstrate that he is forced to break context. In equation 13, we see the result of a sensor message at priority 0 being received by the controller and sent to the actuator.

$$
C_2 := \bar{y}e_1.\mathbf{0} + y(p_1).\mathbf{0}|!C \tag{13}
$$

In equation 15, the controller transmits the signal to the agent and the supervisor sends the set point request to the agent in some order:

$$
\begin{aligned}
S_1 :=& x(u_1).\mathbf{0}|!S \\
M'_2 :=& f(p,d) \rightarrow p'.\mathbf{0} + \bar{y}i'_1.\mathbf{0} + f(e,d) \rightarrow e'.\mathbf{0} \\
& + \bar{x}u'_1.\mathbf{0} + \bar{c}p.\mathbf{0} + \bar{c}e.\mathbf{0} + c(z).\mathbf{0}|!M \\
C_3 :=& y(p_1).\mathbf{0}|!C
\end{aligned}
\tag{14}
$$

In equation 15, the names are substituted:

$$
M'_3 := y(p'_1).\mathbf{0} + x(e'_1).\mathbf{0} + \bar{c}p.\mathbf{0} + \bar{c}e.\mathbf{0} + c(z).\mathbf{0}|!M \tag{15}
$$

Only at this point – again last (cf. sec. 4.1) – is the adversary in a position to receive the information from the system about the mode shift. At this point, either the agent continues to transmit messages for some indeterminate time, considering both message prioritisation and message loss, from the controller using the previous, now inaccurate, transformation, relying on natural variation in the control system to disguise his presence – which we label hiding in the "noise" [12] – until he can replace f by g, with one or more inaccurately manipulated data reaching supervisor functions, or else the agent ceases transmission for some indeterminate time until it can replace the function, being programmed to recognize a significant alteration in control system mode and to await further instructions. If we assume the former, then the control system will move to a state where $f(\overrightarrow{u}) \neq F(v)$ for an indeterminate period of time and hence violate context. If we assume the latter, then the agent will cease communication for an indeterminate period of time - which may violate some context regarding network communication. We also note the requirement to violate an internal context regarding message prioritisation. While any of these conditions may be detectable for a single controller, using a model of its operation, detection is made easier if we deal with groups of controllers related concurrently by context. In section 4.2, we argued that the success of process subversion is limited. It follows that non-agentized processes will provide an accurate set of information about control system state U, while agentized process will provide manipulated results U'.

Hence, even where the adversary uses agents to falsify the data readings from and command instructions to a control system process, his actions may be detected by modelling the expected behavior of a (group of) process(es) in the context of related processes or some model or both. This prediction is underpinned by earlier empirical work in the area [11, 9].

6   Related Work

As an example of a realistic SCADA system structured along the lines we describe, consider [5]. The use of agent processes to subvert messages at network level is predicted in [13]. The manipulation of control systems by adversaries or their agents forms a common theme for attack scenarios [8, 4, 9, 11]. We base our approach on [1]. However, we clearly reject the simplistic use of the Dolev-Yao model in SCADA networks such as in [4]. Indeed, there exists no need for agent subversion within Dolev-Yao type models, while other systems, which do reason about the possibilistic subversion of processes tend to concentrate on proving encryption protocols rather than reasoning about other properties and are monolithic in nature [2]. Our approach enables us to reason about the interactions of both the adversary and corrupt and legitimate agents in the network and is modular in nature, allowing us to separate out the various elements. The model provides a formal underpinning to empirical work on detecting adversary and agent actions from contextual information [11, 9] as well as the necessity for doing so [13, 12] and – on automation – will be a useful resource for testing the viability of various strategies for creating context-based intrusion detection opportunities and for exploring the properties of such features.

7   Conclusion and Future Work

Dolev-Yao and similar adversary capability models imply a network model unsuitable for highly constrained DCS/SCADA environments exhibiting network segmentation and real-time processing requirements and the increasing use of protocol-level security mechanisms providing identification and authentication and hence protection from trivial attacks. Instead, we argue the adversary *must* recruit agents to act on his behalf. These agents provide the adversary with up to supervisory capability over key control systems. They may also provide the power to create denial of service conditions on the network. Even so, the adversary continues to be constrained in its communication. We demonstrate the utility of our approach by showing that the limitations placed on agent-adversary communication will, given certain conditions, reveal (the actions of) agentised processes from contextual information. This finding underpins other research in the area and suggests it as a topic for further research.

Future work will concentrate on developing and testing various strategies for providing contextual information in a SCADA system using automated modelling of the system, so as to provide the basis for a resilient multi-layered approach to monitoring such systems, and the addition of lifting rules in order to supply formal proofs regarding the results of real analysis in combination with discrete events within the system. It is also clear that research into process equivalence in hybrid systems is well-motivated by the analysis of security properties of such systems.

References

[1] Mao, W.: A structured operational modelling of the dolev-yao threat model. In: Christianson, B., Crispo, B., Malcolm, J.A., Roe, M. (eds.) Security Protocols 2002. LNCS, vol. 2845, pp. 34–46. Springer, Heidelberg (2004)

[2] Basin, D., Cremers, C.: From Dolev-Yao to Strong Adaptive Corruption: Analyzing Security in the Presence of Compromising Adversaries. Cryptology ePrint Archive, Report 2009/079 (2009), http://eprint.iacr.org/

[3] Bergstra, J.A., Middleburg, C.A.: Process Algebra for Hybrid Systems. Theor. Comput. Sci. 335(2-3), 215–280 (2005)

[4] Cardenas, A.A., Roosta, T., Sastry, S.: Rethinking Security Properties, Threat Models, and the Design Space in Sensor Networks: A Case Study in Scada Systems. Ad Hoc Netw. 7(8), 1434–1447 (2009)

[5] Dawson, R., Boyd, C., Dawson, E., Nieto, J.M.G.: SKMA: A Key Management Architecture for SCADA Systems. In: ACSW Frontiers 2006: Proceedings of the 2006 Australasian Workshops on Grid Computing and e-Research, pp. 183–192. Australian Computer Society, Inc., Darlinghurst (2006)

[6] Dolev, D., Yao, A.C.: On the Security of Public Key Protocols. In: SFCS 1981: Proceedings of the 22nd Annual Symposium on Foundations of Computer Science, pp. 350–357. IEEE Computer Society, Washington, DC (1981)

[7] Downs, J.J., Vogel, E.F.: A Plant-Wide Industrial Process Control Problem. Computers & Chemical Engineering 17(3), 245–255 (1993)

[8] Gamez, D., Nadjm-tehrani, S., Bigham, J., Balducelli, C., Burbeck, K., Chyssler, T.: Safeguarding Critical Infrastructures. In: DEPENDABLE COMPUTING SYSTEMS: Paradigms, Performance Issues, and Applications, Wiley[Imprint], Inc., Chichester (2000)

[9] McEvoy, T.R., Wolthusen, S.D.: Detecting SCADA Sensor Signal Manipulations in Non-linear Chemical Engineering Processes. In: Proceedings of the IFIP TC 11 25th International Informatin Security Conference, IFIP Advances in Information and Communication Technology

[10] Sangiorgi, D., Walker, D.: PI-Calculus: A Theory of Mobile Processes. Cambridge University Press, New York (2001)
[11] Sheng, S., Chan, W.L., Li, K.K., Xianzhong, D., Xiangjun, Z.: Context Information-based Cyber Security Defense of Protection System. IEEE Transactions on Power Delivery 22(3), 1477–1481 (2007)
[12] Svendsen, N., Wolthusen, S.: The International Federation for Information Processing. In: Modeling And Detecting Anomalies In Scada Systems, 101 (2009)
[13] Verba, M., Milvich, J.: Idaho National Laboratory Supervisory Control and Data Acquisition Intrusion Detection System (SCADA IDS). In: IEEE Conference on Technologies for Homeland Security, pp. 469–473 (2008)

A Cloud Provider-Agnostic Secure Storage Protocol

Nikos Virvilis, Stelios Dritsas, and Dimitris Gritzalis

Information Security and Critical Infrastructure Protection Research Group,
Dept. of Informatics, Athens University of Economics & Business (AUEB),
76 Patission Ave., Athens, GR-10434 Greece
{nvir,sdritsas,dgrit}@aueb.gr

Abstract. Over the last years Cloud Computing has been seen as an emerging technology, which has changed the way computing services are delivered. Cloud computing is not a new technology paradigm, but rather introduces a new way of delivering computing services and resources. On top of its potential value and the several advantages it offers, we can foresee a number of drawbacks of cloud computing, in terms of security and privacy issues. In specific, cloud computing raises the level of expertise needed to protect security and privacy of its stakeholders (i.e. organizations and end-users), mainly due to the fact that the massive concentration of computer resources and data could be a more attractive target to malicious users. In this paper, we present a cloud provider-agnostic model for outsourcing both static and dynamic data to third parties, while preserving their confidentiality and integrity. In addition to a detailed presentation of our model, we also depict an evaluation of it, in terms of its capabilities and weaknesses.

Keywords: Cloud Computing, Security, Storage Services, Confidentiality, Integrity.

1 Introduction

Advances in Information and Communication Technologies (ICT) over the last years, due to the more reliable and pervasive broadband access capabilities, have changed the nature of the Internet itself. Nowadays, Internet is not only a communication network, but it is has already been transformed into a kind of virtual, enormous, and interconnected supercomputer. This has facilitated the introduction, development and adoption of Cloud Computing.

Cloud computing is not a new technology paradigm, but rather a new way of delivering computing resources. There are many definitions of cloud computing; in the context of the specific paper we adopt the definition presented in [1]: *Cloud Computing is an on-demand service model for IT provision that is based on virtualization and distributed computing technologies.* Cloud computing architectures share some common characteristics, such as: highly abstracted and shared resources, near instant scalability and flexibility, near instantaneous provisioning, service on demand-basis, etc. In general, there are three basic categories of cloud computing,

C. Xenakis and S. Wolthusen (Eds.): CRITIS 2010, LNCS 6712, pp. 104–115, 2011.

namely: (a) *Software as a service (SaaS)*, where software is offered by a third party provider, via the Internet (i.e. online word processing tools, web content delivery services, etc.), (b) *Platform as a service (PaaS)*, which facilitates the development of new applications using APIs deployed and configured remotely, and (c) *Infrastructure as service (IaaS)*, which provides abstracted hardware and operating systems capabilities, mainly through virtualization.

In general, cloud computing has changed the nature of computing and it offers significant advantages in terms of reduced cost, increased storage, flexibility and mobility. Moreover, the adoption of cloud by a vast number of individuals/corporations inevitably affects the operation of a large number of infrastructures, including critical ones, which tend to use cloud environments for supporting their every day procedures. In addition to these advantages, cloud computing introduces a number of drawbacks that might impede its further adoption and development (see Fig. 1). Most of these disadvantages are closely related to the security and privacy risks of this technology.

In this context, it is clear that security and privacy may be proved to be a serious obstacle for the further development of cloud computing. Hence, it is necessary to find mechanisms and techniques that will deal effectively with them. In this paper we propose a model addressing confidentiality and integrity of storage services in the cloud. Our model is cloud-provider transparent-agnostic; i.e., it can be used with any cloud provider. Furthermore, the proposed model supports dynamic data management, allowing users to update, delete or append new data, as well as facilitating the file sharing between users.

The paper is organized as follows: In section 2 we present current approaches towards the protection of confidentiality and integrity in cloud computing. In section 3 we present a detailed analysis of our model. In section 4 we analyze the advantages and disadvantages of the model. In section 5 we conclude by presenting thoughts and ideas for further research.

Fig. 1. Main advantages and disadvantages of Cloud Computing

2 Related Work

In this section we will refer to related work, regarding data confidentiality and integrity issues in the cloud environment.

A number of techniques for preserving confidentiality of the outsourced data have been proposed. In [2] the authors propose the use of data fragmentation as a means for ensuring confidentiality. However, their model introduces a significant storage overhead. In [3] a cryptographic cloud storage scheme is presented, which addresses confidentiality and integrity and supports searchable encryption. However this scheme is based on a protocol, which the cloud provider has to support. Similarly in [4] researchers propose a generic scheme for access control to outsourced data, based on a different symmetric key for encrypting each data block. Their approach uses a key derivation method based on key hierarchy in an effort to limit the imposed overhead, but - once more - the model requires the cloud provider to support the proposed protocol. In [5], a file encryption scheme for cryptographic distributed file system is proposed, which is based on optimized Merkle hash trees. In an effort to enhance the performance of the hash tree, the authors propose a universal hash-based MAC scheme that provides confidentiality and integrity of outsourced data. However, this scheme requires a separate, trusted storage among with the untrusted storage where the outsourced data will be stored.

Research effort has been also conducted on Cryptographic File Systems (CFS) [6] [7] [8], which could be used in cloud computing environment for secure storage purposes. However, CFS impose significant computational and network overhead, as they were not designed for remote storage services. Furthermore, CFS might also not effectively address all attack vectors: For example, a cryptographic file system on a laptop computer may only need to be protected against one-time data loss (e.g. theft). But, when the encrypted data is stored on an untrusted storage server, the attacker may potentially observe many encrypted modifications to the stored data and he might also be able to adaptively modify the data [5].

A number of schemes for integrity checking on outsourced data have also been presented. Ateniese et al. have proposed a model for provable data possession (PDP) that enables a client to verify the integrity of his outsourced data, located to a third party, without having to retrieve the whole data set [9]. This is achieved by sampling random sets of blocks from the server, while it only supports static data. In order to enhance their technique, the authors presented an updated scheme [10], which supports some basic dynamic operations on the outsourced data, such as append, modify and delete. Their scheme supports only an a priori number of integrity verifications. In [11], a POR (Proofs of Retrievability) scheme was introduced, by which the server proves to the client (verifier), that an outsourced file F is retrievable with high probability. The proposed approach uses special blocks (called sentinels), inserted between normal data, and asks the server to retrieve randomly the sentinels so as to prove that the file is retrievable. Once more, the sentinel method allows only a fixed number of integrity verifications and supports only static data. A similar technique is presented in [12], which achieves lower storage requirements and a higher level of assurance, with minimal computational overhead, but, as with the previous techniques, it only addresses static data.

Wang et al. [13] proposed a model that supports dynamic data operation, but like the method presented in [10] this takes place in a partial manner. Erway et al. [14] have presented the first fully dynamic PDP model. Their model supports private verification of dynamic data however file updates introduce significant computational overhead. In [15], Wang et al. propose an improved version of their previous scheme, which offers fully dynamic data operation, as well as public verifiability. Finally, some generic and weak schemes have also been presented [16]. These techniques use protocols that enforce the server to provide dedicated storage, at least as big as the size of the outsourced data. They fail to offer any other guarantees.

To sum up, the proposed integrity checking schemes have significant advantages, when it comes to verification of outsourced data - such as reduction in I/O costs to the server [9] - and little (nearly constant) communication complexity [12], but they require data storage (usually metadata) at the client side. Similarly, both integrity and confidentiality schemes proposed so far are based on challenge-response mechanisms requiring the provider's adoption of the protocol.

In practice, the requirement for supporting a special protocol makes the current schemes not directly applicable to existing cloud storage providers (Amazon S3, Microsoft Azure, IBM Cloud Services etc). Even if such a protocol is supported by a provider in the future, the client will be locked-in to that particular provider. This limits the user options on selecting a cloud provider. Hence, the migration to a new provider will be difficult and time consuming, as depending on the scheme, reprocessing of all outsourced data may be needed, according to the new protocol requirements.

Our proposed model addresses effectively the aforementioned issues. It can be used with any cloud provider, without requiring adoption of any specific protocol, avoiding the lock-in issue and keeping migration to a new provider as simple as possible.

3   A Confidentiality and Integrity Ensuring Model

The aim of our model is to protect confidentiality and integrity of data stored in a Cloud Storage Provider, while having the following properties: (a) to be Cloud provider agnostic - without requiring the adoption of a specific protocol by the provider, (b) to be flexible, allowing the user to select the desirable security level she wishes (encryption algorithm, key size, integrity verification), (c) to be mobile, requiring only the private key pair of the user to be stored at the client system, and (d) to support the easy migration of the data to a new provider if the client wishes to do so.

Our threat model considers the cloud provider as self-interested, curious, and potentially malicious. Hence, we assume that the provider will be interested in the contents of the outsourced data and may try passive and active attacks, in an effort to gain access to it. The same assumptions are valid for any other adversary interested in gaining access to the data.

Fig. 2 depicts a macroscopic view of our approach. The basic entity of the model is the *Data Processing Module* (DPM), which runs at the cloud client's system. DPM is responsible for processing the data (i.e. file splitting, encryption etc.), before it will be uploaded to the cloud provider for storage. In general, the main steps taken by DPM, when a user decides to store a file in the cloud, are the following:

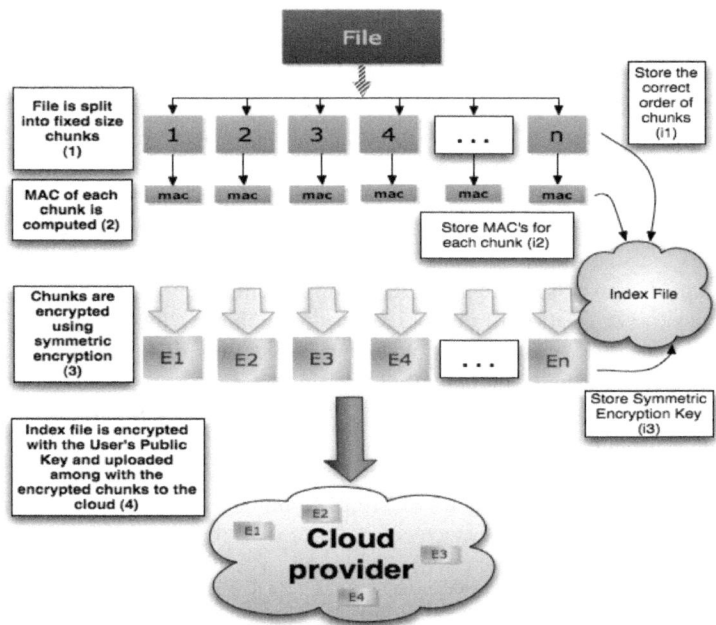

Fig. 2. A model for preserving confidentiality and integrity

Step 1. The file is split into fixed size chunks, and each chunk is given a random filename.

Step 2. A MAC (Message Authentication Code) of each chunk is computed. The key used for the MAC computation is randomly generated, different for each file, while it is common for all chunks of a file.

Step 3. Each chunk is encrypted using a symmetric algorithm and by a second (different from the previous step) randomly generated key, unique for each file. Again all chunks of a file are encrypted using the same key.

Step 4. The links between the correct order of the chunks and the random name they were given are stored on a file called *Index File*. *Index file* also stores the MAC key, as well as the MAC output of each chunk, among with the symmetric encryption key.

Step 5. The *index file* is encrypted using the client's public key.

Step 6. The encrypted chunks and the *index file* are uploaded on the cloud provider in random order.

3.1   File Splitting

As we described in Step 1, every file is split into fixed size chunks and every chunk is given a random file name. Given a case insensitive file system and a filename of 10 characters there are 36^{10} unique combinations[1]. Hence, assuming that the user will

---

[1] Assuming that the cloud provider allows filenames to contain characters a-z and 0-9, case insensitive, for a filename of 10 characters the possible combinations are 36^{10}.

upload 100.000 files with an average size of 1 MB per file and a fixed chunk size of 10KB, a number of 10^7 chunks will be created, so even in a case insensitive environment, several hundreds of thousand files can be stored. Nevertheless, the user can change the size of the filename, according to his needs and/or the cloud provider requirements.

The method of file splitting and chunk filename randomization has several benefits:

- The cloud provider is totally unaware of the real number of files stored on his infrastructure, because he only sees encrypted files of fixed size with random file names.
- Even if the cloud provider had a way of cryptanalyzing the symmetric encryption algorithm used for encrypting the chunks, he would not be able to reconstruct the original file, because the correct order of the chunks is unknown.
- File splitting also addresses (weakly) traffic analysis attacks. A provider receiving data for storage does neither know the exact number, nor the size of the received files.
- By using file splitting, the file operations procedures are optimized. The model adopts an incremental method of file storage, in which a possible change of an outsourced file does not require the retransmission of the overall file, but only the transmission of the updated chunk(s).

In the context of our approach, we do not define the size of the chunks that should be used. However, for optimal performance, the chunk size should be a multiple of the block size of the symmetric encryption algorithm. An appropriate selection of the chunk size is also important for the verification process (see section 3.5).

3.2 Hybrid Encryption

Our model makes use of a hybrid encryption scheme. First of all, we use a symmetric encryption algorithm for rapid data processing. Any symmetric block cipher could be used with a randomly generated key (different for each file) for encrypting each file chunk. On the other hand, the computationally demanding asymmetric encryption is used only for encrypting a single file, the one that contains the required information for file retrieval and decryption (*Index File*).

By using the above hybrid encryption scheme our benefit is twofold: first, the mobility of the scheme is maintained, because the only requirement is the storage of the private key at the client side and at the same time we avoid the performance overhead of asymmetric encryption.

3.3 Chunks Message Authentication Code

A Message Authentication Scheme (MAC) is used for protecting both the message's data integrity, as well as its authenticity. It does so by allowing verifiers, who also own the secret key, to detect potential changes to the message contents. A MAC algorithm generates a fixed amount of data out of an arbitrary long input and a secret key.

We compute the MAC for each chunk by using a randomly generated key, which is different for each file. This way, when a file is retrieved from the storage provider, the chunks are decrypted and the MAC for each chunk is computed and compared with the initial MAC stored in the *index file*. Any difference of the compared values implies an integrity violation.

3.4 Index File

The *index file* is used for storing all information needed for data decryption, verification, and reconstruction. The file contains a record for each outsourced file, which includes all necessary information, as depicted in Table 1. The *index file* is encrypted, with the user's public key. Then, it is stored together with the rest of the encrypted data on the storage provider.

Table 1. An example file record in the index file

Filename: secret-document.doc	
Number of chunks: 10	
Chunk 1: 6d67a1c0f1 *(random filename)*	**MAC (1)**: d8685c1eff3b2276e5da37fd65eea127
Chunk 2: ed3d03d485	**MAC (2)**: f52efa2805789a8d42188341a348c134
Chunk 3: 540641e7ce	**MAC (3)**: 0184830b36ea8bb6a1918ee6f7c18f6a
...	...
Chunk 10: 1509c881b1	**MAC (10)**: 4763339ecd24884d4bc6efe559b7c48c
MAC KEY:	146c07ef2479cedcd54c7c2af5cf3a80
ENCRYPTION KEY:	8c2b76888b0c6f8a8f51da48e67859b788c63a75

Since all the information needed for file decryption and reconstruction is stored in the *index file*, a single point of failure is created. If this file gets corrupted in any way (deliberately or not), it will result to a complete data loss (as there will be no way of decrypting the data). To avoid this drawback, the user could maintain an encrypted copy of the *index file* at the client side, as a kind of backup mechanism.

The *index file* could also be split in fixed size chunks and stored as any other file on the storage provider. The DPM could keep a track of the random filenames for the chunks consisting the *index file* and request those every time it needs to access it. However this countermeasure introduces two issues: First, additional data has to be kept at the client side apart from the secret key. Hence, a problem regarding the mobility and transparency of the model appears. Second, as the *index file* will be accessed every time, either for retrieving of files, storing, or integrity checking, a malicious provider could identify which chunks are the most frequently accessed, and thus identify the specific chunks that consist the *index file*.

3.5 Data Management

Here we present the actions needed for file management processes, namely storage, retrieval, deletion, update, verification, and sharing of files between users.

Let the name of our original file be F and its outsourced form be F^*. The file F is divided into a fixed number of chunks: $F = \{f(0), f(1), (f2), f(3), \ldots f(n)\}$, where $f(x)$ denotes each chunk. Let $MAC_{ki}(f(x))$ be the MAC value computed for each chunk using the symmetric key ki (integrity key), $Enc_{ke}(f(x))$ the encryption of a chunk using the symmetric key *ke* (encryption key), and $Dec_{ke}(f(x))$ the decryption of a chunk using the symmetric key *ke*. Furthermore, let $Enc_{public}(x)$ be the public encryption of the file *x* using the user's public key, and $Dec_{private}(x)$ be the decryption of the file using the user's private key. Finally, let $Ret(f(x))$ be the retrieval of the appropriate chunk, while the uploading of the chunk be $Str(f(x))$.

a) File Storage
The storage process has been also described briefly in section 3.

The steps that are taking place for file storage on the remote server are:

1. The file to be stored remotely is selected.
2. The Data Processing Module (DPM) splits the file into fixed number chunks and issues a random filename to each of them.
3. DPM generates randomly an integrity key (ki) and computes the MACs of the file chunks. $MAC_{ki}(f(x))$
4. DPM generates a new random encryption key (ke) and encrypts all the chunks. $Enc_{ke}(f(x))$
5. The *index file* is retrieved from the remote storage and decrypted using the user's private key. $Ret(index\ file), Dec_{private}(index\ file)$.
6. The encryption key (ke), the integrity key (ki), the MAC of each chunk among with its random file name and the correct order of the chunks are stored in a new file record in the *index file*.
7. The *index file* is encrypted using the client's public key. $Enc_{public}(index\ file)$.
8. DPM uploads the encrypted chunks and the *index file* to remote storage.

a) File Retrieval
The retrieval of a file is the opposite of the storage process. The steps that are taking place for retrieval are:

1. The Data Processing Module (DPM) retrieves the *index file* and decrypts it using the client's private key. $Ret(index), Dec_{private}(index)$.
2. DPM parses the file records in the *index file*, and returns a file listing of all the outsourced data.
3. User selects the file he wants to retrieve.
4. DPM locates the appropriate record in the *index file*, and retrieves the following information:
   a. The number of chunks, their random filenames, as well as the correct order of chunks.
   b. The MAC for each chunk.
   c. The key used for computing the MAC (*ki*).
   d. The key used for symmetric encryption of the chunks (*ke*).
5. The DPM downloads the appropriate chunks from the remote storage server $Ret(f(x))$.
6. DPM decrypts the chunks using the symmetric key $Dec_{ke}(f(x))$.
7. DPM computes the MAC of each decrypted chunk ($MAC_{ki}(f(x))$), and compares it with the MAC stored in the *index file* (integrity check).
8. The chunks are combined in the correct order, in order for the original file to be created.

b) File Update

The update process includes the retrieve process (as the file has to be downloaded locally). The user retrieves and edits the file locally. Following:

1. The Data Processing Module (DPM) checks the filename of the file with the list of files stored on the cloud provider. This is accomplished by searching the *index file*.
2. If a file with the same filename is detected, DPM asks the user if he wants to replace the existing file with the new one (a process including file deletion and file storage) or if he wants to update the file.
3. If the user selects the latter, the DPM will run partially the store procedure, including the division of the file and the MAC computation and will check the MAC computed for each new chunk with the MAC of the chunks stored in the *index file*.
4. For every chunk with a changed MAC, DPM will rename the new chunk to the exact file name as the old chuck, and will upload the new chunk to the provider, replacing the old one. If the modification is such that it results in the change of the total number of chunks, then new chunks will be uploaded or deleted, accordingly, and the file record in the *index file* will be updated.

c) File Deletion

A file deletion includes the following steps:

1. User selects the file to be deleted from the file list.
2. DPM locates the file's record from the *index file*, and notes the chunks that correlate to that particular file.
3. It deletes the appropriate chunks from the remote storage.
4. It deletes the file record for that file in the *index file*.
5. The updated *index file* is uploaded to the storage provider.

d) Verification

When a user uses a cloud provider for storage purposes, we can assume that he will want to verify that specific file(s) - or even all outsourced data is retrievable and the integrity is preserved. As the proposed model is cloud provider transparent, the verification of the integrity of a file requires the chunks linked to that file to be downloaded and verified locally.

This process is costly in network resources. We can not use any of the proposed protocols for remote integrity verification as their requirements contradict with our model objectives (support of specific protocol).

We can limit the communication overhead by checking only a limited number of chunks for each file. By randomly selecting chunks, retrieving them, and verifying their MAC, we may detect corruption. The detection rate depends on the number of chunks we are verifying for a particular file, as well as on the number of verification cycles we run (i.e. executing an integrity check cycle once a day). As the chunks are selected randomly, the provider can neither delete any of the chunks, nor move them to secondary storage (disk tapes or any other not directly accessible media) without risking of been detected, as any of them can be requested for verification in the next verification cycle.

Having in mind the above, the verification process is as follows:

1. The client selects a particular (or multiple) files, or the whole data set, for verification.
2. Based on client's needs, the number of chunks to be checked for each file is set.
3. For each file to be verified, DPM randomly selects the given number of chunks and downloads them from the provider.
4. The chunks are decrypted and their MAC is computed.
5. The new MAC is compared with the stored MAC for every chunk, so as the integrity is checked.

e) File Sharing

The proposed model also supports simple file sharing between users of the same cloud provider. For example, if Bob wants to share a file F, stored in a cloud provider, with Alice, then the following procedure takes place:

1. Bob locates the file record for the file he wants to share from the *index file*.
2. Bob sends Alice the file record, as stored in his *index file*, encrypted with Alice's Public Key.
3. Alice retrieves the data and decrypts the file record using her private key.
4. Alice appends the file record to her *index file*. She can now decrypt and reconstruct the data sent from Bob.

4 Evaluation of Our Model

The proposed model is a provider transparent-agnostic model. It can be used with every cloud provider offering storage services. It should be noted that the model although optimized for cloud environments, it could also be used in every distributed environment, providing secure storage of data. With our model the transition to a different provider is simple and does not require outsourced data to be re-processed neither at client or server side. Since all operations of our model are taking place at the client side, the cloud provider does not need to incorporate any special protocol for supporting it. Moreover, the proposed model is flexible since the only requirement for the client is to store locally her private key (i.e. use of smart card, a TPM (Trusted platform module), etc.). In addition, it does not introduce any storage or processing overhead at the server side, except for the storage overhead, which is due to encryption and to the creation of a single data file, storing the needed information for data retrieval. All data transmitted between the client and cloud provider is encrypted using a hybrid encryption scheme, so as to avoid the performance issues the asymmetric cryptosystems suffer by.

For simplicity reasons, we presented our model by incorporating only one cloud provider, but it is actually trivial to include more providers and split the data and even the *index file* between them. This way the proposed model becomes more robust against cryptanalytic attacks, as a malicious provider does not have the entire information needed to reconstruct a file. Moreover, by using more than two cloud providers, secure secret sharing techniques [17] could be used for further protection of the *index file*. In specific, if one provider is malicious and destroys the *index file*, this can be recovered from the other providers. Additionally, even if a provider is capable of cryptanalyzing the asymmetric encryption used to protect the *index file*, she would be unable to decrypt it, as he would not be able to reconstruct the complete *index file*. Only a small change at the file record of the *index file* is needed, in order for the DPM to know in which provider each chunk is stored to and thus support multiple providers.

The main drawback of the proposed model is that it might be challenging for resource-limited devices to support all the set of operations, since all the operations are done at the client side. Although implementation and benchmark of the model on mobile devices is planned for future work, we can do an estimation based on the following facts: 1) encryption and decryption of the chunks is the most resource intensive operation in our model, 2) the CPU's in modern smart phones range from 260-600Mhz [18], and 3) AES with 128-bit key mode in general requires around 300 clock cycles to encrypt/decrypt each data block (128 bits) [19]. Thus, encryption/decryption of the chunks - even if these are larger than 100kb each, should be trivial for a modern smart phone. The bottleneck of the scheme will most likely be the network connection. However, the effect on battery life due to the demanding CPU operations, when large amount of data is processed, has to be reviewed.

Moreover, the proposed model does not address data recovery (e.g. how to recover a corrupted chuck). In order to address this drawback Error Correcting Codes (ECC) could be used, but this will lead to further storage overhead. Our model does not provide protection against a malicious provider who might delete a large amount of data. Storing all data to multiple providers is the only efficient solution for this problem. Currently it only supports single user access to outsourced data. Finally, as all the information needed for file decryption and reconstruction is stored in the *index file*, this creates a single point of failure. Nevertheless, we have introduced a number of ways for mitigating this problem.

5   Conclusions and Future Work

For future research, we envisage to support multiple user access to outsourced data, and enhance our integrity verification module, while further limiting the communication overhead. Moreover, we would like to address the single point failure issue of the index file, without having to keep a local copy of it, or using multiple storage providers and secret splitting techniques. Finally, we plan to implement our model in a high level language, in an effort to evaluate our model's performance both to desktop computers as well as to mobile devices.

References

1. European Network and Information Security Agency (ENISA), Cloud Computing Security Risk Assessment, Technical Report (November 2009)
2. Stoner, M., Greenan, K., Miller, E., Voruganti, K.: POTSHARDS: Secure Long-Term Storage Without Encryption. In: Proc. of the USENIX Annual Technical Conference, USA, pp. 143–156 (2007)
3. Kamara, S., Lauter, K.: Cryptographic Cloud Storage. In: Proc. of the Financial Cryptography: Workshop on Real-Life Cryptographic Protocols and Standardization, Canary Islands, Spain (2010)

4. Wang, W., Li, Z., Owens, R., Bhargava, B.: Secure and Efficient Access to Outsourced Data. In: Proc. of the 2009 ACM Workshop on Cloud Computing Security, USA, pp. 55–66 (2009)
5. Yun, A., Shi, C., Kim, Y.: On Protecting Integrity and Confidentiality of Cryptographic File System for Outsourced Storage. In: Proc. of the 2009 ACM Workshop on Cloud Computing Security, USA, pp. 67–76 (2009)
6. Blaze, M.: A Cryptographic File System for Unix. In: Proc. of the 1st ACM Conference on Computer and Communications Security, USA, pp. 9–16 (1993)
7. Cattaneo, G., Catuogno, L., Sorbo, A., Persiano, P.: The Design and Implementation of a Transparent Cryptographic File System for Unix. In: Proc. of the USENIX Annual Technical Conference, USA, pp. 199–212 (2001)
8. EncFS Encrypted Filesystem, http://www.arg0.net/encfs
9. Ateniese, G., Burns, R., Curtmola, R., Herring, J., Kissner, L., Peterson, Z., Song, D.: Provable Data Possession at Untrusted Stores. In: Proc. of the 14th ACM Conference on Computer and Communications Security, USA, pp. 598–609 (2007)
10. Ateniese, G., Di Pietro, R., Mancini, V., Tsudik, G.: Scalable and efficient provable data possession. In: Proc. of the 4th International Conference on Security and Privacy in Communication Networks, Turkey (2008)
11. Juels, A., Kaliski, B.: Pors: Proofs of Retrievability for Large Files. In: Proc. of the 14th ACM Conference on Computer and Communications Security, USA, pp. 584–597 (2007)
12. Bowers, K., Juels, A., Oprea, A.: Proofs of Retrievability: Theory and implementation. In: Proc. of the 2009 ACM Workshop on Cloud Computing Security, USA, pp. 43–54 (2009)
13. Wang, Q., Wang, C., Ren, K., Lou, W.: Ensuring Data Storage Security in Cloud Computing. In: 17th IEEE International Workshop on Quality of Service (IWQoS 2009), USA (2009)
14. Erway, C., Kupcu, A., Papamanthou, C., Tamassia, R.: Dynamic Provable Data Possession. In: Proc. of the 16th ACM Conference on Computer and Communications Security, USA, pp. 213–222 (2009)
15. Wang, Q., Wang, C., Li, J., Ren, K., Lou, W.: Enabling Public Verifiability and Data Dynamics for Storage Security in Cloud Computing. In: Backes, M., Ning, P. (eds.) ESORICS 2009. LNCS, vol. 5789, pp. 355–370. Springer, Heidelberg (2009)
16. Golle, P., Jarecki, S., Mironov, I.: Cryptographic Primitives Enforcing Communication and Storage Complexity. In: Proc. of the 6th International Conference on Financial Cryptography, Bermuda, pp. 120–135 (2002)
17. Shamir, A.: How to share a secret. Com. of the ACM, 612–613 (November 1979)
18. Wei, M., Chandran, A., Chang, H., Chang, J., Nichols, C.: Comprehensive Analysis of Smart Phone OS Capabilities and Performance. University of Southern California (2009)
19. Schneier, B., Kelsey, J., Whiting, D., Wagner, D., Hall, C., Ferguson, N.: Performance Comparison of the AES Submissions. In: Proc. Second AES Candidate Conference, NIST, pp. 15–34 (March 1999)

State-Based Firewall for Industrial Protocols with Critical-State Prediction Monitor

Igor Nai Fovino[1], Andrea Carcano[2], Alessio Coletta[1], Michele Guglielmi[1], Marcelo Masera,[1] and Alberto Trombetta[2]

[1] Joint Research Centre, Institute for the Protection and Security of the Citizen,
Via E. Fermi 1, 21027, Ispra, Italy
igor.nai@jrc.ec.europa.eu
[2] University of Insubria, Via Mazzini 5, 21100, Varese, Italy
andrea.carcano@uninsubria.it

Abstract. Traditional cyber-security countermeasures are inadequate for protecting modern Industrial Critical Infrastructures. In this paper we present an innovative filtering technique for industrial protocols based on the state analysis of the system being monitored. Since we focus our attention on the system behavior rather than on modeling the behavior of the possible attackers, this approach enables the detection of previously unknown attacks. Moreover, we introduce the concept of Critical State Prediction, function that is used for anticipating the evolution of the system towards possible critical states. Finally we provide experimental comparative results that confirm the validity of the proposed approach.

Keywords: Security, SCADA systems, critical infrastructures, firewall.

1 Introduction

Critical Infrastructures (e.g. Power Plants, Power Grids, Transportation systems etc.) are increasingly incorporating in a massive way *Information and Communication Technologies* (ICT). This trend enables to optimize the services provided, to implement distributed self-orchestration mechanisms, to manage remote installations in efficient manners, etc. However, the extensive use of ICT has also exposed those infrastructures to a new, never experienced, level of vulnerability to Cyber-attacks. In particular the so called "Industrial ICT" is completely unprepared to face the increasing exposure to Cyber-Threats. In fact, historically, industrial systems have been isolated from the ICT viewpoint, and therefore they have relied on this fact for guaranteeing protection against potential Cyber-attacks. This assumption does not hold anymore and, as showed in several research works [1,3,10], the scenario in which attackers gain control of the process networks of industrial installations cannot be considered anymore implausible. Due to the peculiarities of the industrial communication protocols and systems, the traditional ICT security countermeasures are unable to adequately protect those infrastructures. In this paper we propose an innovative approach for filtering and discriminating between benign and malicious industrial protocol

C. Xenakis and S. Wolthusen (Eds.): CRITIS 2010, LNCS 6712, pp. 116–127, 2011.

flows. This approach relies on the concept of *state analysis*: roughly speaking, we assume that in order to damage an industrial installation, attackers have to force one of the installation subsystems into a critical state. As a consequence, comparing the evolution of the system state with a set of known and unwanted critical states it would be possible to detect whether a chain of locally licit commands sent through the network to the plant devices is indeed able to drive the whole system into a critical state. By blocking the detected traffic, it would be possible to automatically prevent attacks aiming at damaging the installation. As industrial systems are usually designed for minimizing and sharply delimiting the occurrences of potentially harmful scenarios (or, *critical states*), it is a reasonable assumption to hold that critical states of industrial systems are well-known in advance and precisely defined. We note that our approach for intercepting possible attacks focuses on the system behavior rather than on modeling the behavior of the possible attackers. Making no assumptions on attackers (except that – of course – they will try to disrupt the correct behavior of the industrial system), our architecture is able to detect previously unknown attacks. In the present work we also introduce the *Critical State Prediction Monitor*, a function able to measure the proximity of the current state of the monitored system to the set of possible critical states. The idea is to use this additional feature to help operators promptly react to probable critical states.

2 Related Works

Adam and Byres [1] presented an interesting high level analysis of the possible threats affecting an industrial system, a categorization of the typical hardware devices involved and some high level discussion about intrinsic vulnerabilities of the common power plant architectures. A more detailed work on this topic is presented by Chandia et al. [3]. Some work has been done about the security of industrial communication protocols: for example, Majdalawieh et al. [4] presented an extension of the DNP3 protocol, called DNPsec, which tries to address some of the known security problems of such Master-slave control protocols. The DNP3 User group proposed a "Secure DNP3" implementing authentication mechanisms for certain type of commands and packets. Nai et al. [2] presented a secure implementation of the Modbus protocol. Similar approaches have been presented also by Heo et al. [5], while Mander et al. [6] presented a proxy filtering solution aiming at identifying and avoiding anomalous control traffic. Nai et al. presented a first embryonic IDS for Industrial protocols [8] in which a first idea of state based analysis has been introduced; Pothamsetty and Franz (CISCO), released a ModBUS transparent firewall [9] based on Linux Netfilter, however, at the moment it still appears to be in an embryonic stage of development.

3 State Analysis Filtering

Firewalls able to analyze industrial protocols in the traditional fashion (i.e. analyzing the network flow according to "single packet and stream" signatures) cannot

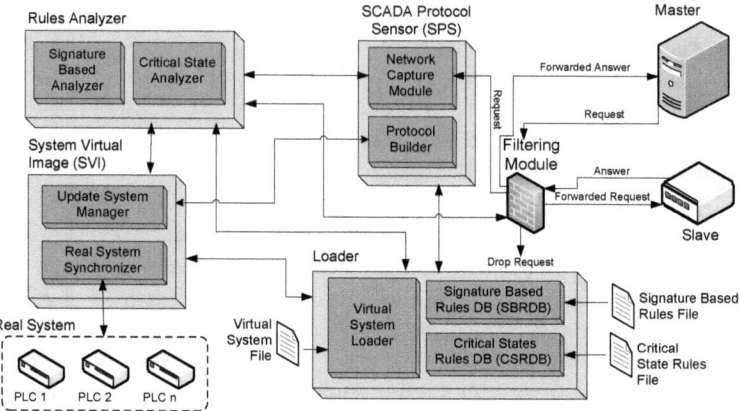

Fig. 1. Critical State Based Firewall Architecture

fully protect process control systems, as there are many dangerous situations that cannot be identified by them. The following example clarifies this statement: consider a system with a pipe P_1 in which flows high pressure steam. The pressure is regulated by two valves V_1 and V_2. If an attacker is able to inject command packets in the process network, he can, for example, send a packet to the PLC controlling valve V_2 to force its complete closure and a command to the PLC controlling valve V_1 in order to maximize the incoming steam. These two operations, taken separately, are perfectly licit. However, if sent in sequence, and if a third security valve V_3 is in the meantime locked, they are able to drive the system into a critical state since the pressure in the pipe P_1 will soon become too high for the pipe specifications. Similar situations cannot be detected by a traditional firewall since it is not aware of the current state of the system.

To solve this problem we developed an innovative filtering technique along the following lines:

1. Since the SCADA (supervisory control and data acquisition) system controls the process running inside the industrial system, by monitoring its activity it is possible to control the activity of the industrial system.
2. Every industrial system is, when designed and deployed, well analyzed and all the possible "unwanted" states are usually identified. These unwanted states can be identified as *critical states*.
3. The data flowing among masters and slaves of a process system can be used to reconstruct the *virtual image* of the state of the monitored system. Comparing the "virtual state" with the critical states to be avoided, it is possible to predict whether the system is evolving into a critical state, and therefore provide early indication of possible critical states.
4. The so defined firewall embedding the virtual system and the state analyzer should, of course, be placed between the SCADA servers and the slaves. In this way, the Critical State detection technique can be used to block the commands which, if executed by the field devices, will put the system into a dangerous state.

In a similar architecture, a not negligible question relates to the "fidelity" of the virtual system. To ensure a tight synchronization between the virtual and real systems, in the proposed approach the firewall embeds a "Master Emulator" able to directly query the field devices when the corresponding virtual elements start to age. Figure 1 shows the block diagram of the prototype developed to implement the described approach. A key point that has a relevant impact on the performance of the firewall regards the way in which *Critical States*, *System Descriptions* and *single packet rules* are provided and organized. The next section provides a thorough description of the languages used to define these elements.

4   Rules Languages

The firewall described in the previous section adopts two detection techniques: (i) a single packet, signature based technique, and (ii) a State Analysis technique. We defined two ad-hoc created languages to describe the signatures of the dangerous packets and to describe the critical states. In this section we provide a formal definition of these languages and an example allowing to understand how they can be used.

4.1   Packet Language

The packet language has been developed taking into account the most used TCP/IP based Industrial protocols. The rules have the form

$$signature \rightarrow DENY/ALLOW$$

where the *signature* expresses exactly the content of a target malicious packet. The "signature" includes two type of fields: (a) TCP/IP related fields, and (b) Industrial Protocol dependent fields. More in detail, in our language a *packet signature* has the following format:

$$\{Source|Destination|SourcePort|destinationPort|SpecificProtocolFields\}$$

Where:

- **Source** is the IP address of the packet sender.
- **Destination** is the IP address of the packet receiver (e.g. the IP address of a PLC).
- **Source Port** is the TCP source port used for the communication.
- **Destination Port** is the TCP Destination port used for the communication.
- **Specific Protocol Fields**: it is a special field containing the list of the specific fields related to different industrial protocols. This prototype at the moment supports two industrial protocols: Modbus and DNP3. In the case of rules regarding the Modbus protocol, this special field will contain two sub−fields: *function code, Payload.* In the case of a rule regarding the DNP3 protocol, this special field will contain elements such as: *DNP3 source address, DNP3 destination address, Function code, Data object, Variation* etc.

4.2 Critical State Language

A rule in the Critical State language has the form *condition → action*, where action can take two values: allow or deny. *Condition* is a logic formula which specifies critical states. Each formula is a conjunctions of predicates defining the critical values of each involved PLC.

A *PLC object* is a set of pairs $plc = \{\langle comp_1, val_1 \rangle, \ldots \langle comp_n, val_n \rangle\}$. Each pair $\langle comp, val \rangle$ denotes the value *val* stored/registered by the plc component named *comp*. PLC and component names are elements of a finite set $\mathcal{N}$ (e.g. C, R, DI, DO). Given names n_1, n_2, ..., values are elements of the corresponding domains $\mathcal{D}_{n_1}$, $\mathcal{D}_{n_2}$, ... A SCADA system *state* is then a set $S = \{plc_1, \ldots, plc_u\}$ of PLC objects. We associate to critical states a set of propositional boolean formulas – called critical formulas – composed of standard predicates connected by the boolean connective "and". We now present the *Critical State language* using a standard BNF notation:

$$\langle rule \rangle := \langle condition \rangle \rightarrow \langle action \rangle$$
$$\langle condition \rangle := \langle predicate \rangle \mid \langle predicate \rangle, \langle condition \rangle$$
$$\langle predicate \rangle := \langle PLCName \rangle \langle relation \rangle \langle value \rangle$$
$$\mid \langle value \rangle \langle relation \rangle \langle PLCName \rangle$$
$$\langle PLCName \rangle := PLC \langle identifier \rangle . \langle comp \rangle \langle number \rangle$$
$$\langle identifier \rangle := \langle ID \rangle, \langle IPaddress \rangle$$
$$\langle action \rangle := Alert \mid Log \mid Look \langle rule \rangle$$
$$\langle relation \rangle := \leq \mid \geq \mid < \mid > \mid = \mid \neq$$
$$\langle comp \rangle := C \mid HR \mid IR \mid DO$$
$$\langle value \rangle := 0 \mid ... \mid 2^{16} - 1$$

Example 1. Consider a system composed of a turbine and a temperature sensor, respectively connected to two PLCs. The PLCs are identified by their *ID number* and *IP address*. The PLC 1 with IP address 10.0.0.10 is connected to a turbine with an holding register set in order to regulate the turbine rotation speed. PLC number 2 (address 10.0.0.22) is connected to a temperature sensor and the temperature value is stored in an Input Register. The system is in a critical state when the temperature is greater than 99 degrees and the turbine rotates at less than 1000rpm. This critical state can be formalized in the Critical State language in the following way:

$$PLC[1, 10.0.0.10].HR[1] < 1000, PLC[2, 10.0.0.22 : 502].IR[1] > 99$$

The firewall will block every packet that will match the previous formula when applied to the virtual system.

5 Critical State Distance

In this section we present a method for predicting whether the system is progressing towards a critical state. The method is based on a notion of *distance* from critical states, which expresses how far the current state of the system is from *any* of the possible critical states CS represented by a set of critical formulas.

Predicting criticality can be achieved by tracking changes of this distance. If the distance decreases, then the system is evolving toward one or more critical states. This information can be used to raise an alert, for instance when the distance is less than a certain threshold. With this technique we can extend the proposed Critical State Based Firewalling, for providing an early-warning monitor.

A *system state* is defined by the state *values* of all system components. These values are usually boolean, integers, or decimal, i.e. they can be represented by real numbers. Thus every state of a system with n total components can be represented by a vector $s \in \mathbb{R}^n$. In this section we assume that the value of every system component is mapped to a specific vector component s_i of s for some $i \in \mathbb{N}$, and it is denoted by v_i. In the following the step-by-step construction of the metric is provided.

Let $d \colon \mathbb{R}^n \times \mathbb{R}^n \to \mathbb{R}^+$ be any metric on $\mathbb{R}^n$. In other words, let d be any notion of distance between two system states, where n is the number of system components. In this work two special distances are of particular interest:

$$d_1(s,t) = \sum_{i=1}^{n} |s_i - t_i| \qquad\qquad d_v(s,t) = \#\{i \mid s_i \neq t_i\}$$

The distance d_1 is also known in literature as the *Manhattan* distance. The distance d_v counts the number of *system components values* which differ between two states.

Given a distance function on $\mathbb{R}^n$ (e.g. as d_1 or d_v previously defined), the notion of distance between a state and a *set of states* can be defined as $d(s,S) = \inf_{t \in S} d(s,t)$. This definition mimics the common sense of distance in daily life.

Given any distance d between a state and a set of states, the notion of distance between a system state s and the set of critical states CS is defined by $d(s, CS)$. It expresses the notion of how distant the current state of a system is from a set of critical states specified by a set of critical formulas.

5.1   Distance Evaluation

The calculation of the distance from critical states is based on a equivalent representation of critical formulas in terms of *range constraints*, described below in the following of this section. Before giving the formal definitions, we show an example of a range constraint. The critical formula $\varphi = v_i \leq 30, v_i \neq 10, v_i \neq 20, v_j \geq 40$, where v_i and v_j are system components values ranging on integer values, can be represented by the equivalent constraint $i \mapsto [-\infty, 9] \cup [11, 19] \cup [21, 30], j \mapsto [40, +\infty]$.

Critical states are specified by a set of critical formulas defined in the grammar introduced in Section 4.2. Each formula has the form $\varphi = p_1, p_2, \ldots$ where p_i are predicates defined in the same grammar. A state s is *critical with respect to* φ if s *satisfies all* predicates p_i. Each predicate has the form $v \bowtie r$, where v is a system component, r is a value, and $\bowtie \in \{<, >, \leq, \geq, =, \neq\}$. Let $I = [a, b]$ be a closed interval on $\mathbb{R}$, where $a \in \mathbb{R} \cup \{-\infty\}$ and $b \in \mathbb{R} \cup \{+\infty\}$. Any predicate $v \bowtie r$ can be represented by an interval or a union of disjoint intervals.

A *range constraint* $C = I_1 \cup \ldots \cup I_n$ is the union of non-overlapping closed intervals. We call $\mathcal{CS}$ the set of range constraints. We call *constraint function* any function $constr\colon \mathbb{N} \to \mathcal{CS}$ mapping the i-th system component value v_i to a range constraint. A constraint function can be easily implemented by a hash map between system components values and range constraints, which are implemented by lists of intervals. In the initialization phase, all critical formulas φ are scanned in order to calculate an equivalent range constraint $constr_\varphi$. In our implementation the size of the hash map implementing $constr_\varphi$ is linear with respect to the total number of predicates of φ.

Restricting the choice of distance only to d_1 and d_v, we show an easy way to calculate the distance $d(s, CS)$. In what follows we use d to denote either d_1 or d_v when not specified. We have that for any value $x \in \mathbb{R}$ and closed interval I

$$d_1(x, I) = \begin{cases} x - \sup I & \text{if } \sup I \leq x \\ \inf I - x & \text{if } \inf I \geq x \\ 0 & \text{otherwise} \end{cases} \qquad d_v(x, I) = \begin{cases} 1 & \text{if } x \notin I \\ 0 & \text{otherwise} \end{cases}$$

Let $C = I_1 \cup \ldots \cup I_k$ be a constraint associated to some system components value. We have $d(x, C) = \min_{j=1\ldots k} d(x, I_j)$ for any $x \in \mathbb{R}$. Moreover, for any state $s \in \mathbb{R}^n$

$$d(s, \varphi) = \sum_{i=1}^n d(s_i, constr_\varphi(i)) \qquad d(s, CS) = \min_\varphi d(s, constr_\varphi)$$

where n is the number of system components. In our implementation, the time complexity for computing $d(s, constr_\varphi)$ is linear with the size of the hash map used for implementing the range constraints. Thus, computing $d(s, CS)$ has a time complexity which is linear with the total number of predicates occurring of all critical formulas.

6   Experimental Tests

In order to test the performance for the CS-Firewall, we established a security test-bed environment composed of a Master, a set of slaves and a prototype of the firewall filtering the network traffic.

In the following we describe each step performed by the CS-Firewall and the Master/Slave simulators:

(a) Master station: sends a Request Message.
(b) CS-Firewall: receives and processes the Request message, updates the virtual system, checks the CS-Rules. If the virtual system status matches at least one critical state, the CS-Firewall blocks the packet, otherwise the packet is forwarded to the Slave Station.
(c) Slave station: receives and processes the Request Message and then executes the command, creates the Response message and sends it back.

Table 1. Time elapsed for each step in the CS-Firewall

N.	Task	Time Min (ms)	Time Max (ms)
2	Process Request	0.08801	0.12101
3	Virtual System Update	0.00339	0.06708
4	Signature Rules Check	0.00083	0,19426
5	CS-Rules Check	0.00093	0.76601
9	Response Forward	0.09202	0.11301
	Total	0.18518	1.19847

(d) CS-Firewall receives and forwards directly the Response message, but in addition it runs, in parallel, another thread which updates the virtual system and calculates the distance between each critical state and the virtual system status. If a critical state distance is zero the CS-Firewall will raise an alert, if a critical state is at close distance of the actual virtual system status, then the CS-Firewall will raise a *"Proximity Alert"*. The Table 1 shows the time elapsed for each step in the CS-Firewall and the total delay introduced by the entire firewall. The showed time values are the result of a large set of tests in which the complexity of the CS-rules varied.

The results show that our architecture does not produce significant effects on the communication through a SCADA network. In what follows we provide a detailed performance evaluation of each single step listed in Table 1.

Process Request Time: It is the time spent by the CS-Firewall to process the packet decapsulation through the TCP/IP stack and to parse the Request application message.

Update Virtual System Time: The CS-Firewall updates the virtual system in two steps: 1) it finds the PLC related to the packet content, 2) it updates the Virtual Object which represents that PLC. The first step does not cause any important effect on the CS-Firewall performance since the list of PLCs is implemented with a Hash Table, therefore the time elapsed to find a PLC (around 0,0042 ms) is almost the same regardless of the number of PLCs. The test of the PLC update time is the following: the Master Station sends 1000 requests with the function code *"Read n coils"* and the Slave Station replies with the proper responses. The CS-Firewall captures the request/response transactions and updates the n values in the virtual system. We performed the test with different n values (Figure 2). The results demonstrate the validity and quality of the proposed approach, since in the worst case, i.e. 2000 coils to update (maximum value allowed according to the Modbus specification), the virtual system update performance is under one millisecond. In addition, the elapsed time increases with the number of coils to update in a linear way as shown in Figure 2.

The results demonstrate the validity and quality of the proposed approach, since in the worst case, i.e. 2000 coils to update (maximum value allowed according to the Modbus specification), the virtual system update performance is under one millisecond. In addition, the elapsed time is linear with respect to the number of coils to be updated, as shown in Figure 2.

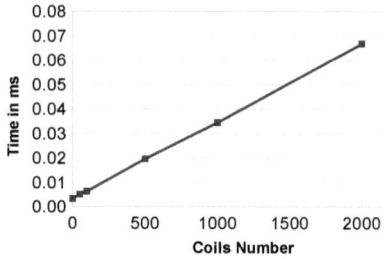

Num Coils	Time (ms)
1	0.003
50	0.005
100	0.006
500	0.019
1000	0.034
2000	0.067

Fig. 2. Virtual System Update Performance Test and graph

Signature Rules Check Time: The performance of the Signature-Based Filter depends on the quantity of rules, therefore the following experiment was carried out: the Master Station sends 1000 generic Request messages and the Slave Station responds with the appropriate responses. The CS-Firewall captures the messages and checks whether they are licit, according to a rules file containing n rules. The test was made with different n values as shown in Table and Figure 3.

The elapsed time increases with the quantity of rules. The growth is linear, and the time is always below 1ms as shown in Chart in Figure 3.

Check Critical State Rules Time: The performance of the Critical State Rules Analyzer depends on two factors: the size of each rule (conditions number) and the quantity of rules. For the first factor (rule size) the following speed test was made: the Master Station sends 1000 generic Request messages and the Slave Station with the appropriate responses; the CS-Firewall captures the messages and checks whether the Virtual System is entering into a Critical State, according to a rules file that contains only one rule with n conditions. We made the test with m different numbers of conditions. For the second factor (quantity of rules) we carried out a similar test, but in this case we used n rules, each one composed of two conditions. We made the test with different n rules. Table and Figure 4 shows the results for both tests.

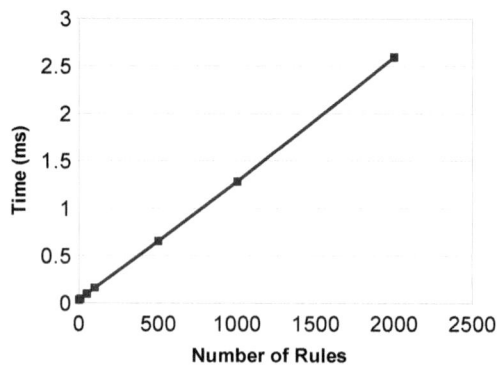

Rules	Time (ms)
1	0.001
10	0.006
50	0.004
100	0.006
500	0.049
1000	0.096
2000	0.194

Fig. 3. Signature Based Rule Filter Performance Test and Graph

Conditions	Time (ms)
2	0.003
4	0.003
32	0.006
128	0.031
256	0.060
512	0.113
1024	0.246
2048	0.554

Rules	Time (ms)
10	0.007
50	0.015
100	0.026
500	0.123
1000	0.330
2000	0.766

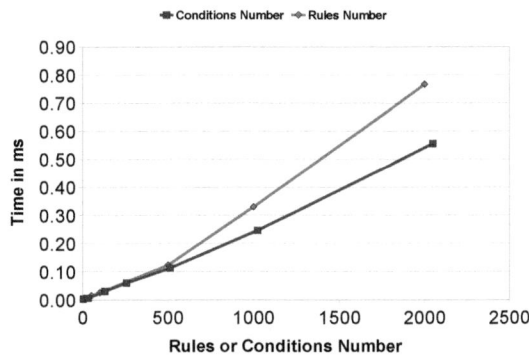

Fig. 4. Critical State Rule Filter Performance Test and Graph

The elapsed time growth is shown in Figure 4 for both tests. The time elapsed is under one millisecond with a number of conditions up to 2048. This is an important result because in a real rules database, it would be difficult to have rules with 2048 conditions. In addition, these tests show that the the critical state rules analyzer performance is high, because the time elapsed is under one millisecond with a number of rules up to 2000, therefore with a large rules set the delay introduced by the CS-Firewall is negligible.

6.1   Distance Performance

While filtering, the CS-Firewall runs a parallel thread calculating the distance between each critical state and the virtual system status. This additional task would provide precious information on the system evolution to the installation operators. In light of what described in Section 5, we have performed the following test:

1. **Intervals Test:** The rule set is composed of one rule with one system component value mapped to a list of n intervals. The range of values for n is from 1 to 2000.
2. **Component Values Test:** The rule set is composed of one rule with n system components values, each one mapped to a list of 10 intervals. The range of values for n is from 1 to 2000.
3. **Rule Test:** The rule set is composed of n rules, each rule contains 10 component values, and each one is mapped to a list of 10 intervals. The range of values for n is from 1 to 2000.

Table 2 shows the results for the three parts of the test.

Table 2. Distance Analyzer Performance Test

Table 2.A

Intervals	Time (ms)
1	0.010
10	0.013
50	0.019
100	0.021
500	0.056
1000	0.093
2000	0.165

Table 2.B

Values	Time (ms)
1	0.013
10	0.037
50	0.147
100	0.270
500	1.308
1000	2.547
2000	5.147

Table 2.C

Rules	Time (ms)
1	0.040
10	0.277
50	1.332
100	2.632
500	13.542
1000	28.967
2000	57.386

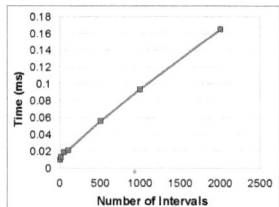 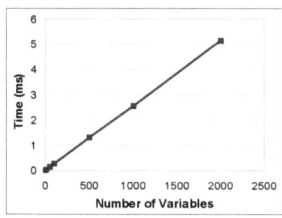 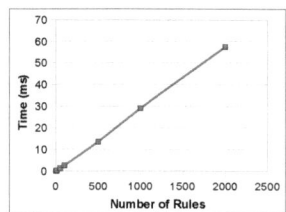

Fig. 5. Distance Test

The time elapsed for calculating the distance in test 2.A is negligible especially considering that a list of 2000 different intervals for a single condition is improbable. The time spent for calculating the distance between the current state and a critical state composed by a single rule with an increasing number of system components values (Table 2.B) is linear, and this time is less than 6ms for a number of components values up to 2000. The time spent for calculating rule distances for the entire rule set (Table 2.C) is linear and the maximum time is less than 60ms for a number of rules up to 2000.

7   Conclusions

In this work we presented a new network filtering approach based on the concept of Critical State Analysis. Relying on the fact that industrial critical systems are usually provided with a well documented analysis of all the unwanted physical critical states, this approach, based upon the behavioral evolution of the system under analysis, and not on the attacker behavior, enables the detection of complex attacks. In addition it has the not negligible advantage of being able to identify not only known attacks but also every type of "zero day" attack aiming at interferring with the physical state of the industrial installation. In this paper we have also introduced the concept of "critical state distance", which is used for implementing an "early warning" system able to provide to the installation operators relevant information about the possible future occurrence of critical states. The comparative tests performed show how the proposed approach can effectively protect industrial systems from ad-hoc crafted ICT attacks.

References

1. Creery, A.A., Byres, E.J.: Industrial Cybersecurity for power system and SCADA networks. IEE Industry Apllication Magazine (July-August 2007)
2. Nai Fovino, I., Carcano, A., Masera, M.: Secure Modbus Protocol, a proof of concept. In: Proc. of the 3rd IFIP Int. Conf. on Critical Infrastructure Protection, Hanover, NH., USA (2009)
3. Chandia, R., Gonzalez, J., Kilpatrick, T., Papa, M., Shenoi, S.: Security Strategies for Scada Networks. In: Proceeding of the First Int. Conference on Critical Infrastructure Protection, Hanover, NH., USA, March 19-21 (2007)
4. Majdalawieh, M., Parisi-Presicce, F., Wijesekera, D.: Distributed Network Protocol Security (DNPSec) security framework. In: Proceedings of the 21st Annual Computer Security Applications Conference, Tucson, Arizona, December 5-9 (2005)
5. Hong, J.H.C.S., Ho Ju, S., Lim, Y.H., Lee, B.S., Hyun, D.H.: A Security Mechanism for Automation Control in PLC-based Networks. In: Proceedings of the ISPLC 2007, IEEE International Symposium on Power Line Communications and Its Applications, Pisa, Italy, March 26-28, pp. 466–470 (2007)
6. Mander, T., Nabhani, F., Wang, L., Cheung, R.: Data Object Based Security for DNP3 Over TCP/IP for Increased Utility Commercial Aspects Security. In: Proceedings of the Power Engineering Society General Meeting, Tampa, FL, USA, June 24-28, pp. 1–8. IEEE, Los Alamitos (2007)
7. Nai Fovino, I., Carcano, A., Masera, M., Trombetta, A.: An experimental investigation of malware attacks on SCADA systems. International Journal of Critical Infrastructure Protection 2(4) (2009)
8. Nai Fovino, I., Carcano, A., Masera, M., Trombetta, A., Delacheze-Murel, T.: Modbus/DNP3 State-based Intrusion Detection System. In: Proceedings of the 24th International Conference on Advanced Information Networking and Applications, Perth, Australia, April 20-23 (2010)
9. http://modbusfw.sourceforge.net/ (last access May 28, 2010)
10. Nai Fovino, I., Masera, M., Leszczyna, R.: ICT Security Assessment of a Power Plant, a Case Study. In: Proceeding of the Second Int. Conference on Critical Infrastructure Protection, Arlington, USA (March 2008)

A Formally Verified Mechanism for Countering SPIT

Yannis Soupionis[1], Stylianos Basagiannis[2], Panagiotis Katsaros[2],
and Dimitris Gritzalis[1]

[1] Information Security and Critical Infrastructure Protection Research Group,
Dept. of Informatics, Athens University of Economics and Business (AUEB)
76 Patission Ave., Athens, GR-10434, Greece
{jsoup,dgrit}@aueb.gr
[2] Dept. of Informatics, Aristotle University of Thessaloniki
Thessaloniki, GR-54124, Greece
{basags,katsaros}@csd.auth.gr

Abstract. Voice over IP (VoIP) is a key technology, which provides new ways of communication. It enables the transmission of telephone calls over the Internet, which delivers economical telephony that can clearly benefit both consumers and businesses, but it also provides a cheap method of mass advertising. Those bulks unsolicited calls are known as SPam over Internet Telephony (SPIT). In this paper we illustrate an anti-SPIT policy-based management (aSPM) mechanism which can handle the SPIT phenomenon. Moreover, we introduce a formal verification as a mean for validating the effectiveness of the aSPM against its intended goals. We provide model checking results that report upper bounds in the duration of call session establishment for the analyzed anti-SPIT policy over the Session Initiation Protocol (SIP) and prove the absence of deadlocks.

Keywords: Spam over Internet Telephony (SPIT), Policy management, Model checking, Formal verification, Voice over IP (VoIP).

1 Introduction

VoIP (Voice over Internet Protocol) is the general term that describes two-way transmission of voice over the Internet in real (or near-real) time. Adoption of VoIP as a mainstream communication mean brings huge benefits to organizations, like a reduced call cost as well as smooth integration with the current internet infrastructure and the provided services. In VoIP, the voice signal is digitized and then transmitted over the Internet in packets, as it happens when sending an email with a sound file attachment.

Therefore, VoIP can be thought as an evolution of the email service and it seems that it also faces the same problems and challenges as its predecessor. The main problem of the email is SPAM. The term used in VoIP instead of SPAM is SPIT [1, 2] and it is derived from ''Spam over Internet Telephony''. SPIT [2] refers to all unsolicited and massive scale attempts for initiating a session that establishes voice communication with an oblivious user. If the user answers the call, the "spitter" broadcasts his message in real time. SPIT comes in three different types, namely: (a) call SPIT, (b) instant message SPIT and (c) presence SPIT. SPIT is expected to

C. Xenakis and S. Wolthusen (Eds.): CRITIS 2010, LNCS 6712, pp. 128–139, 2011.
© Springer-Verlag Berlin Heidelberg 2011

become a serious threat to the spread of VoIP in the forthcoming years. This threat stems from the well known email spam problem and existing botnets that in addition to SPAM emails are re-programmed for initiating VoIP calls. This is the reason why companies, like NEC and Microsoft, invest into developing mechanisms for tackling SPIT [3, 4]. Currently, several SPIT prevention methods have been proposed, but research on SPIT prevention is still in its infancy.

In a recent article [5], an anti-SPIT Policy Management (aSPM) mechanism for detecting and handling SPIT calls was proposed. This paper introduces formal verification as a mean for validating the effectiveness of an anti-SPIT Policy against its intended goals. Moreover, we provide model checking results with upper bounds in the duration of call session establishment, which show that the aSPM mechanism does not affect dramatically the time needed for session establishment and prove the absence of deadlocks.

Model checking communication protocols like SIP is based on a finite state model representing at a suitable level of abstraction the behavior of a system where the protocol runs in one or more concurrent protocol sessions. Correctness properties are expressed as assertions or temporal logic formulae that are algorithmically validated by state exploration across all possible execution paths. Operational errors or security flaws can be detected in the form of safety or liveness property violations that reflect unexpected behavior. For a violated property, the analyst gets a counterexample, i.e. an execution path to the detected invalid state that provides valuable feedback for redesigning the system. To the best of our knowledge, our work is the first attempt towards formal verification of anti-spamming countermeasures.

In Section 2 we describe the methodology for formally verifying the anti-SPIT policy mechanism at hand. Section 3 outlines the analyzed anti-SPIT policy called aSPM. In section 4 we report results obtained from a real-time SIP session experiment, in order to formulate valid modeling assumptions and property specifications. Section 5 introduces the SIP-aSPM model developed in the SPIN model checking tool [6] and the correctness properties that are validated. In section 6 we provide the obtained verification results and the paper concludes with a critical view of the outcomes and a discussion on future research prospects.

2   Methodology

Figure 1 provides an overview of the adopted methodology for formally verifying the anti-SPIT policy at hand.

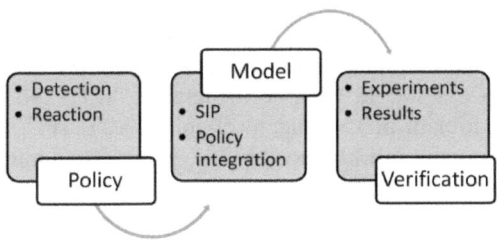

Fig. 1. Methodology for formally verifying anti-SPIT policy

The first step towards the development of an anti-SPIT policy is the detailed design of the detection and the reaction processes that comprise the policy. It is also necessary to describe how the policy is integrated into a SIP VoIP environment.

The next step involves the development of a finite state model for the SIP protocol that in our case takes place within the SPIN model checking tool [6]. SPIN is an automated model checker that aims to efficiently verifying (distributed) software systems. Its success has been proved through several case studies [7, 8], where SPIN is used to trace design errors in distributed systems. It provides the capability of reporting flaws like model deadlocks, unspecified receptions, flags incompleteness, race conditions, unwarranted assumptions about the speeds of processes [9] and others.

In our problem, one of the research goals is to verify that the anti-SPIT policy does not create "invalid" states in the SIP communication process and for this reason our model reflects in detail the call session establishment and the SIP message exchanges.

The anti-SPIT policy is then integrated into the model by implementing the behavior of entities that enforce the policy, as well as the message overload incurred by the policy reaction process. Model parameters concerning the cost in time for the exchanged messages have been derived from the measurements made in the conducted call session experiments.

Finally, we verify property specifications like the absence of deadlock in execution scenarios with one or more concurrent protocol sessions and the requirement of timely session establishment.

3 Policy Description

While SIP is considered to be one of the most widespread protocols for multimedia session maintenance there are reports [10] that describe SIP security errors and therefore raise the need for a security policy mechanism. Our work on the anti-SPIT Policy Management (aSPM) mechanism [5] is based on identifying potential threats that can exploit protocol weaknesses. The SIP protocol provides a connection-based technology, i.e. a call setup phase has to take place before any voice traffic is carried across the IP network. Signaling commands are used in establishing and terminating a call, as well as in providing some special features such as call forwarding and call waiting. Therefore, the nature of SIP only allows for proactive countermeasures against SPIT, like for example policy rules, which can properly adjust the reaction of the elements that participate in the negotiation and the communication process. Based on this assumption, the anti-SPIT policy takes the form of an obligation policy [11] that includes a set of rules and the appropriate countermeasures obeying the condition-action model [12]. Therefore, aSPM consists of the detection and the reaction processes.

The detection process should be able to detect a SPIT call or message, when it reaches the callee's domain or User agent client (UAC). SPIT detection depends on pre-identified criteria and it is influenced by the preferences-interests of the callee, in terms of the attributes of the call or message, or the anti-SPIT policies of the callee's domain. In order to define the detection rules (conditions) the SIP-targeted SPIT threats were identified by an in-depth analysis. The result of the SIP analysis was a number of well-defined SPIT-related threats and vulnerabilities, in accordance with the SIP RFC [13]. Afterwards, attack scenarios were created based on SPIT-oriented attack graphs. The attack scenarios were converted into specific attack signatures, which formed the base for the condition creation (policy key element).

The reaction process applies specific actions in case a call or a message has been detected as SPIT. These reactions, i.e. the application of specific anti-SPIT measures, are enforced by the anti-SPIT policies of the callee's domain. Most of them are SIP messages [14, 15], because the policy should: (a) be transparent to the administrators and users and (b) keep to a minimum the participation of other applications during message handling. An example of a proposed condition - action is illustrated in Table 1.

Table 1. A condition and its suggested countermeasures

Caller's device (UAC) receives a response with message code 300 (Multiple Choices) and there is a SIP header in *Contact* field which is not part of the *From*
1. The UAC rejects the call and returns a message 403 (Forbidden)
2. The UAC rejects the call and returns a message 606 (Not Acceptable)

The countermeasures that are taken into account in this research work are the proposed SIP messages. The SIP message response codes, which are used by the policy, are the 4xx request messages and the 6xx global failures. These messages direct the caller or his/her domain to resend the previously dispatched message so as to meet the necessary requirements of the callee or his/her domain.

3.1 Policy Integration in a VoIP Environment

In this section we describe how the anti-SPIT policy can be integrated in a SIP infrastructure in order to measure the anti-SPIT policy impact to the overall SIP signaling phase. For this purpose, the policy is formally described with an XML schema that includes the attack scenarios (conditions) and the applied countermeasures (actions).

The implementation approach is depicted in Figure 2 and includes two additional modules:

1. The XML parser which reads the XML policy instance into memory and provides easy access to tag values of the document.

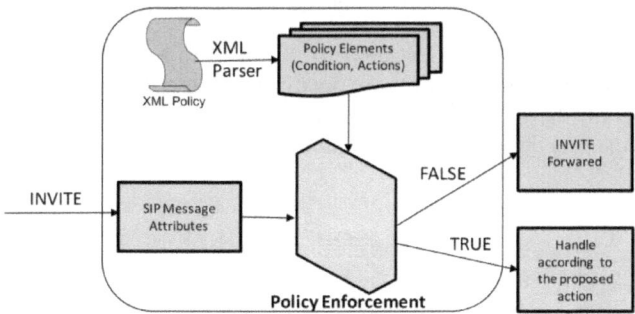

Fig. 2. The aSPM Architecture

2. The policy enforcement, which has as input the parsed xml document, together with the message attributes. The module checks all the policy conditions, so as to find out which are fulfilled (first a SIP message is received and parsed, and then the message attributes are checked against the policy element) and if one or more conditions are met, then the associated action (described in the fulfilled policy element) takes place.

The proposed policy integration will obviously incur time delays to call establishment. Therefore in the next section we report the results obtained in an experiment scenario, which illustrate that the additional time needed due to the aSPM infrastructure is a minor effect on the call establishment procedure.

4   Experiments

In order to evaluate the impact of policy enforcement in terms of the cost in time for the SIP negotiation process, a laboratory environment was deployed. The SIP server where the policy was implemented is the SER server [40] one of the most widely used SIP servers. It is an open source software product, currently used by organizations including Columbia University, Swiss Federal Institute of Technology, etc. [16, 17].

The laboratory (Figure 3) that we have installed consists of the following fundamental entities:

1. Two (2) SIP SER servers. They have been customized in order to register users, redirect SIP messages and establish calls. The PCs used for setting up the SER servers were a Pentium 4, 2.8GHz with 1GB RAM running the Fedora 9 operating system.
2. A policy module. It has been installed in the SIP server, at the "logical" entrance of the network environment and includes the domain XML policy.
3. Two (2) soft phone clients that have been part of the VoIP callee's domain. These clients are active, which means that they are ready to interact with incoming calls. The used soft-phone software is called twinkle [18] and it is an open-source product.
4. An external client. This client is programmed to make new calls to the internal clients. The calls are initiated by using SIPp [19] which establishes calls as well.

The experimentation scenario is related to our goal to verify all possible execution paths in a SIP setting with one to two concurrent protocol sessions. Since our policy module accepts all the incoming and outgoing SIP traffic of the VoIP infrastructure, we made two tests: a) the aSPM was enabled and b) the aSPM was disabled.

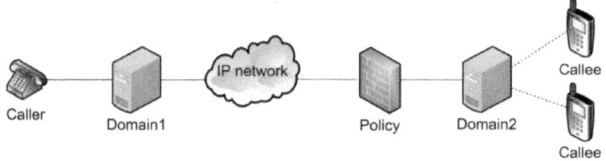

Fig. 3. Laboratory Environment

Table 2. Time needed for exchanging messages

Channel Time (msec)	UAC – D	D –D	UAC –UAC	UAC – aSPM	D- aSPM
Minimum	97	153	97	286	321
Average	102	154	98	387	428
Maximum	106	162	98	432	642

The total number of initiated calls was 10.000 and the needed time for the message exchanges between the participating entities is illustrated in Table 2. The participating entities are the two domains (D), the User Agent Client (UAC) and the policy module (aSPM). The first two columns show the time costs when the aSPM is disabled, and the last two when the aSPM is enabled. The third column shows the time needed for the caller's UAC to send the final CK message, where the policy does not interfere.

The main assumption is that the time needed to send a message between two communication entities does not depend on the role of the involved entities in the communication, i.e. whether they are the sending or the receiving entity. For example the same time is needed to send a message from Domain1 to Domain2 with the time needed to send a message from Domain 2 to domain 1.

The times shown have been used as parameters in the formal verification model in order to assess how the message exchange affects the requirement of timely session establishment. The reported times may be altered depending on the hardware features that are assumed in the described experiment. However, the proposed verification approach is still effective for other parameter sets.

5   Formal Verification

Formal verification took place in five successive steps:

1. First, we developed a model for a single SIP protocol session according to the protocol specification in [13]. While SIP entities may interact with a significant number of messages, we aimed to an abstract representation of the protocol operation. More precisely, we omitted message manipulation functions that can have a negative impact to the model's state space, without being within the scope of the intended aSPM analysis.
2. From the experiment of section 4, we collected data values for the parameters representing time in the modeled SIP message exchanges. These values were attached to executable actions that reflect the expected behavior in a single protocol session.
3. We created a second protocol entity (Callee) that participates in a parallel SIP session with the protocol initiator (Caller).
4. The aSPM policy was then integrated into the SIP model.
5. SPIN's state exploration functions allowed model checking for a possible deadlock, for reachable states that potentially violate SIP functional properties (therefore called invalid states), as well as for a Linear Temporal Logic [9] formula encoding the requirement of timely session establishment.

5.1 Assumptions and Property Specification

We assumed that in all cases SIP messages are delivered to the intended recipient, thus excluding the presence of a man-in-the-middle intruder entity, which is an open research prospect. The initiator of the communication (Caller of the SIP) belongs to Domain1 and both responders (Callees of the SIP) belong to the same domain, namely Domain2.

Since we intended to verify a system execution scenario with two concurrent protocol sessions and in order to avoid the possible state space explosion [23], we focused only on the SIP messages that are related to the behavior of the aSPM policy. Thus, we omitted the message manipulation functions after having checked that they do not affect the SIP execution outcome and they are not affected by the policy reactions. For each protocol participant, we encoded the messages that can be sent and might be received in all protocol steps. These messages are:

1. INVITE messages that are created by the Caller
2. 2xx successful response message created by the Callee
3. 3xx redirection response messages created by the Domain 2 server
4. 4xx request failure messages created by the Domain 2 server
5. 6xx global failure messages created by the Domain 2 server
6. ACK messages created by the Caller

The developed protocol model was verified for the absence of deadlocks, i.e. the resulting executions either terminate with successfully completed initiated sessions or with failed sessions, due to dispatched messages that declare an error. Thus, the produced state space includes error execution paths that are possible in a real SIP communication. Formal analysis can either take into account these paths or not, depending on property specifications that are model checked.

Apart from the absence of deadlock we also studied call establishment timeliness for all error-absent execution paths and for both versions of the model, i.e. the SIP model and the model with the aSP policy. In this way, we aim to verify that the aSP mechanism does not incur unacceptable message overload that can undermine call establishment timeliness.

5.2 SIP-aSPM Model Description

The SIP-aSPM model was encoded in SPIN's model description language called PROMELA [9] and comprises six interacting processes (proctypes): i)the Caller (UAC) who initiates one or two protocol sessions, ii) the Domain1 where the Caller belongs to, iii) two (2) Callees namely UAC_1 and UAC_2 that communicate with the initiator, iv) the Domain2 where the Callee belongs to and (v) a proctype stopwatch Timer that measures the time for SIP call establishment with and without the aSPM policy. The model also defines rendezvous communication channels, in order to allow synchronous message passing between the aforementioned processes.

Based on the experiment results of Table 2 we defined discrete time values for each message delivery action. Values time_i with i={1,2,3,4,5} determine the global timer updates implemented by proctype Timer that take place in every message exchange.

For example, every message exchange between the UAC and UAC_1 or UAC2 results in a time_3 increase (98 msec) of the global timer. By tagging the modeled message exchanges with time values we can derive verification results for all possible execution paths that depend on the decisions of the aSPM policy.

The model allows model checking properties over the combined execution of up to two parallel sessions, which can be non-deterministically initiated at any time by the caller's UAC. In the two-session execution scenario shown in Figure 4, the UAC entity eventually selects both UAC_1 and UAC_2 for establishing distinct SIP media sessions. More precisely, UAC non-deterministically selects the first Callee (UAC_1 or UAC_2) and dispatches an INVITE message (named INIVTE_1 if the recipient is UAC_1 and INVITE_2 if the recipient is UAC_2). The caller's Domain 1 simply forwards the message to Domain 2. Upon arrival of an INVITE message to Domain 2, there are three possible responses, namely: (i) redirection of the Callee entity (message 3xx), (ii) request failure (message 4xx) or (iii) global failure (message 6xx). Redirection involves reform of the received INVITE message, in order to incorporate the new Callee's address. Caller responds only to the two mentioned failure messages (4xx and 6xx) by resending a new INVITE message, but this happens only when he has not already received more than three (3) error messages. In the latter case Caller drops the call and session establishment fails.

If there is no error, Domain 2 forwards the INVITE message to the Callee's address and waits for the callee's approval. Callee produces a 2xx response message (shown as m200_OK in Figure 4) and sends it to the Caller via the Domain 2 server. Domain 2 forwards the message to Domain 1 and consequently the server handles it to the Caller.

When Caller receives the expected 2xx message, he sends an ACK message directly to the Callee, thus establishing a new media session. At any time of the described call establishment procedure, the Caller may non-deterministically initiate a second SIP session with the other Callee. Both sessions may be completed successfully or otherwise any of them can terminate due errors reported from Domain 2, upon receipt of the dispatched INVITE messages.

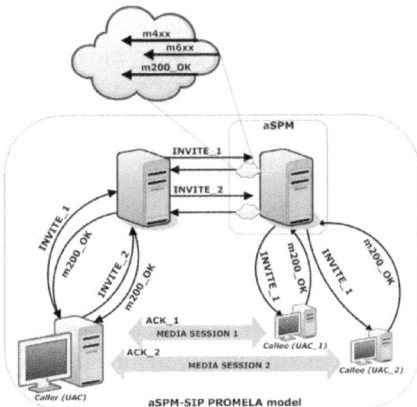

Fig. 4. Message exchanges in the SPIN SIP-aSPM model

5.3   Verification Results

In order to verify the previously specified properties (section 5.1) we have, at first, to define them using the appropriate temporal logic. SPIN model checker [6] is an automated on-the-fly model checker that is used to trace logical errors in distributed systems, i.e. communication protocols. It also supports the verification of user-defined properties as formulations of the Linear Temporal Logic (LTL). Using LTL we are capable of model checking the developed SIP-aSPM model for correct-ness requirements such as, properties relating timeliness. In detail, we a) create appropriate LTL formulas describing the desired SIP properties, and b) define system process invariants (using assertions) that are validated throughout the verification process.

Timely completion of media session establishment was checked by formula Q1, where:

$$Q1: \quad [] (q \rightarrow p)$$

with $\rightarrow$ representing the left associative implication, `[]` for the temporal operator `always` and `p`, `q` user-defined symbols with the following values:

`#define p time<4000, #define q (sessions==0)`

Model variable sessions – with initial value 2 – changes with the number of sessions that are successfully completed. If sessions==0 then both SIP sessions end with success. Value 4000 represents the allowed duration in msec for successful call establishment. Formula Q1 is therefore interpreted as:

"If in a reachable state both sessions have finished with success, this happens in less than 4.000 msec".

For Q1, SPIN generated the corresponding never claim and verified that the property holds in all possible executions. Table 3 reports the obtained model checking results for a series of properties that are expressed as variants of formula Q1. Shown results are accompanied by state space statistics under various state exploration strategies with or without partial order reduction (an optimization for ignoring all superfluous interleavings). We observe that when the antiSPIT mechanism is enabled, the verification analysis produced no error across execution paths, where at least one session is successfully completed in less than 6,5 sec. Similarly, there were no errors across paths where both sessions are successfully completed in less than 10 sec.

When aSPM is disabled, the provided results report upper time boundaries for successfully establishing one or two call sessions.

Apart from the Q1 LTL formula, we also used assertions (defined as active monitor proctypes), in order to derive additional verification results. With assertions we can detect invalid end-states, like when sending more than two error messages of type 4xx or 6xx. We detected an invalid end state, which is reported in Table 3 in the state space with 13172 states, thus realizing that the Domain 2 can send more than two 4xx or 6xx messages. This result validates the error prone design of our model, i.e. a realistic representation of all cases where there is an unexpected termination of the SIP protocol due to multiple error messages 4xx or 6xx. If no error messages are produced by entity Domain 2, the SIP-aSPM model terminates correctly.

Table 3. Results of the SIP-aSPM Formal Verification

Property Description	States	Transitions	Memory (MB)	Property Definition	Verification Result
At least one (1) Session Successful Completion before 6500 msec (aSP Enabled)	3.8e+06	7.181e+06	585.309	Q1	Valid
Parallel Session Successful Completion before 10000 msec (aSPM enabled)	3.8e+06	7.246e+06	616.11	Q1	Valid
Full State Space with no errors (Deadlock absence)	3.8e+06	7.181e+06	585.309	-	Valid
Partial State Space Search before 6000 msec (with invalid end-states)	13172	13172	0.924	Assertion	Invalid
Full State Space Search for one (1) successful session completion before 3000 msec (aSPM Disabled)	3.8e+06	9.238e+06	600.712	Q1	Valid
Parallel Session Successful Completion before 6000 msec (aSPM Disabled)	3.8e+06	7.246e+06	616.114	Q1	Valid
Partial State Space Search with more than two (4xx or 6xx) message dispatches (unexpected errors)	956	2163	0.149	Assertion	Invalid

Finally, we successfully verified the absence of deadlocks by using the corresponding SPIN model checking option.

6 Related Work

In this section, we briefly survey some relevant techniques and approaches, which focus on modeling policy infrastructure and verification of SIP protocol properties.

Zave [20] has presented three formal, state-oriented models for SIP and has discussed five cases where the SIP standards are incomplete. She proposed solutions to all detected problems, but her work concerns different SIP messages from those studied in our work (e.g. the update message that concerns the re-negotiation session establishment).

Liu [21] has modeled and analyzed SIP INVITE transactions over an unreliable medium. Then by examining the state space of the model it was found that the INVITE transaction is not free of livelocks and dead codes, as it is in the case of a reliable medium. The results of this work are not directly connected to our work, since with the SIP messages involved it is not possible to produce SPIT. As a consequence, this approach cannot be used for studying the behavior of our policy implementation.

Finally, Schaeffer-Filho et al. [22] have modeled a specific policy interaction, but for a totally different system. They defined a formal model for the design of Self-Managed Cells (SMCs) with a consistent policy which assists to the collaborations across SMC. The created model allowed them to verify the correctness of the anticipated SMC interactions based on policy decisions before these interactions are implemented or deployed in physical devices (e.g. PDAs, mobile phones, sensors).

7 Conclusions

The Session Initiation Protocol has become a popular communication system in Voice over IP applications, as it is widely used for establishing and maintaining multimedia sessions over the Internet. One of the obvious potential problems of VoIP applications is the growth of the SPIT phenomenon [2]. This work proposes a formally verified SPIT policy mechanism over the SIP protocol. We used the SPIN model checking environment, in order to fully analyze the temporal behavior of the policy and protocol interactions.

The paper discusses the proposed aSPM methodology and the SIP-aSPM model development. We define the basic properties where the verification was focused. The obtained model checking results provide evidence that the aSPM mechanism does not affect dramatically the time needed for call establishment in two concurrent SIP sessions. We note that the parameters used depend on the hardware features assumed in the conducted laboratory measurement.

The proposed analysis can be used for deriving upper bounds in the duration of media session establishment for SIP-aSPM systems. Also, it is open to extensions that will provide additional verification results. We consider studying error scenarios that will be generated with a powerful intruder model entity over the SIP session establishment. In this way, we will be able to validate whether the proposed aSPM mechanism over SIP is vulnerable to intruder attacks that may subvert the SIP protocol's functionality. Further experimentation and improvements in the proposed policy may be done, but in any case the formal verification method seems to be a valuable mean for the design of effective antiSPIT policies.

References

1. Sawda, S., Urien, O.: SIP security attacks and solutions: A state-of-the-art review. In: Proc. of the IEEE International Conference on Information and Communication Technologies: From Theory to Applications (ICTTA 2006), vol. 2, pp. 3187–3191 (April 2006)
2. Rosenberg, J., Jennings, C.: The Session Initiation Protocol (SIP) and Spam, Network Working Group, RFC 5039 (January 2008)
3. Quittek, J., Niccolini, S., Tartarelli, S., Stiemerling, M., Brunner, M., Ewald, T.: Detecting SPIT Calls by Checking Human Communication Patterns. In: Proc. of IEEE International Conference on Communications (ICC 2007), United Kingdom, pp. 1979–1984 (2007)
4. Graham-Rowe, D.: A Sentinel to Screen Phone Calls Technology. MIT Review (2006) (accessed November 8, 2009)

5. Soupionis, Y., Dritsas, S., Gritzalis, D.: An adaptive policy-based approach to SPIT management. In: Jajodia, S., Lopez, J. (eds.) ESORICS 2008. LNCS, vol. 5283, pp. 446–460. Springer, Heidelberg (2008)

6. Holzmann, G.: The model checker SPIN. IEEE Transaction on Software Engineering 5/23, 279–295 (1997)

7. The SPIN model checker website, http://spinroot.com/ (last access: May 23, 2010)

8. Basagiannis, S., Katsaros, P., Pombortsis, A.: Intrusion Attack Tactics for the Model Checking of e-Commerce Security Guarantees. In: Saglietti, F., Oster, N. (eds.) SAFECOMP 2007. LNCS, vol. 4680, pp. 238–251. Springer, Heidelberg (2007)

9. Holzmann, G.: The SPIN Model Checker - Primer and Reference Manual. Addison Wesley, Reading (2003)

10. Walsh, T., Kuhn, D.: Challenges in securing voice over IP. National Institute of Standard and Technology (NIST), USA

11. Sloman, M., Lupu, E.: Security and management policy specification. IEEE Network, Special Issue on Policy-Based Networking 16(2), 10–19 (2002)

12. Strembeck, M.: Embedding policy rules for software-based systems in a requirements context. In: Proc. of the 6th IEEE International Workshop on Policies for Distributed Systems and Networks, POLICY 2005 (June 2005)

13. Rosenberg, J., et al.: Session Initiation Protocol (SIP), RFC 3261 (June 2002)

14. Cisco Systems, Session Initiation Protocol gateway call flows and compliance information SIP messages and methods overview,
http://www.cisco.com/application/pdf/en/us/guest/products/ps4032/c2001/ccmigration_09186a00800c4bb1.pdf

15. Cisco Systems, SIP Messages and Methods Overview,
http://www.cisco.com/univercd/cc/td/doc/product/software/ios122/rel_docs/sip_flo/preface.pdf

16. SER server version 2.0, http://www.iptel.org/ser (retrieved March 20, 2009)

17. Example SER deployments,
http://mit.edu/sip/sip.edu/deployments.shtml

18. Twinkle softphone, http://www.twinklephone.com (retrieved August 25)

19. SIPP traffic generator for the SIP protocol, http://sipp.sourceforge.net/ (retrieved September 30, 2009)

20. Zave, P.: Understanding SIP through model-checking. In: Schulzrinne, H., State, R., Niccolini, S. (eds.) IPTComm 2008. LNCS, vol. 5310, pp. 256–279. Springer, Heidelberg (2008)

21. Liu, L.: Verification of the SIP Transaction Using Coloured Petri Nets. In: Proc. of the 32nd Australasian Computer Science Conference, New Zealand, January 19-23, pp. 63–72 (2009)

22. Schaeffer-Filho, A., Lupu, E., Sloman, M., Eisenbach, S.: Verification of Policy-based Self-Managed Cell Interactions Using Alloy. In: Proc. of the 10th IEEE International Symposium on Policies for Distributed Systems and Networks (Policy 2009), UK (July 2009)

23. Godefroid, P.: Partial-Order Methods for the Verification of Concurrent Systems: An Approach to the State-Explosion Problem, p. 142 (1996)

Trust and Reputation for Information Exchange in Critical Infrastructures

Filipe Caldeira[1,2], Edmundo Monteiro[1], and Paulo Simões[1]

[1] CISUC - DEI, University of Coimbra, Coimbra, 3030-290, Portugal
{fmanuel,edmundo,psimoes}@dei.uc.pt
http://www.dei.uc.pt
[2] Polytechnic Institute of Viseu, Viseu, 3504-510, Portugal
http://www.ipv.pt

Abstract. Today's Critical Infrastructures (CI) are highly interdependent in order to deliver their services with the required level of quality and availability. Information exchange among interdependent CI plays a major role in CI protection and risk prevention for interconnected CI were cascading effects might occur because of their interdependencies. This paper addresses the problem of the quality of information exchanged among interconnected CI and also the quality of the relationship in terms of trust and security. The use of trust and reputation indicators associated with the information exchange is the proposed solution.

The proposed solution is being applied to information exchange among interconnected CI in scope of the European FP7 MICIE project, in order to improve information accuracy and to protect each CI from using inconsistent and non trustable information about critical events.

Keywords: Critical Infrastructures, ICT security, Trust and Reputation Management.

1 Introduction

The human society is becoming more and more dependent on services provided by Critical Infrastructures such as telecommunications, electricity and water supply. As stated by former USA President Bill Clinton, "Critical infrastructures are those physical and cyber-based systems essential to the minimum operations of the economy and government. These systems are so vital, that their incapacity or destruction would have a debilitating impact on the defense or economic securit" [1]. Growing interest on this matter is clear from governments initiatives such as the Critical Infrastructure Protection (CIP) Program, started in 1998 by USA Administration, the European Programme for Critical Infrastructure Protection (EPCIP) in 2006 and the European initiative to establish a Critical Infrastructure Warning Information Network - CIWIN.

There are several models in the literature that provide the means to understand the interdependencies occurring among heterogeneous CI, and highlight the relevance of a system able to use these models to provide concrete instruments to CI owners in order to reduce the risk of service unprovisioning. This is

C. Xenakis and S. Wolthusen (Eds.): CRITIS 2010, LNCS 6712, pp. 140–152, 2011.

the main goal of MICIE (Tool for system̲i̲c risk analysis and secure mediation of data exchanged across linked C̲I̲ information infrastructure̲s̲) an FP7-ICT project aiming at the design and implementation of a real-time risk level dissemination and alerting system [2].

As ongoing research in this area is mainly focused on understanding interdependencies among CI, on the development of secure communication systems and on the use of received information for risk prediction models, we have identified the lack of mechanisms that allow reasoning on the trust level of received information and on the partnership behaviour. In this paper we present a framework that incorporates trust and reputation mechanisms on information exchange among Critical Infrastructures, describing the developed framework, presenting validation results and a discussion on foreseen results.

The rest of this paper is organised as follows. In Section 2 we discuss related work. The key components of the MICIE Alerting System (including the Secure Mediation Gateway) are presented in Section 3 as being the application scenario. Section 4 presents our approach to trust and information management. Section 5 presents validation work and Section 6 concludes the paper.

2   Related Work

In current research in ICT areas a growing interest in trust and reputation [3] can be found. In particular, current research is focusing on the development or refinement of trust models, usually developed for specific application areas like e-commerce web sites or more generally for the use in distributed environments where electronic transactions occur between persons and computer systems.

Among existing definitions for trust, we adopted a definition from [4] - " Trust: a subjective expectation an agent has about another's future behaviour based on the history of their encounters." Also we can refer that trust is the opinion of one entity (services, computer, person, etc.) about another single entity, while reputation is the community opinion about one entity.

Most of the research work in this area is focused on P2P systems [5,6,7], wireless sensor networks [8,9,10], on-line personal interactions, software agents, and generic models and formalisms for trust and reputation systems [11,12,13,14].

While most work integrates observed trust with reputation information received from partners, we are, for the moment, focusing our work on building trust information based on observed services and on deriving trust from evidences directly related with the entity whose trustworthiness is being evaluated. In this context, most of the work reviewed evaluates trust using the amount of positive or negative transaction experiences [11,13,15]. Our aim is to improve those models allowing that observed events can have a value in a defined range (e.g. [0..100]) for each transaction, introducing more detail about each transaction.

Some existing models give only a single value for trust. This value can be binary (trustee or not trustee) or can also be represented by more than two discrete values using either discrete or continuous numbers or labels. We consider that a trust model should, at least, give the user a value of trust in a defined discrete range allowing them to be used as more precise indicators. Another important aspect related to trust models, with particular importance when we need to make decisions, is that they should provide measures to express uncertainty, reliability or confidence associated with a trust value. Some authors propose models that are able to express uncertainty [16,17,18].

Trust may be quantified and computed in many ways. In particular, several methods are proposed to derive trust from the collected evidence [14]. Authors propose simple probability [19], Fuzzy Approaches [20] or Bayesian networks [9]. There are substantial differences among the proposed methods, mainly related to the information used to evaluate trust, the use of reputation information, the use of parameters and the use of inactivity periods [7], etc.

There is also a growing interest on CI Protection, with recent projects such as CRUTIAL [21] and IRRIIS [22] providing significant contributions to the field. However, to the best of our knowledge, none of these projects fully addresses the problem of real-time information exchange for on-line CI risk prediction (or the security issues associated with the related exchange of information).

In our work we will address the usage of trust and reputation indicators in the process of information exchange between interdependent CI. More specifically, we will follow the approach of [19,7] (the use of ageing factors and time slots) on building trust from past experience and use a statistical approach to evaluate trust values. Since trust is evaluated as a simple probability, we can infer that trust value expresses the probability that an entity will behave as expected according to the trust definition we use.

3   Application Scenario

The MICIE project is in line with European developments in the Critical Infrastructure Protection (CIP) field, contributing in three main areas: the identification and modelling of interdependencies among CI; the development of risk models and risk prediction tools; and the development of a framework enabling secure and trustfully information sharing among CI [23]. The main goal of MICIE is to provide, in real time, each CI operator with a CI risk level, measuring the probability that, in the future, one CI can loose the capacity to provide or receive some services. Figure 1 describes the MICIE overall architecture[24].

The status of the CI components is collected, in real-time, in order to have all relevant information for the alerting system. The information is used by the Prediction Tool to assess the risk level of monitored services providing, in real-time, the status of the CI. Internal and external information is associated with the risk models used by the Prediction Tool, allowing the incorporation of interdependencies. Status information can be exchanged across partner CI using a Secure Mediation Gateway (SMGW), allowing CI to work in a fully cooperative distributed environment for risk prediction [24].

Regarding the sensitive nature of exchanged information, MICIE project has dedicated special attention to the security requirements such as confidentiality, integrity, availability, non repudiation and auditability/traceability. The usage of trust and reputation indicators by the Prediction Tool and the SMGW

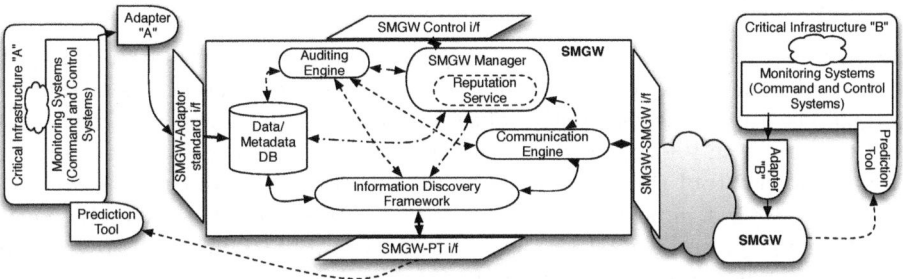

Fig. 1. MICIE overall system and SMGW architecture

Manager, contributes to improve information accuracy and to protect each CI from receiving and use inconsistent information.

The Trust and Reputation Service (TRS) evaluates information exchanged between CI in order to infer a trust level for each transaction. This service incorporates a level of trust on the data received from each partner, allowing that trust levels are incorporated in risk assessments as a mean to improve its accuracy and its resilience to inconsistent information. It will be possible, for instance, to give more weight to highly trusted data or to ignore data provided by low-trust partners.

The information needed to evaluate trust and reputation is gathered and evaluated from multiples sources, namely:

Analysis of past data provided by partner / service: The TRS will compare the risk estimates provided over time, for each service, against the current service levels, in order to infer the trustiness of future estimates.

Analysis of partner behaviour: Based on the knowledge gathered by the SMGW the TRS can analyse the partner behaviour in terms of ICT security. For instance, if the partner CI behaves abnormally (for example trying to access non-authorised data or using non-authorised credentials) the TRS should downgrade the level of trustiness associated with that partner CI as this could indicate that the partner is faulty or does not have good intentions.

Human factor: Operator perception about each partner/service. The operator can have information about each partner/service that can be incorporated in the Reputation Service.

Shared reputation services: The TRS can use the intelligence from multiple CI collectively to define the reputation of a specific partner based in each own partner trust in that partner. This aspect is under preliminary research and needs special attention on a way to maintain source confidentiality.

Trust evaluation can be achieved at two levels: Service Level, where each service subscribed to remote CI is evaluated, reflecting our trust in a particular service; At Global CI Level, where an indicator is added to each interconnected CI. This indicator represents the reputation of that particular CI. Presented Trust indicators can be used to produce interdependency security indicators.

4   Trust and Reputation Service

The Trust and Reputation Service (TRS) framework presented in Figure 2, gathers needed information using two agents. The Risk Alerts Trust Agent that detects and calculate the risk alert event accuracy and the Behaviour Trust Agent used to receive and normalise behaviour events. Each agent sends events to the TRS Discovery Tool that computes in real-time the trust and reputation indicators. Computed indicators are provided to external entities, namely the CI SMGW manager and the CI Prediction Tool. A graphical interface provides the CI operator with an overall view about trust and reputation indicators.

4.1   TRS Agents

Risk Alerts Events -   In interconnected CI scenarios, one CI can subscribe alert information regarding dependent services and use it to compute its own risk level. To be able to evaluate trust aspects related to receive risk alerts, the first goal is to define an accuracy value for each received risk alert. For this purpose, the concept of Risk Alert Event is introduced as one of the following situations: (1) A service decreases its Quality of Service (QoS) (this event ends when the QoS exceeds the threshold or, if an alert is received, the event ends when the alert is removed); (2) After the reception of a risk alert message.

The Risk Alerts Trust Agent is monitoring, in real-time, received risk alerts levels (Rl_t) and the current service levels (Sl_t) in order to detect events. Both Rl_t and Sl_t belong to the $[0..100]$ range.

For each event $A(Event_n)$, the accuracy is defined as the average of all comparisons made during the event (value T), between observed service level and announced risk level (1). Function $f(Sl_t, Rl_t)$ is a discrete function so we need to use a sample rate for regarding the time factor. This sample rate can be different for each service and will depend on the information available on the system. One small sample rate yields more realist observations.

$$A(Event_n) = \frac{\sum_{t=1}^{T} (f(Sl_t, Rl_t))}{T} \quad , \tag{1}$$

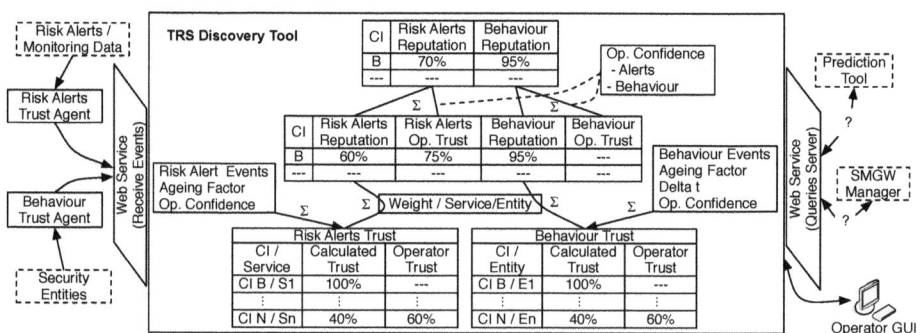

Fig. 2. Trust and Reputation Service (TRS)

where $f(Sl_t, Rl_t) = |Sl_t - Rl_t|^\kappa$, $\kappa \in R^+$. The value k allows to penalise the larger differences or the small differences and should be assigned considering the degree of importance of each service. In this approach, the duration of an event is not considered as we are, for now, only focusing on the accuracy of the alert.

Behaviour Events - The SMGW provides the collection and analysis of data related to security aspects used to infer a trust indicator for each peer behaviour.

As data is gathered from heterogeneous sources and can be received in different formats, the information is normalised based on a security model that identifies relevant behaviour patterns. This system consists, basically, of tables mapping possible received values and trust indicators. For instance, it is possible to define that four authentication failures in less that a minute produce a confidence level of twenty on our security model as exemplified in Table 1. This model acts as an adaptor between heterogeneous sources and the trust estimator algorithm. By employing these adaptors it is possible to infer trust indicators, as all security events are quantified and can be used in a common calculation.

Table 1. Adaptor Table Example

Failed Authentication Attempts/Minute		
Trust Indicator Level	Description	Received Values
100	No Failures	0
80	One/Three Failures	1-3
20	Four/Ten Failures	> 3 and < 10
0	More that 10 Failures	>= 10

The events used to evaluate trust on CI behaviour are all the interactions among peer CI in terms of ICT security (internal or external). For instance, the events can be Intrusion Detection Systems (IDS) alerts, failed connection attempts, attempts to read/write information without permission.

The Behaviour Trust Agent receives security alerts from the CI SMGW and, based on the defined security model, normalise the received information and send the event to the TRS Discovery Tool.

4.2   TRS Discovery Tool

The TRS Discovery Tool is responsible for the calculation, in real-time, of the trust and reputation indicators. For each type of indicator (risk alerts and behaviour trust), the TRS Discovery Tool maintains current and past indicators in a database in order to provide them to the CI operator and to the SMGW Manager and Prediction Tool. In the next sections, the methodology used for trust evaluation is presented.

Trust and reputation indicators on received risk alerts - The trust that CI A has in alerts received for service X provided by CI B is represented by $T_{(A,B,X)}$ and can be calculated by the average of the accuracy of each past event between those two CI for that particular service.

As stated in previous works [7,19], this solution has already identified weaknesses, for instance, one peer can behave correctly for a series of events and then capitalise gained trust to send false alarms. This problems occurs mainly due to the fact that the trust value will change very slowly as it depends equally on all the past transactions. This weakness can be minimised introducing the concept of ageing, using a discount factor D, to give more weight onto recent events. The ageing factor should always depend on the context. In our model the ageing factor needs to be defined on a per peer/service basis. In this context, $T'_{(A,B,X)}$ can be computed for the Nth event as:

$$T'_{(A,B,X)} = \frac{(D * (N-1) * T_{(A,B,X)}) + A(Event_N)}{D * (N-1) + 1} \quad . \tag{2}$$

D will be a value in the $[0..1]$ interval and a small value of D will raise the importance of the last events while a value of D near 1 will provide less ageing to oldest events. A large ageing factor will bring progressively the previous identified problems that lead us to introduce ageing. There are several approaches for choosing the ageing parameter D, for instance, a fixed value, make it decay exponentially using a $D = f(t) = x^t$ $(0 < x < 1, t = 1..N)$ or, as presented in [19], observe the partner behaviour instability and focus on more recent alerts when observed behaviour reveals strong time correlation.

As discussed in section 3, a Human Factor is also considered in trust evaluation. This factor can be used in two ways: To initialise the trust indicator when there are no past observations available; by the operator reflecting his opinion and contribution to the trust calculations. In the second case the contribution weight needs to be specified. Considering the Human Factor, the final trust value for a specific CI/service is defined in (3).

The α factor is assigned by the CI Operator depending on the confidence he or she has in the opinion $(TO_{(A,B,X)})$. $T(final)_{(A,B,X)}$ represent the TRS confidence in alerts for each service individually taking into account also the CI operator perspective. In order to understand how services evolve over time, and to define a relation among them, a time value is associated with each $T(final)$.

$$T(final)_{(A,B,X)} = (1 - \alpha)(T_{(A,B,X)}) + \alpha(TO_{(A,B,X)}) \,, (0 < \alpha < 1) \ . \tag{3}$$

Using a weight factor for each service, the reputation of each CI can be evaluated using (4), where $GT'_{(A,B,t)}$ represents the reputation that CI A as about CI B on time t. $GT_{(A,B)}$ represents the last evaluated indicator. W_i is the weight associated to service i provided by CI B. N is the number of evaluations. S represents the services that A receives from B and D is the ageing factor. Indicator in (4) should be evaluated every time a service indicator changes. $T(final)_{(A,B,i)}$ represents the last indicator calculated for service i.

$$GT'_{(A,B,t)} = \frac{(D * (N-1) * GT_{(A,B)}) + \frac{\sum_{i=1}^{S}(T(final)_{(A,B,i)} * W_i)}{\sum_{i=1}^{S} W_i})}{D * (N-1) + 1} \quad . \tag{4}$$

The CI operator also contributes to the reputation indicator with a subjective value as described in (5) where θ is assigned by the CI operator and demonstrates the confidence concerning the subjective reputation value $TO_{A,B}$.

$$GT(final)_{(A,B,t)} = \theta(TO_{A,B}) + (1-\theta)(GT_{(A,B)}) \ , (0 < \theta < 1) \ . \qquad (5)$$

Trust and reputation indicators on peers behaviour - From the security monitoring systems, we expect to receive events when a misbehaviour is detected. This fact leads to a situation where almost only negative events are received. Considering only the events on a simple statistical approach, it is expected to have always a low value for the indicator, not representing the complete peer behaviour. To avoid this problem the concept of Inactivity was introduced.

The fact that events are not received during a given time period - Inactivity - indicates that, during this period, the peer CI behaviour is correct. In order to use inactivity periods, time is divided into a set of time slots [7], each slot with Δt duration. Inactivity in one slot means that the peer behaviour has the maximum value. If information is received during one slot, the slot value becomes the average of all events received during that slot. Trust values for each time slot are calculated using (6).

$$Event_{(Slot\ s)} = \begin{cases} 100, \ \text{if} \ NEvents_{(Slot\ s)} = 0 \\ \\ \frac{\sum_{i=1}^{N} Event_i}{N}, \ \text{if} \ N = NEvents_{(Slot\ s)} > 0 \end{cases} \qquad (6)$$

The Δt value needs to be defined for each security entity (behaviour monitoring systems, e.g. firewall, IDS, etc.) and can represent a period of only a few seconds to hours. A larger Δt implies slow changes on the trust indicator, being more evident when few events are received over time.

For the s time slot, the trust on entity E for CI B $(T'_{(E,B,s)})$ is calculated using (7) where D is the ageing factor, $T_{(E,B)}$ is the indicator evaluated for the slot $(s-1)$ and $Event_{(Slot\ s)}$ is the event value of the slot s. The indicator and the time when evaluation occur are stored in the TRS database.

$$T'_{(E,B,s)} = \frac{(D*(s-1)*T_{(E,B)}) + Event_{(Slot\ s)})}{D*(s-1)+1} \ . \qquad (7)$$

Using (8) operator trust can be included. The θ factor is assigned by the CI operator representing the confidence on the subjective trust $(TO_{(E,B)})$ that he or she has on CI B behaviour concerning security entity E.

$$T(Final)_{(E,B)} = \theta(TO_{(E,B)}) + (1-\theta)(T_{(E,B)}) \ , (0 < \theta < 1) \ . \qquad (8)$$

As the event values are already normalised (has described in section 4.1), it is possible to evaluate an indicator encompassing all types of events. Using a weight factor for each entity, the behaviour reputation is known using (9), where $TBehaviour'_{(B,t)}$ represents the reputation of CI B behaviour on time t and W_i is the weight associated to security entity i. $TBehaviour'_{(B)}$ represents the last evaluated reputation indicator. Each weight must be defined along with the definition of the security model, representing the relevance of each entity in maintaining security. An ageing factor D is also included. In a similar way used in (8) it is possible to consider the operator information, including his confidence and reputation opinion related to the CI behaviour.

$$TBehaviour'_{(B,t)} = \frac{(D * (t-1) * TBehaviour_{(B)}) + \frac{\sum_{i=1}^{E}(T(Final)(i)*W_i)}{\sum_{i=1}^{E} W_i})}{D * (t-1) + 1} .$$

(9)

5   Validation

Trust in Received Risk Alerts -   The events are generated using a normal distribution and the following parameters are used: penalisation factor $k = 2$; ageing factor $D = 0.3$; a threshold of 10%. The scenarios presented in Table 2 represent the following situations: (S1) The system behaves as expected with only small errors with the event accuracy always above 60% and mainly above 90%; (S2) System is not accurate but can still be trustworthy, as evaluated event accuracy is always above 40%; (S3) Received alerts are not as expected with above 40% of inaccurate indications; (S4) System in inaccurate.

Table 2. Simulation Scenario (% of events for each range of event accuracy values)

Scenarios	Event % of occurrence									
	[0-10]	[10-20]	[20-30]	[30-40]	[40-50]	[50-60]	[60-70]	[70-80]	[80-90]	[90-100]
S1	0	0	0	0	0	0	5	5	10	80
S2	0	0	0	0	10	10	10	10	20	40
S3	40	20	10	10	10	10	0	0	0	0
S4	80	10	5	5	0	0	0	0	0	0

Figure 3 presents the simulation results obtained from 1000 events of each defined scenario. It is clear that the trust indicator for each service will tend to the average of the generated events. It is also possible to see, that in worst scenarios (S3 and S4) the trust indicator drops below the average as those events are more penalised due to the chosen value of $k = 2$.

Figure 4 represents an attack or faulty component situation. Two different scenarios are presented in order to demonstrate that the framework behaves as expected, independently of the number of events. In Figures 4(A) and 4(B), the first, 2000 events (20 in Figure 4(B)) belong to S1. Next, received alerts become inaccurate (S4) during 100 (10 in Figure 4(B)) events returning to its normal behaviour after that (S1). It is visible that the trust indicator decreases rapidly and next starts to grow gradually. Figure 4(B) describes the use of the Human Factor. In this case the operator assigned a value of trust as being 90% and defined a contribution of 0.8 to final value. With this Human Factor, the operator can rapidly change the trust in a service.

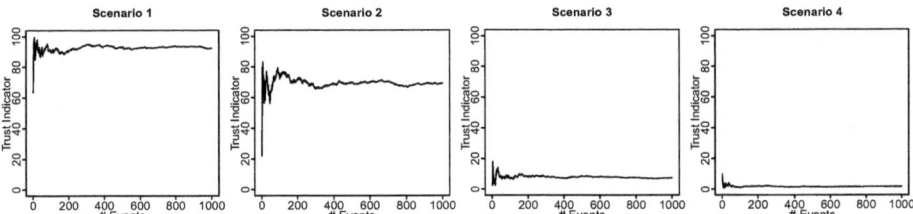

Fig. 3. Simulation for each defined scenario

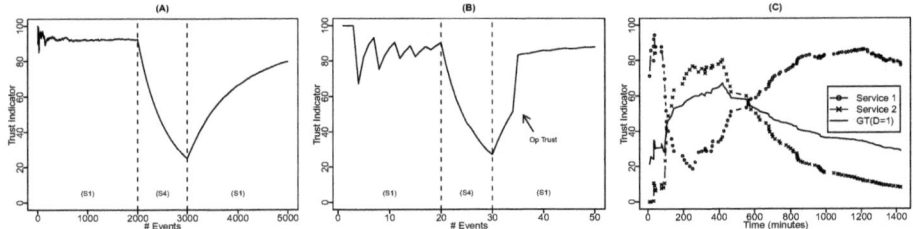

Fig. 4. Simulation - Trust on Received Alerts

In Figure 4(C) a simulation was performed using information observed from two services. Each service received an average of 5 events/hour from a mixture of scenarios one to four. The operator assigned a weight of 0.7 to service 2 and 0.3 to service 1. A value of $D = 1$ was used to calculate the Reputation indicator. In this simulation, when the service more important is becoming unreliable, then the CI reputation is decaying even when the other service is trusty.

Trust on Peers Behaviour - In order to validate behaviour trust indicators, the arrival times of the events are generated using an exponential distribution, with an average of x per hour. Event values are generated from the scenarios defined in Table 2.

Figure 5 shows the results of four different simulations with common parameters $\Delta t = 10$, ageing $D = 0.05$ and simulation period=24 hours. Chosen ageing factor allows trust indicator to incorporate rapidly new situations.

In Figure 5(A), events from scenario S3 arrive at a rate of 5/hour. As the arrival rate is small, the trust indicator starts with no defined tendency but will tend gradually to around 50%. This simulation also demonstrates that even with some incorrect behaviour, the indicator raises in the periods without events.

In the simulation presented in Figure 5(B), the first half of the events belongs to S2 and the last half belong to scenario S3. The event rate is 5/hour. In this simulation it is possible to observe that due to the ageing value each half of the simulation seems independent from the other demonstrating that the trust value rapidly incorporates changes in the peer behaviour.

The 3rd simulation (Figure 5(C)) has a rate of 1 event/hour in all the scenarios, namely, S1, S3 and S4. In this simulation, with few events, the trust indicator does not drop below 60% due to influence of the slots where the

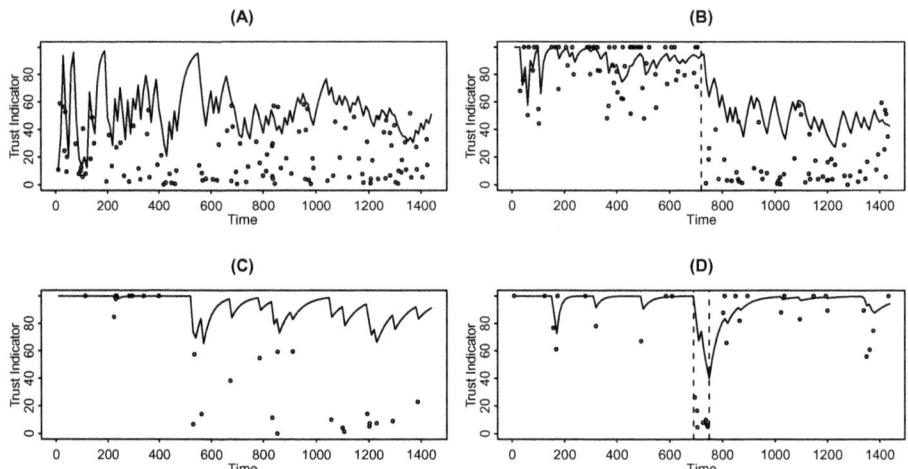

Fig. 5. Security service behaviour simulation

system is behaving well. This situation can also demonstrate how important the values defined for Δt are. In this case, a larger value of Δt would lead to a lower trust indicator. It is also important for the CI operator to know how to interpret the received indicators, in order to properly configure the system.

A situation of a possible attack or misbehaviour in a small period of time is demonstrated in Figure 5(D). In this case, during the first 11,5 hours, events from scenario 1 arrive with a rate of 1/hour. During a period of one hour, the scenario changes to S1 (the worst scenario) with an event rate of 5/hour. In that moment, our trust indicator rapidly decays below 50% clearly indicating that something is wrong. With this indicator, the SMGW manager can act, for instance blocking the access from that CI or that Service. The last simulated hours represent the S2 at a rate of 1/hour. On S2 and with a lower event rate, the trust indicator clearly indicates the resolution of the past situation.

6   Conclusions

The MICIE system aims to provide, in real-time, risk levels measuring the probability that a CI will loose the capacity to provide services. This information is based on CI own data and on data received from peer CI. The proposed framework intends to enhance contributions expected from the MICIE project helping to answer questions like "how much can we trust in received risk alerts or in the peers CI behaviour?".

Trust and Reputation indicators can be incorporated in CI risk assessment as a means to improve its accuracy and its resilience to inconsistent information provided by peer CI. The proposed indicators are also used by the MICIE SMGW Manager, allowing a more dynamical and adaptable management, reacting autonomously when trust indicators change. For instance, if one peer trust decreases below a defined threshold, a new policy can be triggered and the SMGW stops accepting connections from that peer.

The Trust and Reputation Service prototype was developed allowing an easy integration with the MICIE SMGW. The TRS collects information via its Agents and computes in real-time the trust and reputation indicators, providing them to external entities. A graphical interface has been built providing the CI operator with a overall view about trust in all services/CI.

Results from the validation process are promising, demonstrating the ability to improve CI interoperation security. Authors expect to evaluate this proposal with MICIE project starting with a simple reference scenario that encompasses a small portion of an electricity distribution network and an interdependent telecommunications network [23]. Planned validation work for the MICIE project will also include more complex scenarios, provided by the Israel Electric Corporation and including multiple CI.

Acknowledgments. Work partially financed by FP7 ICT-SEC MICIE project [2] grant agreement no. 225353, and by the Portuguese Foundation for Science and Technology (SFRH/BD/35772/2007).

References

1. Clinton, W.J.: Presidential decision directive 63 (May 1998)
2. Micie: Micie - tool for systemic risk analysis and secure mediation of data exchanged across linked ci information infrastructures. FP7-ICT-SEC-2007.1.7 – 225353 – Annex I – "Descrition of Work" (2008)
3. Artz, D., Gil, Y.: A survey of trust in computer science and the semantic web. Web Semantics: Science (January 2007)
4. Mui, L., Mohtashemi, M.: A computational model of trust and reputation. In: 35th Hawaii International Conference on System Science, HICSS (2002)
5. Chen, J., Lu, H., Bruda, S.: Analysis of feedbacks and ratings on trust merit for peer-to-peer systems. In: International Conference on E-Business and Information System Security, EBISS 2009, pp. 1–5 (2009)
6. Chen, S., Zhang, Y., Yang, G.: Trust and reputation algorithms for unstructured p2p networks. In: International Symposium on Computer Network and Multimedia Technology, CNMT 2009, pp. 1–4 (2009)
7. Spitz, S., Tuchelmann, Y.: A trust model considering the aspects of time. In: Computer and Electrical Engineering, ICCEE 2009, vol. 1, pp. 550–554 (2009)
8. Ganeriwal, S., Balzano, L., Srivastava, M.: Reputation-based framework for high integrity sensor networks. Transactions on Sensor Networks, TOSN (2008)
9. Momani, M., Challa, S., Alhmouz, R.: Bnwsn: Bayesian network trust model for wireless sensor networks. In: Mosharaka International Conference on Communications, Computers and Applications, MIC-CCA 2008, pp. 110–115 (2008)
10. Zahariadis, T., Ladis, E., Leligou, H., Trakadas, P., Tselikis, C., Papadopoulos, K.: Trust models for sensor networks. In: 50th International Symposium on ELMAR 2008, vol. 2, pp. 511–514 (September 2008)
11. Jøsang, A., Ismail, R., Boyd, C.: A survey of trust and reputation systems for online service provision. Decision Support Systems 43(2), 618–644 (2007)

12. Malik, Z., Bouguettaya, A.: Reputation bootstrapping for trust establishment among web services. IEEE Internet Computing 13(1), 40–47 (2009)
13. Ray, I., Ray, I., Chakraborty, S.: An interoperable context sensitive model of trust. Journal of Intelligent Information Systems (January 2009)
14. Sabater, J., Sierra, C.: Review on computational trust and reputation models. Artificial Intelligence Review (January 2005)
15. Hussain, F., Chang, E., Hussain, O.: State of the art review of the existing bayesian-network based approaches to trust and reputation computation. In: Internet Monitoring and Protection, ICIMP 2007, p. 26 (2007)
16. Huynh, T., Jennings, N., Shadbolt, N.: An integrated trust and reputation model for open multi-agent systems. Journal of Autonomous Agents and Multi-Agent Systems 13(2), 119–154 (2006)
17. Jøsang, A., Ismail, R.: The beta reputation system. In: Proceedings of the 15th Bled Electronic Commerce Conference (January 2002)
18. Teacy, W., Patel, J., Jennings, N., Luck, M.: Travos: Trust and reputation in the context of inaccurate information sources. Autonomous Agents and Multi-Agent Systems 12(2), 183–198 (2006)
19. Aime, M., Lioy, A.: Incremental trust: building trust from past experience. In: World of Wireless, Mobile and Multimedia Networks (WoWMoM), pp. 603–608 (2005)
20. Ludwig, S., Pulimi, V., Hnativ, A.: Fuzzy approach for the evaluation of trust and reputation of services. In: IEEE International Conference on Fuzzy Systems, FUZZ-IEEE 2009, pp. 115–120 (August 2009)
21. Crutial: Crutial project web site (2008), http://crutial.cesiricerca.it
22. IRRIS: Irriis project web site (2008), http://www.irriis.org/
23. Capodieci, P., et al.: Improving resilience of interdependent critical infrastructures via an on-line alerting system. In: COMPENG 2010 (2010)
24. Caldeira, F., et al.: Secure mediation gateway architecture enabling the communication among critical infrastructures. In: Future Network and MobileSummit 2010 Conference (2010)

A Modelling Approach for Interdependency in Digital Systems-of-Systems Security - Extended Abstract

Adedayo Adetoye, Sadie Creese, Michael Goldsmith, and Paul Hopkins

International Digital Laboratory, University of Warwick, Coventry, CV4 7AL, UK

There is little doubt that the proper functioning of our modern society depends upon cyberspace, and that the continued growth in appetite for new technology and the potential benefits associated with it shows little sign of abating. Unfortunately the reality of modern information and communications systems involves a complex array of hardware, middleware, software, communications protocols and services, operated by a diverse set of stakeholders (users and providers each with a heterogeneous set of changing motives (including personal, enterprise, or societal gains). Everyday services that we take for granted often rely on complex interdependent systems, with the result that a seemingly unrelated failure in one of the subsystems, invisible to the service consumer, may lead to an all too visible collapse of the service that they expect. In the context of information and network risk management this complexity means that it is currently very difficult to predict how an organisation might be impacted by vulnerabilities being exploited or failures accidentally manifesting elsewhere in a system. Additionally, organisations responsible for subsystems are likely to evolve different risk-management cultures and practice, making their adoption and use of network and information risk controls (and consequences for other interdependent subsystems) difficult to predict.

We propose conceptual models and analysis techniques which seek to study the impact of subsystem information and network risk control mechanisms at the micro – system – level (within a single organisation) and the macro – system-of-systems – level (across organisation interfaces), and to understand the sensitivities to control decisions witnessed at both levels. As well as enabling critical national infrastructure (CNI) organisations to understand their sensitivity to risk controls deployed elsewhere in the CNI, our methodology is aimed at facilitating collaborative information and network risk management across the CNI (where trade-offs may need to be made in order to maintain some services in preference to others, in order to enable a maximally beneficial outcome for the CNI as a whole). This CNI macro-level risk management is something which is simply not possible at the moment. There are many reasons for this, but two predominate: firstly, it reflects the potentially conflicting priorities of subsystem operators whose risk managers' primary responsibility is to their own organisation and who are unlikely to embrace an approach which could result in their organisation becoming a loser in a global optimisation; and secondly, the lack of methods to understand and implement system-wide strategies makes it hard to demonstrate the value of joined-up risk management across organisations, whereas if it could be demonstrated to an organisation that being optimised against for a short period of time will enable robustness and confidence in the macro-system (sector, society, etc) as a whole, which if allowed to fail would ultimately harm their organisation, then they might be more inclined to consider such an apparently altruistic behaviour for selfish reasons! However, it is not clear that independent actors will always work towards that end.

C. Xenakis and S. Wolthusen (Eds.): CRITIS 2010, LNCS 6712, pp. 153–156, 2011.

This paper essentially lays out our direction of travel within the *SATURN* project[1]. Specifically, we are concerned with understanding how risk-management practice can affect the exposure of the information and computing infrastructure to threats propagating across a CNI. Our analysis methods should be generically applicable to systems-of-systems, and we are developing a risk ontology which should apply to any organisations within the sectors studied, and be extendable to others. Our approach is firstly to understand how organisations within heterogeneous CNI sectors deploy controls to mitigate risks; then, secondly, to explore the impact of these risk-control decisions across a CNI system-of-systems. We will need to address a variety of research questions including:

1. **Relating controls and vulnerability:** How do information risk controls relate to vulnerabilities within the CNI and what is the nature of the mitigation?
2. **Heterogeneity of practice:** How does deployment of information and computer risk controls differ across sectors and organisations?
3. **Interdependency arising from control decisions:** In what ways can a control decision taken in one organisation impact the threat exposure of other CNI organisations? Could there be subtle dependencies which are not currently known?
4. **Predictability of control decisions:** Is it possible to predict how likely an organisation is to activate a particular control or control configuration? If so, can we devise probabilistic analysis methods in order to explore the spectrum of likely outcomes for other organisations in the CNI and for the CNI as a whole?
5. **Situational awareness:** How might we enable enhanced situational awareness and decision making in the face of threats propagating across a CNI?
6. **joined-up CNI risk management:** How might this enhanced understanding of the impact of risk practice across a CNI be used to enable joined up risk management, and what are the limiting factors?
7. **Analysis methods:** Which analysis techniques are best suited for our needs and how might they drive situational-awareness enhancements?

Modelling and Analysis Methodology. Our focus is on the resilience and robustness of information infrastructures, and in particular the interdependencies which might exist within and between organisations. To enable us to reason about such interdependencies we require a model of our universe, appropriately scoped (abstracted) to make analysis tractable, but rich enough to identify potential sensitivities. Our approach to generating such a model is to create an initial framework upon which to base our analysis techniques, to validate the results of the analysis techniques via practical experimentation on a cyber-range (a facility which possesses enough resources to model a scenario including a full stack of applications accurately), and then to evolve our model as necessary. Here we present our initial conceptual model.

We abstract the universe into four layers: *physical* (which would contain power, water, physical infrastructures, etc); *technology* (which would contain computers, applications, base stations, routers, any network architecture, etc); *information* (which contains data, meta-data, content, etc); and *enterprise* (which contains employees, enterprise

---

[1] A collaboration between UK industry and academia sponsored by the Technology Strategy Board and the Engineering and Physical Sciences Research Council, whose support is gratefully acknowledged; http://www.saturn-project.info

policies and processes etc). We have chosen these layers because they differ markedly in terms of the nature of the assets requiring protection, the vulnerabilities within them, and the risk controls deployed at each. We view organisations as stacks (vertical slices) through these layers, which will each have their own configuration of components and actors within each layer. It is important to note that we expect that in general all organisations will contain elements of all four layers within them, and that there are dependencies between the layers as represented by the stack. In this way layers rely on certain behaviours from layers above and below them, except for the top and bottom layers, where we model externalities.

Our analysis techniques will initially explore how we might detect sensitivities in one layer to changes in behaviour within other layers in a single organisation, and also in that layer between organisations. Our working hypothesis is that there are likely to be some subtle interdependencies as well as the obvious couplings (such as that we need power to switch the computers on), and that such subtleties may exist both between and within organisations, particularly between layers. We expect that vulnerability exploits might be witnessed at any particular layer, but that there will be consequences for the layers above and below (where the behaviours and properties they are relying on change in some way due to the attack). In this way attacks will propagate to organisations across a single layer (so technology to technology for example) and within organisational stacks (so a technology level exploit leads to a compromise of data integrity which leads to a poor decision being made at the human layer). We treat natural disasters in much the same way as an attack. The propagation of the effect of an accidental fault will move both across a layer (so a flood may effect many organisational stacks) and also within an organisational stack.

Risk-Culture Context. Any analysis we make will need to be within the context of a set of risk controls deployed within the organisations being examined, since the risk controls will directly impact upon the presence of vulnerabilities and the nature of response in the face of a perceived attack or disaster scenario. Risk controls take many forms, and unfortunately many controls can seek to address many vulnerabilities. This will add some complexity to our analysis, and directly motivates the need to devise possibilistic techniques in order to explore the sensitivities to differing assumptions regarding behaviour and adoption of controls (as opposed to attempting to fix controls and their precise impact). In this way we can explore whether, for example, there are particular controls which, if adopted, would have a much greater impact upon some single organisation or system of organisations than another control.

The selection of a business control to reduce the level of risk for any organisation is dependent upon the business, its structure, its objectives, its processes, the technology it uses, and the business and regulatory environment in which it operates. While we will predominately concern ourselves in this project with IT-based controls, we must recognise that it is those risks that a business faces at an enterprise level that drive the choice and operation of specific risk controls.

Within the area of IT security, management systems and standards have already emerged to provide a relatively uniform set of security controls that can be applied within an organisation. In particular, ISO 27001/27002 [1] and NIST SP 800-53 [2], group controls around a particular control objective, such as *access control* or *auditability*. In each case, the standards identify the principles and map (in the case of NIST SP 800-53) objectives to recommended baseline control measures. The intention is always that the business has a set of guidelines on which it can construct the specific controls that it needs to implement either for the business unit or for an individual system, as determined by the risk assessment. While such controls are related to IT security, they can be oriented towards both people and processes as well as towards technology and may be applicable at any point in the lifecycle, as preventative, detective, corrective or recovery measures. We observe and question several aspects of the application of these controls that require examination both within the enterprise and between enterprises:

– **Freedom of Choice:** Controls may be implemented in many different ways, indeed the appropriate choice of one control in preference to another and its effectiveness initially and throughout its life form an active area of research. When assessing the overall effectiveness of controls in a system-of-systems, how do we ensure that we have comparable measures of effectiveness?
– **It depends upon your point of view:** Various risk-assessment methodologies can result in a different viewpoint on risk and adoption of controls. What risks are we really trying to mitigate with a control, and might the same control applied within another business be intended to mitigate a different risk?
– **Two for one:** While controls may be focused on addressing a particular risk they potentially have the ability either to address other risks simultaneously or to supplement other controls. How do we assess the supportiveness of control mechanisms between enterprises?
– **You can have any colour as long as its black:** Organisations' internal standards and best-practice guides generally reduce the range of controls selectable by an enterprise. Does this create significant homogeneity between controls implemented within certain sectors, or do organisations really have a choice in their application?
– **What's in a name?:** Apparently similar controls do not necessarily focus on achieving the same effect; [2] provides a illustrative example contrasting similar control objectives in itself and ISO 27001, noting the difference in focus between information flow between end-points on the one hand and boundary domains on the other. How different are the perceived semantics of the controls within organisations and standards and how difficult will it be to reconcile those differences?
– **Some controls are more equal than others:** Security controls applied in one sector may require significant tailoring for another. For example, protection of information in transmission is considered essential in protecting privacy in finance and retail sectors, but considered secondary in the utility sectors, where it is industrial process control in question and the availability and integrity of the data takes precedence over its confidentiality. Do these competing priorities lead to controls which are practically in competition, and if so how do the conflicts get resolved?

References

1. BS ISO/IEC 27000:2009. Information technology-Security techniques - Information security management systems - Overview and vocabulary. ISO/IEC, Switzerland (July 2009)
2. Ross, et al.: Recommended security controls for federal information systems. NIST Special Publication 800-53, National Institute of Standards and Technology, Gaithersburg, MD, USA (December 2007)

Risk Ontology and Service Quality Descriptor Shared among Interdependent Critical Infrastructures

Matthieu Aubigny[1], Carlo Harpes[1], and Marco Castrucci[2]

[1] itrust consulting s.a.r.l., Ecostart Bât 2, Rue du Commerce,
L-3895 Foetz, Luxembourg
{aubigny,harpes}@itrust.lu
[2] Sapienza Università Di Roma, Via Ariosto 25,
00185 Roma, Italia
castrucci@uniroma1.it

Abstract. This paper presents first an ontology of risk for interdependent and heterogeneous Critical Infrastructures (CIs). It defines a data structure called Service Quality Descriptor (SQD) specifying the degradation of QoS over time, which should be shared between interconnected CI. SQD are shared in real time and contain a precise prediction of the future quality of service, so that this sharing can be useful to avoid failures, identify interdependencies, or accelerate and coordinate power failure recoveries and service restoration. Finally, the paper proposes a simplified method to determine the SQD of a delivery service as a linear function of the SQD of supporting services and parameters depending on the service delivery infrastructure. The approach has been defined within the European FP-7 project MICIE, in line with the EU initiative to establish a Critical Infrastructure Warning Information Network (CIWIN).

Keywords: Risk analysis, Security Quality Descriptor, Quality of Service, Risk ontology, Interdependency risk, Critical infrastructure Protection, Risk Level.

1 Introduction

To improve the security of European Critical Infrastructure Protection capability, the European Commission has launched a research program called MICIE (whose extended title is "Tool for systeMIc risk analysis and secure mediation of data exchanged across linked CI information infrastructurEs"). The main purpose of this project is to design and to implement an online alerting system for interdependent and heterogeneous Critical Infrastructures (CIs), "providing a real time combined risk level indicator" [1]. This combined risk level describes the ability level of a CI to deliver its services with a defined target Quality of Service (QoS) despite the degradation of its own environment and despite the degradation of the QoS of supporting services provided by interdependent CIs.

2 Risk Description

2.1 How to Describe Risk?

To describe the risk, we consider every CI as service provider [2], deploying a specific process (composed of a set of process items) to provide its main service

C. Xenakis and S. Wolthusen (Eds.): CRITIS 2010, LNCS 6712, pp. 157–160, 2011.
© Springer-Verlag Berlin Heidelberg 2011

(composed of a set of service items offered entirely or partially to, at least one single user, i.e. one CI). According to the specification of a specific risk ontology applied to service, we characterised the risk from two points of view: classically, as the combination of a (negative) event which impacts and harms one or more service items of the service provider; and secondly as a degradation of QoS. In the case of autonomous service provider, the risk, called *environmental risk*, is classically caused by environmental events (local accident, dysfunction or attacks) on the service processing. However, in our study for interdependent CIs, the threat can also be directly due to the QoS degradation of, at least, one interdependent service. This type of threat leads to a specific risk which is called here *interdependency risk*.

In our study, we use a formalised approach of risk description based on the notion of dependability. We consider that the description of the concept of dependability [3], i.e. the attributes of dependability, the threats on dependability and the implemented safeguards to reach dependability, allows describing at the same time the environmental and interdependency risk. The attributes of dependability are the availability, reliability, safety, integrity, maintainability, confidentiality, authenticity, non-repudiation, accountability and auditability [4]. The threats on dependability are fault, error, and failure, which can occur in service process. And the implemented means to reach dependability are fault prevention, fault tolerance, fault removal and fault forecasting, included in the service process. The risk level can be comprehended according to:

a. The description of external threats and internal dysfunctions on the service item provided by the description of threat on dependability, mitigated by the implemented fault treatment on service item, which allows describing the environmental risk.

b. The description of the dependability attributes for every interdependent service item (i.e. the state of services item used by the targeted service) and for the targeted service item, which allows assessing the QoS of the targeted service.

2.2 Service Quality Descriptor

According to our risk ontology, we defined a data structure to describe the state of the QoS provided by the CI: the Service Quality Descriptor (SQD). The SQD is defined as a

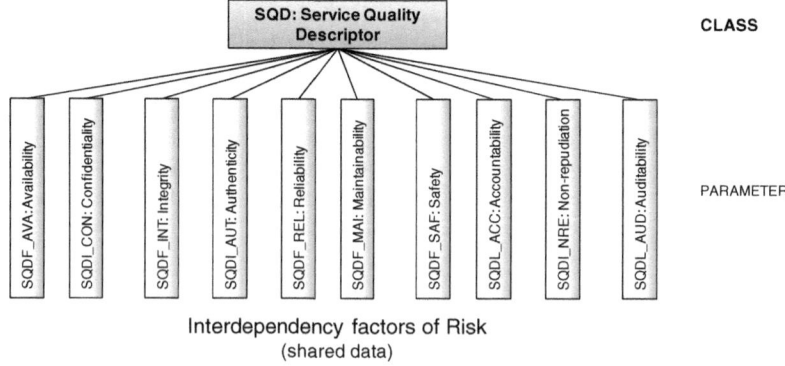

Fig. 1. Break-down overview of the *SQD Class*

list of temporal functions drawing the state of the risk of a service. The SQD is used to assess the influence of the QoS degradation of this service on interdependent services. Indeed, the parameters of this class (cf. Fig. 1), which allow quantifying the degradation of QoS, are intended to be shared with related CIs to predict their own risk.

2.3 Value Assignment to SQD

For each time t, each SQD is the random variable taking the value 1 if the property is fulfilled and 0 if it is missing. The SQD is characterised by the expected values noted $sqd_i(t)$ and by its variance $\sigma_i(t)$, both functions of time. To simplify the description of $sqd_i(t)$, we replace it by a linear approximation for different segments of time, i.e. $sqd_i(t) = a_{i,j} t + b_{i,j}$, for time t between t_{j-1} and t_j. Note that $t_0=0$ is considered current time and we consider m time intervals, i.e. $j \in \{1,\ldots,m\}$. For the variance, a simple model with one single time slot could be enough: $\sigma_i^2(t) = c_i t + d_i$. This variance expresses errors from the model itself, the assessment error, and uncertainties of dependent services. To conclude, the Service Quality is well described by the tuple SQD = (A, B, C, D, T) where A and B are $10 \times m$ matrices containing the parameters $a_{i,j}$ and $b_{i,j}$, C, D and T are vectors of length 10 containing c_i, d_i, and T is the vector describing the m time slots t_j.

3 Simplified Method of SQD Assessment

The theoretical idea is to compute the random variable SQD as complicated function of the SQD_k of n supporting services: $SQD = f(SQD_1,\ldots,SQD_n)$. The function f describes the behaviour of the whole infrastructure producing a new service with the help of n supporting services. But characterising this function is very complex because it depends of many various factors. Therefore we decided to simplify the computation according to the following assumptions.

3.1 Assumptions

First, we suggest considering each sqd_i parameter as a function only of the i-th parameters of the SQDs of the supporting services, e. g. the availability of the delivered service depends on the availability of the n supporting services, but not on their integrity. Second, we propose to use the same time slots for every SQD parameters. We suggest that in an interconnected environment, time slots should be standardised and chosen according to a logarithmic scale: more slots within near future (minutes), a large slots for far future (days). Third, as every complex function can be replaced by a linear approximation, we consider modelling the infrastructure linearly to determine very quickly the effect of a change of risk of a supporting element to the risk of the produced service to be shared. The dependencies are thus described by n real values p_k, so that

$$SQD = p_1 SQD_1 + \ldots + p_n SQD_n$$

3.2 SQD Parameters Computation

The tuple (A,B,C,D,T) describing the services can be computed by $A = p_1A_1 + \ldots + p_nA_n$ and $B = p_1B_1 + \ldots + p_nB_n$ supposing that $T = T_1 = \ldots = T_n$, where the tuple (A_1,B_1,C_1,D_1,T_1) is the tuple of the supporting service $SQD_1, \ldots$ The formula for C and D indicating the standards deviation are somewhat more complex and require approximation. Note that the above equation suggest that the parameter p_1, ... are the same for all 10 interdependency factors, but the model can easily be extent to consider a matrix P of $10 \times n$ parameter.

Note also that for different circumstances, e.g. in case of major supplier missing, a different set of parameters should be used, as dependencies are inherently non-linear. To scope with obvious non-linearities, a different matrix P can be used for different circumstances. Finally, the above formulas need one addition extension as past events generally influence future, to model e.g. recovery time. The availability at time t does not only depend on the availability at time t of the supporting service, but maybe on the availability of a supporting service in previous time slot.

References

1. Capodieci, P., Ciancamerla, E., Minichino, M., Diblasi, S., Foglietta, C., Panzieri, S., Lefevre, D., Oliva, G., Setola, R., De Porcellinis, S., Delli Priscoli, F., Castrucci, M., Suraci, V., Lev, L., Shneck, Y., Iassinovski, S., Khadraoui, D., Aubert, J., Jiang, J., Simoes, P., Caldeira, F., Spronska, A., Harpes, C., Aubigny, M.: Improving Resilience of Interdependent Critical Infrastructure via an on-line Alerting System. In: Conference COMPENG (Février 2010)
2. Flengte, F., Beyel, C., Rome, E.: Towards a Standardised Cross-Sector Information Exchange on Present Risk Factors. CRITIS Congress (2007)
3. Avizienis, A., Laprie, J.-C., Randell, B., Landwehr, C.E.: Basic Concepts and Taxonomy of Dependable and Secure Computing. IEEE Trans. Dependable Sec. Comput. 1(1), 11–33 (2004)
4. Hu, J., Bertok, P., Tari, Z.: Taxonomy and Framework for Integrating Dependability and Security. In: Quian, Y., Tipper, D., Krishnamurthy, P., Joshi, J. (eds.) Information Assurance Dependability and Security in Networked Systems, ch. 6. Morgan Kaufmann, San Francisco (2007)
5. Aubigny, M.: Risk Modelling and Simulation for Critical Information Infrastructure Protection, Master Thesis, University of Luxembourg – itrust consulting (2009), http://www.itrust.lu

Author Index

Batch number: 09474016

Printed by Printforce, the Netherlands